Across the margins

MANCHESTER
UNIVERSITY PRESS

Across the margins

Cultural identity and change in the Atlantic archipelago

EDITED BY GLENDA NORQUAY
AND GERRY SMYTH

Manchester University Press
Manchester and New York
distributed exclusively in the USA by Palgrave

Copyright © Manchester University Press 2002

While copyright in the volume is vested in Manchester University Press, copyright in individual chapters belongs to their respective authors, and no chapter may be reproduced wholly or in part without the express permission in writing of both author and publisher.

Published by Manchester University Press
Oxford Road, Manchester M13 9NR, UK
and Room 400, 175 Fifth Avenue, New York, NY 1000, USA
www.manchesteruniversitypress.co.uk

Distributed exclusively in the USA by
Palgrave, 175 Fifth Avenue, New York, NY 10010, USA

Distributed exclusively in Canada by
UBC Press, University of British Columbia, 2029 West Mall, Vancouver, BC, Canada V6T 1Z2

British Library Cataloguing-in-Publication Data
A catalogue record for this book is available from the British Library

Library of Congress Cataloging-in-Publication Data applied for

ISBN 0 7190 5749 3

First published 2002
10 09 08 07 06 05 04 03 02   10 9 8 7 6 5 4 3 2 1

Typeset in Caslon and Frutiger Condensed
by Koinonia Ltd, Manchester
Printed in Great Britain
by Bookcraft (Bath) Ltd, Midsomer Norton

Contents

Notes on contributors

Sean Campbell is a lecturer in the Department of Communication Studies at Anglia Polytechnic University, Cambridge. A graduate of the Universities of Glasgow and Strathclyde, he is currently researching the second-generation Irish in post-war England, focusing specifically on cultural production and identity-formation. His publications include articles in *Immigrants and Minorities*, *Irish Studies Review*, and *The Great Famine and Beyond: Irish Migrants in Britain in the Nineteenth and Twentieth Centuries* (2000).

Peter Childs has published articles on Paul Scott, E. M. Forster and Hanif Kureishi. He has also edited a reader in *Post-Colonial Theory and English Literature* for Edinburgh University Press and written, together with Patrick Williams, *An Introduction to Post-Colonial Theory*. Currently lecturing at Cheltenham and Gloucester College of Higher Education, he is the author or editor of eight books, of which the most recent are *Modernism* (2000) and *Reading Fiction* (2001).

Aileen Christianson is a senior lecturer in the Department of English Literature, Edinburgh University, specialising in nineteenth- and twentieth-century Scottish literature and women's writing. She has been on the editorial team of the Duke–Edinburgh edition of *The Collected Letters of Thomas and Jane Welsh Carlyle*, vols 1–28, 1970–200, since 1967. She was a member of the Edinburgh Rape Crisis Centre Collective, 1978–96.

Colin Graham is Lecturer in Irish Writing at Queen's University Belfast. He is the author of *Ideologies of Epic: Nation, Empire and Victorian Epic Poetry* (1998), *Deconstructing Ireland: Identity, Theory, Culture* (2001), and co-editor with Richard Kirkland of *Ireland and Cultural Theory: The Mechanics of Authenticity* (1999).

Murdo Macdonald is Professor of History of Scottish Art at the University of Dundee. His recent publications include *Scottish Art* in Thames and Hudson's *World of Art* series and 'Patrick Geddes and Scottish Generalism' in Welter and Lawson (eds) *The City after Patrick Geddes*. He was editor of *Edinburgh Review* from 1990 to 1994.

Willy Maley is Professor of Renaissance Studies at the University of Glasgow. He has published widely on aspects of early modern and modern Scottish and Irish culture, and is the author of *Salvaging Spenser: Colonialism, Culture and Identity* (1997), and editor (with Andrew Hadfield) of *A View of the Present State of Ireland* (1997). He has been a Visiting Professor at Dartmouth College, New Hampshire (1997), and was the first recipient of the Gerard Manley Hopkins Visiting Professorship at John Carroll University in Cleveland (1998). He is presently working on a number of projects concerning the 'British Problem' in the sixteenth and seventeenth centuries.

Glenda Norquay is Reader in Literary Studies at Liverpool John Moores University. She has published widely on Scottish women's writing. Other publications include *Voices and Votes: A Literary Anthology of the Women's Suffrage Campaign* (1995), and *Stevenson on Fiction* (1999). She is currently working on a monograph on Stevenson's reading practices.

Linden Peach is Professor of Modern Literature at Loughborough University. His publications include booklength studies of Virginia Woolf (2000), Toni Morrison (2000) and Angela Carter (1998). He is also the author of *Ancestral Lines: Culture and Identity in the Work of Six Contemporary Poets* (1993), and has written extensively on Welsh writing in English. He is co-author (with Angela Burton) of *English as a Creative Art: Literary Concepts Linked to Creative Writing* (1995).

Shaun Richards is Professor of Irish Studies at Staffordshire University, specialising in the cultural politics of Irish Literature, specifically that of the drama. He has published widely in this area, most notably *Writing Ireland* (1988) which he co-authored with David Cairns. Among his current projects is the editing of the *Cambridge Companion to Modern Irish Drama*.

Berthold Schoene is Senior Lecturer in Literary Studies at Liverpool John Moores University. His research interests include postcoloniality, Scottish literature, and literary representations of masculinity. Besides publishing essays on Iain Banks, Hanif Kureishi, Meera Syal, and Scottish culture and postcoloniality, he is the author of *Writing Men: Literary Masculinities from Frankenstein to the New Man* (2000). His current research is on 'Autism and the Subject of Masculinity'.

Gerry Smyth is Reader in Cultural History at Liverpool John Moores University. He has published widely on various aspects of Irish cultural history. His most recent book is *Space and the Irish Cultural Imagination* (2001), and he is currently working on a critical history of Irish rock music.

Acknowledgements

The idea for this book emerged from two conferences organised between Liverpool John Moores University and its then ERASMUS partner, the University of the Basque Country. We are grateful to all the contributors to those events, in particular to Roger Bromley and Linden Peach for their help and sustained interest. Edna Longley and Cairns Craig made valuable comments on early proposals. We would also like to thank Aileen Christianson and Shaun Richards for helpful comments and suggestions, and particularly Timothy Ashplant who gave generously of his time and support. Thanks are due also to the editors' colleagues within the Department of English Literature and Cultural History at Liverpool John Moores University for their support of the sabbatical programme which facilitated work on this project. Glenda Norquay acknowledges the financial support of the Carnegie Trust for the Universities in Scotland, during a Research Fellowship at the Institute for Advanced Studies in the Humanities, University of Edinburgh, at which some of this work was carried out. The prompt responses of contributors, the insights of Matthew Frost and the anonymous readers at Manchester University Press, and the efficiency of editorial staff at various stages, made this project much pleasanter that it might otherwise have been.

Introduction:
crossing the margins

GLENDA NORQUAY AND GERRY SMYTH

'So there it was, our territory', writes the narrator in Seamus Deane's novel-cum-memoir *Reading in the Dark* (1997: 59), claiming his own particular domain with all the confidence of childhood. We are drawn to the identification of places, impelled to categorise our territory. It is, however, only movements within and across space that actuate, modify, transform it; as Michel de Certeau puts it, 'space is a practised place' (1988: 117). Any identification of boundaries is in itself an act of construc-tion, a spatial practice that recognises its mutability. From this paradox emerges the need for what Homi K. Bhabha terms 'travelling theory' (1990b: 293), a way of understanding movement and migration, of what it means to be 'in-between' but also of recognising how important the sense of belonging to a place has been. The organisation of space has functioned to impose centralising power structures; but the claiming or reclaiming of territory has also offered a means of resistance for those pushed to the edges. In this volume we are exploring such paradoxes in relation to different definitions of 'the margins', a spatial concept which has had much currency but which might increasingly be questioned on theoretical, geographical and political grounds.

Among other things, we are interested in the geographical edges of the cluster of islands in which we live, the terrain historically described as the 'United Kingdom of Great Britain and Northern Ireland and the Republic of Ireland'. To use 'margins' in this context suggests a spatial and definitional grouping of 'nations', organised around a putative English 'core' often operating as a substitute for 'Britishness'. Until recently, the elision of English into British (and *vice versa*) seemed to occupy an unproblematic position at the core of this construction, although the ideological implications of this process are now questioned on a number of fronts. The concept of 'margins' also indicates that in Scotland, Northern Ireland, the Republic of Ireland and Wales, countries of small and sparse populations have been seen as struggling to preserve political and cultural identities in the face of increasing demographic and economic concentration in England and, more recently, in the south of England. Historically these areas have been positioned, through linguistic markers of difference, as the 'Celtic margins'. This term has perhaps more resonance for Ireland and Wales than it does for Scotland, in that a large part of the Scottish population was never in possession of the Gaelic language; it nevertheless encapsulates the processes both of representation and self-representation of different cultural and racial inheritances from that of England. The concept of 'margins' denotes therefore geographical, economic, demographic, cultural and political positioning in relation to a perceived centre.

One aim of this book, however, is to move away from rather than replicate this core/periphery model – to question the term 'marginal' itself, to hear voices talking 'across' borders and not only to or through an English centre. Even as a reclaimed term, the idea of 'marginality' still appears to give some priority to a notional centre; while this has some bearing on historical and geographical structures of power, it can also occlude lines of connection which do not move from centre to margin, or from margin to centre. It ignores the fact that in some contexts the margins may occupy central positions: as W. N. Herbert notes in his 'Mappamundi' – a poetic map of the world: 'Ireland's/bin shuftit tae London, whaur/oafficis o thi Poetry Sock occupeh fehv/squerr mile' (O'Rourke 1994: 146).

Challenges to an unhelpful margins/centre binarism and to the centripetal forces of metropolitan culture have also emerged in new questions about the constitution of Englishness itself – as demonstrated most obviously in the Runnymede Trust report. We also want, therefore, to examine the possible intersections between geopolitical markers of supposed 'marginality' and other boundaries and hierarchies operating in identity politics – gender, ethnicity, class and sexuality in particular. In this arena we believe that insufficient attention had been placed to the relationship between 'Celtic spaces' and other areas of 'difference', even within the context of emerging concerns around a 'New Britishness'. As Robert Crawford notes in the afterword to his influential *Devolving English Literature*:

> [Only] two months before the election which brought to power a
> British government committed to devolution and the most significant

constitutional changes to the British nation for three centuries, Homi Bhabha with the British Council presented a major conference-cum-festival called *Reinventing Britain*. Incredibly, the project contained nothing whatsoever about the devolution debate, or how the changing relationships between Scotland, England, Wales, not to mention Ireland, might contribute to 're-inventing Britain'. (2000: 309)

One focus, therefore, is on the dynamics between old and new identity groupings in this changing context. A third and related aim is to engage with the extremely rapid changes in Scotland, Ireland, Wales and England through specific attention to cultural practices. The countries we are concerned with are undergoing transformations in both culture and politics. Since the book was first conceived, Scotland and Wales have gained devolved parliamentary powers; in Ireland the setting up of new forms of cross-border power sharing combined with rapid economic growth in the Republic to redraw social and political patterns. Irish and Scottish writing, moreover, gained unexpected 'mainstream' and metropolitan recognition, while Welsh popular music suddenly (finally!) attained the subcultural kudos traditionally attendant upon other minority communities. It is only through detailed analysis of cultural products and traditions that the intricacies of these changes can be understood: it is our intention, therefore, that the book operates on both a specific and a general level, not only in the movement within each essay from a particular case study to the broader issues raised, but also across the volume as a whole.

With these aims in mind we chose to work with the term 'Atlantic Archipelago' as most representative of the particular organisation of space, people and identity with which we were concerned. This term is primarily associated with the historian J. G. A. Pocock, whose 1975 call for a less nation-centred history was answered over the following quarter century by the emergence of a school specifically dedicated to 'Archipelagic history'.[1] Influenced in some important respects by the French *Annales* and by the rise during the 1960s of 'history from below', and motivated in part by the crisis attending established political structures, historians (especially of the medieval and early modern periods) became concerned to trace the evolution of a disparate set of cultural and political factors which has impacted upon island life, factors which are not apprehensible, or *alone* apprehensible, in terms of the established national identities. As John Morrill writes: 'Englishness is self-evidently the product of the complex interactions of peoples and cultures (Britons, Romans, Saxons, Norsemen, Normans). Scottishness, Irishness, Welshness too are the product of complex interactions of peoples, one of them the English' (1996: 2).

The prioritisation of the political in this particular account remains problematic; likewise, the retention in some influential interventions of certain loaded terms, such as the 'Britannic' or 'Four-nations' history favoured by Hugh Kearney (1989, 1991), is not something to which we would necessarily subscribe. Nevertheless, the present volume represents a response to the ongoing, contentious practice of 'archipelagic historiography', offered in the belief that, whatever its limitations, such a subject at least acknowledges the inadequacy of earlier paradigms, and recognises that new models need to be developed to engage with the matrix of overlapping identities and practices that have traditionally functioned, and continue to function, throughout what used to be known as 'the British Isles'.

This book makes no claims to provide a comprehensive, or indeed a coherent, model of what an archipelagic cultural studies should look like. That will be the task of individuals and groups from many backgrounds working over time in many different institutional and intellectual circumstances. There has been one development, however, which because of its ubiquitous nature may prove enduring, and which because of its influence upon all the essays gathered here is worth signalling. It is a development implicit in the new history that, we have suggested, provides the *imprimatur* for an archipelagic cultural criticism.

What we are alluding to here is the initiation of a new *historical* (and, in this volume, a new *critical*) subject in terms of a new *geographical* perspective. The complexity of this refraction is evident in the issue of definition: the term 'British' has clearly evolved to the point where it cannot be used unproblematically, and there have been various attempts to invent alternative geographical definitions which might signify the issues at stake in clearer ways. The term we favour here – Atlantic archipelago – may prove to be of no greater use in the long run, but at this stage it does at least have the merit of questioning the ideology underpinning more established nomenclature. It is, moreover, essentially a geographical term – both locational and descriptive – and this provides a clue as to the manner in which a cross-marginal cultural criticism might set about identifying appropriate archives and methodologies. For at roughly the same time as 'the history of the Atlantic archipelago' was emerging in Britain and Ireland, the field of what has come to be known as 'new' or 'postmodern' geography was also in the process of consolidation, much of the time in different departments of the same institutions.

The last decades of the twentieth century witnessed the emergence of what we might call the 'spatial imagination' and the growing realisation of its absolute centrality to human experience (Soja 1989). This development is not only connected with the growth of widespread scepticism towards history in general and institutionalised historiography in particular, but also with a number of factors which have combined to put pressure on the historicism which has dominated western critical/cultural institutions since the nineteenth century. Besides reinvigorating fields (such as geography and built environment) traditionally concerned with the social, cultural and political organisation of spatial practices, the spatial imagination also began to make itself felt in less obvious disciplines. Although its natural home may turn out to be cultural studies, other fields such as philosophy, sociology and (even) literature have rediscovered a spatial imagination informing their most basic assumptions and practices (Fitter 1995; Gregory 1994; Keith and Pike 1993; Naess 1989; Schama 1995; Smyth 2001). Working within this context our aim is to bring together a number of essays which would work across marginal territories but which will also allow for a re-imagining of these spaces.

There were certain areas in which this process of talking across seemed imperative: language, gender, sexuality and ethnicity. The first section of the book, therefore, includes: an essay by Willy Maley which examines debates on the political and poetic choice of language, drawing attention to significant differences between Irish and Scottish strategies; a discussion of the complicated dynamic of woman and nation by Aileen Christianson, which explores the work of twentieth-century Scottish and Irish women writers and assesses the relevance of a postcolonial context in understanding the 'debatable' boundaries arising from that intersection; an exploration of masculinities in both English and Scottish writing from Berthold Schoene, which also deploys sexual difference as a means of testing postcolonial theorising, but does so within the context of a discourse in which bodily, social and national-cultural spaces overlap and compete; and a chapter by Peter Childs which offers a different perspective on the notion of marginality by addressing 'Englishness' in relation to 'migrant' writing in prose concerned with India and England after Independence. In each case specific intersections of identity are used to explore the wider configurations of space and self. In this section we also include an essay by Colin Graham which offers a mediation on the broader critical implications of postcolonial theory through analysis of its application in a specific context. Taking the reader from Michelet, via Barthes and Bataille, to Joyce, Graham explores the dilemma of 'speaking Ireland' when the very articulation of that marginality itself involves an intellectual 'crossing' from the margins.

We also seek to develop comparative work within the archipelagic framework in analysis of particular cultural forms. The second part of the book therefore contains essays which are directed towards specific readings: a chapter on poetry by Linden Peach which draws on a wide range of new poetry to question simplified margin/centre relations; a historicising perspective on the work of cultural studies and its responses to the relationship between ethnicity and second-generation Irish musicians from Sean Campbell; and our own comparison of contemporary Irish and Scottish fiction which identifies similarities and differences in recent developments. In each instance the writers take on the task of examining and assessing points of connection and diversity across a particular body of work, while moving away from contrasts which focus on an English 'norm'. A recurring feature of the essays is a concern with reception as well as production, emphasising the significance of location within specific cultural maps. This second part of the book also includes chapters which test definitions of 'marginality' through concentration on even more specific instances of the relationship between a cultural tradition and a changing political context. Thus, Shaun Richards uses Welsh drama to explore the cultural politics of South Wales, while Murdo Macdonald examines previous frameworks in which Scottish art has been defined and understood and offers a rethinking of what nationality means in the context of the visual arts.

Within this disparate range of interests and material, we are aware of a tension under negotiation: contributors and editors are working with the recognition that in a sense all national identities are 'constructed', that divisions of space – geographical, historical, cultural – exist mainly in our minds but are also operating with an awareness that culture nevertheless continues to be practised and, perhaps more significantly, understood, in terms of national affiliations. Cultural criticism has traditionally relied (albeit grudgingly for the most part) upon other disciplines – specifically geography, history and politics – for the categories which animate its intellectual vision. It would be difficult to write a book about 'Scottish poetry', say, if history had not provided us with a paradigm of Scottishness (incorporating among other things aspects of character, language and narrative) in terms of which specific individual phenomena might be considered. Arnold Kemp, for example, reviewing a new anthology of Scottish poetry, can assert: 'What makes a poet

Scottish comes down to voice and identity rather than linguistic choice. Yet more than anything else language is the anvil on which Scottish poetry and its "flytings" … have been forged' (2000). Although echoing Joyce in his use of the term 'forged' (but apparently without Joyce's sense of ironic ambiguity), Kemp glosses over the fact that 'Scotland' also requires geopolitical definition; otherwise we encounter all sorts of problems involving domicile, borders, generations, and a host of other potentially embarrassing complications. But if 'Scotland' as a geopolitical possibility is changing, as it palpably is, any analysis of 'Scottish' poetry is necessarily compromised. By the same token, if historiography is changing then the fields and disciplines which rely in the main upon history for their constituent categories must also be obliged to change. In the light of developments both within and outwith the academic institutions, in other words, our study of Scottish poetry risks being unfashionable at best, inappropriate at worst. If history has a new subject – the history of the Atlantic archipelago – then so too must cultural criticism.

Our aims, however, present certain challenges. For a start, many academics are reluctant to leave behind the comforting paradigms of national literatures and cultures, even more so to abandon their own comforting places within those paradigms. The contributors to this volume show bravery in stepping into such debatable terrain. Writing our own chapter on fiction we were conscious of 'authority' when each speculated on things Irish or Scottish: we were comfortable within our own 'established' national and disciplinary locations, but we also instinctively felt some (unspoken) right to a voice within those boundaries. Yet (against all our theoretically anti-essentialist inclinations) we were reluctant to enter the other's territory without the confidence of a 'blood' connection. A second difficulty lies in our sense of being overtaken by events: our 'margins' were becoming, in political terms at least, 'centres'. In 1999 Joyce Macmillan commented that '[post-devolution], political Scotland is behaving like a newly-formed volcanic island, its topography still heaving and shifting so rapidly that only a fool would attempt to map it' (286). Her remarks might be applied, on a larger scale, to the terrain we are trying to map out here. The essays offer, therefore, thoughts from a particular moment in time, just as they offer only a 'slice' of space. Thirdly, in developing this book we have been forced to recognise the contradictory nature of our own aims, to work across margins while at the same time questioning not only ideas of marginality but also of nationality. We both feel some unease with this: in a postcolonial context we are all being encouraged to see ourselves as 'mobile mongrel islanders' (Kearney 2000: 34), part of a postnationalist world, and – in some respects – this has provided a liberating impulse for the book. Yet we also acknowledge the desire to belong, which pulls us into identifications with geographical and historical spaces, and recognise that this desire still holds possibilities of allegiances that may be empowering and enlightening.

In negotiating these contradictory impulses we have again found theories of spatial practice helpful. The rediscovery of a spatial imagination attends to the *narrative* and the *structural* imagination of space – attends, that is, to the conceptual invocation of the subject within a range of spatial contexts, but also (and more challengingly) to the organisation of discrete texts, genres and practices in terms of what we might call 'spatial poetics' or 'spatial form'. Analysis which articulates politics *with* poetics is capable of engaging with the wide variety of ways in which cultural phenomena have been and continue to be ordered across a wide variety of social and political contexts. As a brief example, consider what many believe to be the most essential(ist) of Irish cultural practices: traditional music. This subject might appear on first glance to be unamenable to analysis in terms of spatial politics/poetics. Such analysis, however, might begin by addressing 'external' social and political issues, such as the function of the pub as 'a space that hovers between the private and the public spheres in Ireland' (Gibbons 1997: 268); the erosion of session culture under pressure from tourism and other commercial considerations; the relocation to larger venues such as the pub-club, the theatre and the stadium; and what might be referred to as 'the general economy of noise' obtaining within contemporary Irish society. The critic would also want to consider, however, what might be referred to as 'soundscape' or the 'spatial form' of specific texts and performances. This would encompass a wide range of factors, including the speed of the music, rhythm, attack, volume, counterpoint, timbre, the positioning of soloists and/or different instruments. Crucially, analysis would also need to engage with the potential for traditional music to create 'spatial illusions' (Tuan 1977: 14) – for example, the association (in much contemporary cinematic discourse) of certain instruments with certain landscapes.

The methodological economy of politics/poetics has its parallels in other critical and cultural fields. But the real point is that, as this example shows, the spatial imagination might prove beneficial for archipelagic studies. Traditional Irish music could be profitably compared in these terms to other 'traditional' musical practices – whether Celtic, Caribbean, sub-continental, or whatever – throughout the archipelago.

The idea is not to replace an historical imperative with a geographical one, but to relieve the intellectual hegemony of the former while pointing out the complete interpenetration of each by the other.[2] For on consideration it turns out that the wide variety of power structures extant throughout 'the British Isles' has always been as much about the desire to master space as about the drive to order time. The Marxist critic Aijaz Ahmad argues that imperialism and its late capitalist logic cannot be resisted by recourse to a fatally derivative nationalism, but by means of a rejuvenated post-Soviet socialism (1992: 287–318). Colonialism's other, however, was never merely nationalism and/or socialism, but a spatial imagination which it had to reconfigure in its own controlling terms. Its ally in this ideological task was an historicism which naturalised colonialism's own way of seeing and which blocked oppositional discourses. But a backwards glance at the cultural history of domination/ subordination in the Atlantic archipelago reveals a deep, widespread fascination with the organisation of cultural and political identity around a series of spatial problematics.

While a number of recent books have addressed the historical and political framework of the Atlantic archipelago, the focus of this volume is on cultural practices within that context – an area in which there is less work done. Although both the Scots–Irish Research Network (based at the University of Strathclyde) and the Research Institute in Irish and Scottish Studies (based at the University of Aberdeen and to be known from January 2001 as the AHRB Centre for Irish and Scottish Studies in recognition of an impressive grant from that body) have produced excellent multidisciplinary research, it would appear that scholars are still most confident when working with identifiable cross-border connections – such as neglected political networks in Scottish and Irish history, for example, or in shared cultural frameworks – than tracing intersections in contemporary culture and literature. We hope therefore that this book contributes to critical analysis which, whilst acknowledging the hard-won specificity of concerns in writing from different geographical locations, also moves beyond the diachronic formation of national literatures and cultures.

The Irish cultural critic Luke Gibbons suggests that:

> [another] way of negotiating identity through an exchange with the other is to make provision, not just for 'vertical' mobility from the periphery to the centre, but for 'lateral' journeys along the margins which short-circuit the colonial divide ... Hybridity need not always take the high road: where there are borders to be crossed, unapproved

roads might prove more beneficial in the long run than those patrolled by global powers. (1996: 180)

If the archipelago's disparate marginalities have tended to have little to say to each other, this is by and large also true of the scholarly disciplines engaged with cultural manifestations of these marginalities. If, however, cultural criticism, history and geography can come together across disciplines in a way which proves mutually beneficial, then the same might also be true of those many groups (self-)identified as marginal to a putative mainstream culture. We should be talking; we should be seeking out those 'unapproved roads' imagined by Gibbons if we are to dispense with the by now superannuated category of 'marginality' and move on to more useful, and ultimately more enabling, positions.

Notes

1 See for example Bradshaw and Morrill 1996; Connolly 1999; Elcock and Keating 1998; Grant and Stringer 1995; Osmond 1988. These studies vie for intellectual space alongside others which, if not actually pursuing what one commentator is still disposed to call 'the Whig interpretation of English history' (Cannadine 1995: 13), still practise a kind of history more or less in terms of received political and cultural discourses – see for example Colley 1992; Crick 1991; Davies 1999; Foster 1993; Hechter 1975; Levack 1987; Nairn 1981; Robbins 1997; Samuel 1989.

2 As Soja says: 'Geography may not yet have displaced history at the heart of contemporary theory and criticism, but there is a new animating polemic on the theoretical and political agenda, one which rings with significantly different ways of seeing time and space together, the interplay of history and geography, the "vertical" and "horizontal" dimensions of being in the world freed from the imposition of inherent categorical privilege' (1989: 11).

PART I

Theorising identities across the Atlantic archipelago

1

'Ireland, verses, Scotland: crossing the (English) language barrier'[1]

WILLY MALEY

> The very problem of the national and the individual in language is basically the problem of the utterance (after all, only here, in the utterance, is the national language embodied in individual form). (Mikhail Bakhtin, cited Wesling 1997: 81)

> The Irish mix better with the English than the Scotch do because their language is nearer. (Samuel Johnson, cited in Boswell 1906 [1791]: 473)

> Why Scotland and Ireland? What is marginal, one might ask, about cultures that have produced writers like Burns, Boswell, Stevenson, and Scott, on the one hand, and Wilde, Shaw, Yeats, and Joyce, on the other? (Reizbaum 1992: 168–9)

One measure of the strength of a new subject is its capacity to attract major funding. With this in mind it is worth noting that the Irish Government recently gave its largest ever grant in the humanities – £400,000 – to Trinity College Dublin to develop Irish–Scottish Studies. At the same time, the UK's Arts and Humanities Research Board (AHRB), from a list of 145 applications, published a shortlist of twenty-five that included only one Scottish University for its Research Centre funding. Aberdeen University, whose Research Institute in Irish and Scottish Studies (RIISS) piloted the UK's first postgraduate programme in Irish–Scottish Studies, netted an award of £870,000, the largest ever grant in the humanities in Scotland. What is evident from these institutional awards and innovations is that Irish–Scottish Studies has officially arrived as a new (inter) discipline.

The pioneering work of critics such as Marilyn Reizbaum is now being followed through (Horton 1997; Reizbaum 1992). Reizbaum justified her own cross-marginal approach in the following way:

I feel I can talk about Scotland and Ireland together in this context, without homogenizing them and thereby further marginalizing them (all Celts are alike), because they have comparable 'colonial' histories with respect to England (unlike Wales) and because their status as minority cultures, which has more or less continued in psychic and/or political ways, has had a similar impact not only on the dissemination of their respective literatures but on the nature and means of the writing. (1992: 169)

Ireland and Scotland are marginalised and minoritised, but this experience has provoked different reactions from writers in the two countries.

My title suggests a contest of some kind, a battle of the bards, and it would be tempting to referee some stiff competition in the dead poets society by reading Yeats in the light of Burns, and MacDiarmid in the wake of Joyce. But despite my title, the intention is not to draw up bardic battle lines. My essay aims at comparison rather than conflict. As Edna Longley writes:

If unionists want their Scottish ties to yield more than a baronial blazon, an ancestral and atavistic title to 'Ulster Britishness', they must explore contemporary Scotland while Scotland itself explores the ratio between pluralistic cultural self-consciousness and gradations of political independence. The Scottish debate has more to offer than the English muddle about British nationalism. Belonging to the UK means engaging with what might be its crisis, what might be its mutation. To behave otherwise is to admit a 'colonial' status. (1997: 114–15)

Of course, there are very good historical reasons for Scotland and Ireland being averse to one another, to do with Empire and Union, and I have written elsewhere on that aversion (Maley 2000a; 2000b). Here, I want to accentuate the positive. In this essay I shall explore the missing middle of the vernacular in Irish writing, drawing on Edna Longley's perceptive remarks about Tom Paulin's poetic project and the vexed issue of Ulster-Scots. I propose to take in other kinds of writing than just poetry, though the chief part of what I have to say does relate to verses.

A few years ago, I was preparing to teach a course on contemporary Scottish and Irish writing, and I sat down to select the poetry and drama options. Since the Renaissance was my own period I found three plays I thought would work well together: Brian Friel's *Making History* (1989), the story of Hugh O'Neill, the Gaelic chieftain whose flight to the Continent left a vacuum into which a nascent Catholic nationalism was born; Frank McGuinness's *Mutabilitie* (1997), the story of Spenser's Irish sojourn, weaving in a visit by Shakespeare and an analogy between the theatre

and Catholicism that effectively dramatises Stephen Greenblatt's essay
on 'Shakespeare and the exorcists' (1985); and, finally, Liz Lochhead's
Mary Queen of Scots Got Her Head Chopped Off (1989), whose nursery
rhyme title is undercut by its adult theme. All three plays were set in the
1580s or 1590s, and all addressed gender, history and national identity,
focusing on a loser of one kind or another: the embattled and ultimately
exiled Hugh O'Neill; the English poet burned out of his adopted home;
and the Scottish monarch executed by her English cousin. All three also
obsessed about England, and this interested me because I was concerned
with the ways in which the hyphen between Anglo-Irish and Anglo-
Scottish concealed a third term – Scotland and Ireland respectively.
Another thing that struck me was the fact that while Friel and McGuinness opted for an English poetic voice – with a brief and unconvincing
lapse on O'Neill's part – Lochhead's language was resolutely Scots.

This last feature was even more striking when it came to the poetry.
I had picked up two anthologies that I admired, Fallon and Mahon's
Penguin Book of Contemporary Irish Poetry (1990), and Donny O'Rourke's
Dream State (1994). When I looked at the two together I was astonished
at the difference. While the Scottish anthology offered poetry in all the
languages and dialects of Scotland, and displayed a richness and diversity
of voice that I had come to expect, the Irish volume, by contrast, was
much more monologic, full of the samey and the sonorous, with very few
exceptions. There was a tendency, to quote Beckett's Winnic in *Happy
Days*, 'to speak in the old style'. Why was this so? What gave the Irish
anthology a less 'contemporary' feel? The answer lies in the language
question as it impinges, unevenly, on the literature of the two nations.

Edwin Muir, Scottish poet and critic, made light of Irish immigration in his travelogue, *A Scottish Journey*, published in 1935, but in his
literary history, *Scott and Scotland*, published the following year, he held
Ireland up as a model of national cultural revival. Muir's argument,
simply put, was that Scottish writers had lost the ability to speak to the
nation as a whole by their refusal of English – Muir was attacking Hugh
MacDiarmid in particular – and he labelled their local efforts 'parochial',
citing Yeats as an example to be followed of a truly national figure. Muir
was arguably reacting against such influential accounts as that of T. S.
Eliot, who in 1919 had pronounced Scottish Literature 'provincial':

> The first part of the history of Scottish literature is part of the history of
> English literature when English was several dialects; the second part is
> part of the history of English literature when English was two dialects –
> English and Scottish; the third part is something quite different – it is

the history of a provincial literature. And finally, there is no longer any tenable distinction to be drawn for the present day between the two literatures. (cited in Dunn 1992: xvii)

For Muir, who was determined to see a Scottish literature develop that was worthy of a nation rather than a region, such remarks were anathema. Muir's argument, which concludes his study of Scottish literature, is worth quoting in full, since it captures the complexity of the modern debate around language and national identity:

> Scotland can only create a national literature by writing in English. This may sound paradoxical: in support of it I can only advance my whole case in regard to the Scots language … and the contemporary case of Ireland. Irish nationality cannot be said to be any less intense than ours; but Ireland produced a national literature not by clinging to Irish dialect, but by adopting English and making it into a language fit for all its purposes. The poetry of Mr Yeats belongs to English literature, but no one would deny that it belongs to Irish literature pre-eminently and essentially. The difference between contemporary Irish and contemporary Scottish literature is that the first is central and homogeneous, and that the second is parochial and conglomerate; and this is because it does not possess an organ for the expression of a whole and unambiguous nationality. Scots dialect poetry represents Scotland in bits and patches, and in doing that it is no doubt a faithful enough image of the present divided state of Scotland. But while we cling to it we shall never be able to express the central reality of Scotland, as Mr Yeats has expressed the central reality of Ireland; though for such an end the sacrifice of dialect poetry would be cheap. The real issue in contemporary Scottish literature is between centrality and provincialism; dialect poetry is one of the chief supports of the second of these two forces; the first can hardly be said to exist at all. And until Scottish literature has an adequate language, it cannot exist. Scotland will remain a mere collection of districts. (Muir 1982 [1936]: 111–12)

The irony is that the 'Mr Yeats' whom Muir praised had himself looked to Scotland for inspiration, and to a Scottish writer who helped establish the vernacular as a truly international language. At the turn of the century Yeats characterised Synge as 'truly a National writer, as Burns was when he wrote finely' (Yeats 1962: 157).

It is ironic that at a time when Edwin Muir was arguing for a Yeats-ian model of national literature for Scotland, Irish writers were pursuing a more local/regional line, but with one difference from Scottish writers. Irish writers appear to have adhered more to Muir's insistence on English as the proper language of literary renaissance and resistance than to the

opposing view of Hugh MacDiarmid, who championed the vernacular.
The letter of Yeats lives on, if not the spirit.

Douglas Dunn is one of many Scottish critics who have argued for
the degree to which MacDiarmid's was a project of recovery and renewal,
a cultural enterprise that was national as much as linguistic or literary:

> MacDiarmid was trying to make a nation as well as poetry. He did so
> with a language that through disuse had become the victim of an inbuilt
> preterite. Vernacular, Doric, Braid Scots, Synthetic Scots, Plastic Scots,
> Aggrandized Scots, or Lallans, were and are (but, by and large, they are
> all one) instruments with which to cleanse the Scottish psyche of
> generations of English influence. It was for decades, and remains, a
> language unexposed to actual contact with changing intellectual and
> domestic life. It is a language with very few, if any, new words. Indeed,
> it is a language in which old words are used in poetry with the force of
> neologisms, the shock of the unfamiliar. (Dunn 1992: xxi)

While MacDiarmid looked to the Modernist experimentation of Joyce,
Muir looked to the potent public oratory of Yeats.

As Dunn points out: 'Only in recent years has [Edwin Muir's]
insistence on English as the only authentic language of Scottish poetry
been proved mistaken through developments which have brought about
a healing in the controversy that used to be described as "the language
question"' (1992: xxxi). But Muir's mistake had implications for Irish
poetry, for if Scottish writers defied his call and continued to write in all
the languages of Scotland, then across the water in Ireland a 'central
reality' would be forged at the expense of 'dialect poetry'. And this
despite the arguments of a formidable figure like Patrick Kavanagh.

For, curiously, at the same time that Muir was deriding Scottish
dialect poetry for creating a Scotland that was 'parochial and conglom-
erate', reducing the country to 'bits and patches', 'a mere collection of
districts', Kavanagh was defending parochialism. There was in Ireland at
this time a move afoot – still visible today – to resist the overweening
influence of Yeats and to celebrate specificity, locality and region rather
than nation. But – and here is the rub – to do so in the anglicised accents
of Yeats. Kavanagh's famous distinction is instructive:

> Parochialism and provincialism are direct opposites. The provincial has
> no mind of his own; he does not trust what his eyes see until he has
> heard what the metropolis – towards which his eyes are turned – has to
> say on any subject. This runs through all activities.
>   The parochial mentality on the other hand is never in any doubt about
> the social and artistic validity of his [sic] parish. All great civilizations

are based on parochialism – Greek, Israelite, English. Parochialism is universal; it deals with the fundamentals.

To know fully even one field or one lane is a lifetime's experience. In the world of poetic experience it is depth that counts, not width. A gap in a hedge, a smooth rock surfacing a narrow lane, a view of a woody meadow, the stream at the junction of four small fields – these are as much as a man can fully experience. (cited in Fallon and Mahon 1990: xviii)

If MacDiarmid won the day in Scotland, as writers became increasingly confident about using Scots, then Muir saw his vision materialise in Ireland. As Declan Kiberd points out:

> The story of Irish poetry after the 1950s is the tale of how a new gener-ation of men and women sought once again – as Yeats had at the start of the century – to free Ireland from provincialism by an exacting criticism and a European pose … The poetry of those postwar decades was characterized also by a growing engagement with foreign – and specifically English – authors. One way of fighting free of the awesome legacy of Yeats, after all, was to set up shop under the sign of Eliot or Auden. (1991: 1311–12)

It is in this context, the context of a shift towards an English-oriented poetry, that Edna Longley refers to the poetry of the North of Ireland as exerting a necessary complicating force:

> 'Ulster poetry' – in the totality of its relations and publications – is an ideal focus for inter-disciplinary study. It breaks up Ireland as a unitary subject. It breaks up Britain as a unifying affiliation. It subverts the 'discourses' of Englishness and Irishness. It upsets poetic canons in two countries at once. (1988: 18)

Longley's call for a transgressive cultural poetics is salutary: 'In tandem with the inter-disciplinary and the inter-national, we need the inter-sectarian, and the cross-border' (1988: 22). Comparing Scottish and (Northern) Irish poetry should prove productive, though the differences may turn out to be as significant as the similarities.

Provincialism persists in Ireland, not least of all in the so-called 'Province'. In 1998 I asked Seamus Deane why he had not chosen to write his novel, *Reading in the Dark* (1996), in the Derry dialect that he so clearly still speaks. I had some idea as to why this might be. One was his own interest in the literature of an earlier period, hence his facility for the reflective, high tone suited to a memoir. A second, more problematic hunch I had was that Deane shared an Irish Catholic antipathy to the 'bad example' set by Protestant playwrights like Synge and O'Casey, and a suspicion of anything that smacked of stage Irish or peasant parlance dressed up as 'poet's talking'. A third was market conservatism. I found his answer – that he had seen unsuccessful efforts to render that speech into print – somewhat evasive. If you look at the couple of instances where Derry speech is invoked in *Reading in the Dark* it is in the kind of comic-cut way that Scottish writers like James Kelman have argued against, wearing the clothes-pegs of dialogue rather than being integrated into the narrative. Accent is almost always apostrophised in contemporary Irish poetry, trapped in a speech bubble, denied the oxygen of publicity.

Apart from the expression 'gom' (meaning 'fool'), Deane's novel contains two clear instances of accented Irish English . In the first case, the narrator and his brother are laughing at the accents of the male relatives at their Aunt Ena's funeral:

> We would listen and then move away, choking with laughter at their accents and their repetitions. For it wasn't talking; it was more like chanting.
> 'Man dear, but that's a sore heart this time o' year, wi' Christmas on top o' us and all.'
> 'It is that, a sore heart indeed.'
> 'Aye, and at Christmas too.'
> 'Och ay, so it is. Sore surely.'
> 'Did ye see Bernadette, now; the younger sister?'
> 'Was that Bernadette? She's far changed now.'
> 'Far changed indeed. But sure she'd be shook badly now by that death.'
> 'Aye, the manner o' it. So quick.'
> 'Still, you can see the likeness to the brother. The dead spit o' him.'
> 'Which brother d'ye mean?'
> 'The lost one. Eddie. The wan that disappeared ...'
> Liam and I had stopped laughing. We both listened, but they said little before my father appeared. He motioned us over to him.
> 'Now there's a double sore heart,' said one of them as we moved off. 'The oldest boy gone and now the youngest sister. Never had good health, God help her.' (41)

'Tis a double sore heart indeed, says I. To be sure. Ironically, the narrator's own phrase – 'For it wasn't talking; it was more like chanting' – is not only dialect itself, but in its evocation of 'chanting' it recalls the etymology of 'accent', which derives from the 'chant' or 'accompanied song'. Irish writers prefer to sing unaccompanied.

The second occurrence of accented Irish English – or Ulster Scots – comes when the narrator is mapping out his territory, 'with the border writhing behind it':

> We would walk out there into Donegal in the late morning and be back
> in the city by six o'clock, in time to see the women and girls streaming
> home from the shirt factories, arms linked, so much more brightly
> dressed, so much more talkative than the men, most of whom stood at
> the street corners. We would call to them, but they would dismiss us as
> youngsters.
>   'Wheel that fella home in his pram. His mother'll be lookin' for him.'
>   'You and your wee red cheeks. Teethin' again!'
>   We'd retreat in disarray. (60)

Disarray indeed. In this array, Deane, like many Irish authors, adopts a
priestly tone, the high style, for first-person narrative. Like others too he
laments the loss of Irish and upholds the idea of an oral tradition, yet still
he opts in the end for a language that by and large uses an Irish accent
only for comic effect or to represent speech. The narrative voice remains
resolutely anglicised.

Recently, one Irish critic, interviewing Patrick McCabe, asked why
this anomaly arose between dialogue and narrative in Irish writing: 'how
is it that so many writers, writers living and writing in this country today,
when they come to the descriptive passages or the thoughtful passages
and so on, it goes into a sort of scholastic prose and it's quite different
from the dialogue?' (FitzSimon 1998: 186)

This is a good question, and while the power of the Church, the
history of colonialism, and the ill-fated experiments of Protestant
playwrights may constitute the beginnings of an answer, it is worth
attending to McCabe's immediate response:

> you describe and then suddenly you're back into God-mode, you know,
> the omnipotent narrator sort of stuff and you think 'Ah, this is wrong'
> … there does certainly seem to be a sense where the scholastic, dispas-
> sionate prose has disconnected you, or you don't want to be connected
> with the real pain of life or the real joy of life. Somehow, it's a
> fingernail-paring kind of thing, and ultimately it's not rewarding really
> for reader or writer. (186)

Compare the comments of Liz Lochhead, a performance poet and
playwright who plays with varieties of Scots, current and historical: 'I
don't write in standard English. I write in Scots English and sometimes
actually in Scots … but there's also that prose voice one feels one's got to
master, that English-male-posh-grown-up-dead speech'. (1990: 10–11)

It is precisely 'that English-male-posh-grown-up-dead speech' that
predominates in Irish poetry, not to mention plays and prose, what Mc-
Cabe calls the 'God-mode' but I prefer to think of as the priestly high

tone. Irish writers have a tendency to confine accent to quoted speech. Take Seamus Heaney's moving tribute to his mother, 'Clearances'. One verse in this powerful poem tells of Heaney's mother's anxiety about her speech:

> Fear of affectation made her affect
> Inadequacy whenever it came to
> Pronouncing words 'beyond her'. *Bertold Brek.*
> She'd manage something hampered and askew
> Every time, as if she might betray
> The hampered and inadequate by too
> Well-adjusted a vocabulary.
> With more challenge than pride, she'd tell me, 'You
> Know all them things'. So I governed my tongue
> In front of her, a genuinely well-
> adjusted adequate betrayal
> Of what I knew better. I'd *naw* and *aye*
> And decently relapse into the wrong
> Grammar which kept us allied and at bay.
>
> (Fallon and Mahon 1990: 169–70)

Little wonder Heaney's mother affected inadequacy in the presence of such an exacting and corrective attitude. For Heaney's terms here – 'hampered and askew', 'inadequate', 'the wrong Grammar' – betray an approach to language that is normative to say the least. In 'Man and Boy', a poem about his father and grandfather, Heaney cites his father describing a salmon 'As big as a wee pork pig by the sound of it' (1991: 14). The comical colloquialism – 'big as a wee' – is in sharp contrast with the sombre and serious tone of the rest of the poem. In this scenario, as in Deane's novel, it is the older generation that have accents. The narrator knows 'better', and speaks perfect English, or imagines himself so to do.

Roddy Doyle and Patrick McCabe are exceptions in fiction, but as Edna Longley argues, employing what for me is a strange sort of logic, 'prose writers, particularising character and scene, can perhaps do more than poets to preserve local words' (1991: 651). Conversely, one might say that contemporary Irish poetry, though Irish in content, is very English in form, and for good historical reasons – translation, a longer inter-action with English culture than Scotland, and a different education system to the Scottish one, the latter allowing more readily for bidialec-talism. In Scotland, writers are comfortable with both English and Scots. In Ireland, the politics of pronunciation is much more problematic.

There is a double bind, and Longley points to it, perhaps unwitting-ly. Unionist writers, in their desire to be British, underplay Ulster Scots, or, if they promote it, they do so for political rather than cultural reasons: 'The inflated and politicised claims made for Scots, which copy Sinn Féin's exploitation of the Irish language, both discredit a real case and epitomise the selective unionist use of Scotland' (1997: 114). Nationalists are likewise resistant to dialects since Irish English sounds too much like English, and recalls an earlier Anglo-Irish tradition. Irish writers would rather be priestly and classical and high in tone, or write in Irish. Sticking with Longley (who is a wonderful close reader of poetry and a marvellous polemicist), she takes issue with Tom Paulin's call for writing in Ireland's 'three fully-fledged languages – Irish, Ulster Scots and Irish English' (Paulin 1984: 191). Paulin's look at the language question throws back a marginal mirror image:

> Many words which now appear simply gnarled, or which 'make strange' or seem opaque to most readers would be released into the shaped flow of a new public language. Thus in Ireland there would exist three fully-fledged languages – Irish, Ulster Scots and Irish English. Irish and Ulster Scots would be preserved and nourished, while Irish English would be a form of modern English which draws on Irish, the Yola and Fingallian dialects, Ulster Scots, Elizabethan English, Hiberno-English, British English and American English. A confident concept of Irish English would substantially increase the vocabulary and this would invigorate the written language. A language that lives lithely on the tongue ought to be capable of becoming the flexible written instrument of a complete cultural idea. (191)

Paulin touches a nerve here. 'A confident concept of Irish English' is exactly what is missing in modern Irish literature, though recent work has gone some way to restoring confidence, at least in terms of critical credibility (Todd 1989; Wales 1992). Edna Longley takes issue with the alleged novelty of Paulin's look at the language question:

> In fact, since Yeats, such an idea, shorn of Paulin's totalitarianism, has informed the practice of the best poets. Nor can Ulster Scots, either for conversational or literary purposes, be cordoned off in some linguistic zoo-park as a backward species whose robust primitiveness may one day contribute to the national bloodstock. The natural spectrum of Seamus Heaney's vocabulary shows the way that Paulin would harshly flood-light with academy or dictionary. Moreover, Paulin has invented a new form of poetic diction by sprinkling his poems with dialect, or would-be dialect, words (in Edward Thomas's phrase) 'like the raisins that will get burnt on an ill-made cake': scuffy, choggy, glooby, claggy, biffy, keeks, glup, boke. If that's meant to be Ulster-Scots idiom, the implications are almost racist. As Thomas maintained: 'Only when a word has

become necessary can a man use it safely; if he try to impress words by force on a sudden occasion, they will either perish of his violence or betray him'. Even Synge went a bit far in the matter of idiomatic vitamin-injections. And prose-writers, particularising character and scene, can perhaps do more than poets to preserve local words. Lallans poetry, in the mouth of Hugh MacDiarmid, was virtually a one-man show. On the political front, Paulin's advocacy of a 'confident concept of Irish English' has met with some amazement among Nationalist Irish-language enthusiasts, who refer scornfully to 'the creole dialects of English'. (1991: 651)

MacDiarmid was not a one-man show. Other writers – like Lewis Grassic Gibbon, Nan Shepherd, Marion Angus, Violet Jacob and Neil Gunn – cultivated Scots in influential ways. And in any case, MacDiarmid did instil confidence in the Scots tongue. Does Longley share the scorn of 'Nationalist Irish-language enthusiasts' for 'the creole dialects of English'? Longley concludes that distance from the domestic scene gives rise to a cultivated nostalgia: 'Since Heaney, Deane and Paulin no longer live in Northern Ireland, it may be inevitable that they should fall into the tropes of stylised retrospect' (1991: 652). But 'the tropes of stylised retrospect' are far from being confined to exiles. They pervade Irish culture.

Paulin fails to mention among his 'three languages' the one that arguably exerts most pressure on Irish poets, namely 'English English', or just plain English. Longley considers Paulin's version of Ulster Scots to be impoverished and she contrasts Seamus Heaney's use of phrases like 'the body o' the kirk' (1991: 654), which strikes me as no less token-istic and clichéd, akin to Deane's 'wee red cheeks'. (Moreover, in an odd move, Longley appears to endorse Irish-language advocates who resist Paulin's notion of Irish English, which they refer to scornfully as 'the creole dialects of English'.) Well, double sore heart indeed. Hampered and askew, I ask you.

If Longley can tar Paulin with the brush of racism for proposing that 'Ulster Scots' be deliberately cultivated in such a coarse manner then something is rotten in the state of Irish letters. The 'three languages' debate in Scotland has different connotations. Douglas Dunn points to the unique Scottish achievement whereby national unity is imagined through linguistic diversity: 'Despite the survival of poetry in three langu-ages (and it was far from guaranteed) there seems a hunger for unity, not through a single language, but through one nationality that sanctions a tripled linguistic and poetic experience' (1992: xxvii). This flexibility of language choice allows for a freedom of expression and a richness of representation that makes a mockery of Muir's arguments against depicting Scotland in 'bits and patches'. Thus, for a poet like Dunn, the availability of accents is the key to accommodating variation: he maintains that the language question in Scotland has essentially been resolved through a three-way dialogue:

> That poetry in Gaelic should not only have survived, but enjoyed a renascence, is little short of miraculous. At one time a Scottish poet writing in English could be bullied into believing that his or her language was not a native tongue. Similarly, the translating-back-in-time feeling of the Scots language, with its sometimes extruded diction, could generate unsettling questions about the authenticity of what seemed an archaizing mode. Hectoring issues such as these now appear to have been settled, and the liberty of three languages established. (1992: xlvi)

Perhaps I am guilty of hectoring here, but it strikes me that 'the translating-back-in-time feeling ... with its sometimes extruded diction', a feature of some Scots writing, applies across the board – and across the water. Irish poetry is clearly marked by 'an archaizing mode'.

Before one gets too carried away with Scotland's inclusiveness it is worth pointing out that black Scottish poets such as Jackie Kay and Maud Sulter, who have contributed considerably to Scotland's literary culture, have made their homes in England. There may be openness in the languages on offer, but there is still a residual monoculturalism that mitigates against difference that is visible as well as vocal. There is further work to be done on the effects of such vocal interventions on patterns of gender and national identities.

Of course, 'English' is itself an Anglo-Latin Creole, and there are only varieties that rally round an unsettled standard, but while other varieties, such as Indian English, jockey for position, Irish English remains problematic, at least in a literary context, not least of all because Ireland's writers are self-conscious about its use. Irish English is spoken by a majority of Irish citizens, but it is a language that is devalued, and largely absent from literature, from poetry and from public life. When Roddy Doyle said that he 'wrote *The Commitments* because there are probably a million people living in suburbs in Dublin who did not exist in TV content and literature' he indicates an accentual absence (1996). What Doyle marks in some ways is the return of the vernacular. He also marks a reaction to an attitude of intellectual snobbery that disparages accentual variation from the so-called standard. There's nothing more amusing – and sad – than people with accents pontificating about purity of diction. Scottish poet Tom Leonard has parodied this stance:

> thi langwij
> a thi
> intillect hi
> said thi lang-
> wij a thi intill-
> ects Inglish.
>
> (Dunn 1992: 336)

Irish writers with strong accents that are absent from their work do not appear to see the irony. Hyper correction, the tendency to overcompensate for any possible accented deviation from the perceived standard; downright snobbery; lip service to an oral tradition that they overlook in favour of a scholastic style, a preferred academic mode that will get them recognition beyond their shores, and to hell with the homeys. Old English in new clothing, more sermon than song. Accents allowed for funny stuff and light-hearted interludes, for dialogue and quaint colloquial colour. More English than the English themselves, hence their success.

But enough of Irish poets – what about the Scots? And is there something about the profession of poetry in Ireland that rules out the working class in a way that this form of literary expression does not exclude speakers of the middle tongue in Scotland? Ireland, verses, Scotland. But let us build bridges, for if there is a different attitude to the middle tongue in the two countries, then at the level of content and theme there is much to be gained from close comparative reading. Irish and Scottish poets share the loss of a native language, the loss of land that accompanies the loss of language, the gap that opens up between fathers and sons and mothers and daughters as older forms of expression yield underfoot to more anglicised modes, the pain of exile, anger, hunger, and uprooting.

Robert Crawford, one of several Scottish poets to mix marginalised modes of speaking with cutting-edge poetic technology, has written at length in Bakhtinian terms of the in-betweenness of Scots: neither English nor Other:

> Scots is likely to strike the majority of international readers as a deliberate variation on English, which frequently quotes, re-accents, and realigns elements of English vocabulary, mixing them in a rich impurity with alien elements (in the same way that some 'Black English' works). Such Scots is a form of 'dialogized heteroglossia', which is why the use of it affects not only Scottish but English identity, in much the same way as does the superbly impure language of James Joyce and the other Modernists. (1993: 7)

In 'Mappamundi', W. N. Herbert, a poet closely linked with Crawford (they were contemporaries at Oxford doing doctorates respectively on MacDiarmid and Eliot), touches on the Scottish perception of the place of Irish poetry in the world:

> Eh've wurkt oot a poetic map o thi warld.
> Vass tracts o land ur Penntit reid tae shaw
> Englan kens naethin aboot um. Ireland's
> bin shuftit tae London, whaur
> oafficis o thi Poetry Sock occupeh fehv
> squerr mile. Seamus Heaney occupehs three
> o thon. Th'anerly ither bits in Britain
> ur Oaxfurd an Hull. Thi Pool, Scoatlan,
> an Bisley, Stroud, ur cut ti cuttilbanes in
> America, which issa grecht big burdcage wi
> a tartan rug owre ut, tae shaw
> Roabirt Lowell.
>
> (from O'Rourke 1994: 146)

Herbert hails from Dundee, a city which itself has a long and complicated history of Irish immigration and trade links with the Indian subcontinent; his views on language are worth quoting at length:

> My experience of being Scottish in England was the discovery of suppressed contrasts. Unlike Ireland, Scotland is not supposed to be 'different' or 'foreign'. It is the country which is not quite a country, possessing a language which is not really a language. To use only English or Scots, then, seems to cover up some aspect of our experience, to 'lie'. The truth about Scotland, perhaps, can only be situated between the dominant and suppressed parts of language, in the realm of the forked tongue.
>
> So I write in English and Scots. In each of these I could be accused of lying. In Scots I pretend that my basic speech – Dundonian – hasn't been atrophied by cultural neglect, and still has access to the broad vocabulary of the Scots dictionary. This creates the language of a quasi-fictional country, one which offers a critique of the present status of 'Scotland'.
>
> In English I don't lie so much as hope: that an English audience is engaged by the depiction of a challengingly 'other' culture, and that my Scottish audience has a mind of its own. (cited in O'Rourke 1994: 144)

Interestingly, Donny O'Rourke, the editor of the *Dream State* anthology, and himself an engaging Scottish poet, says: 'What is lacking in Scotland, as opposed to Ireland, is much sense of young writers using an ancient language to grapple with the present'. (1994: xxxvii) Is it perhaps that where Scottish poets resort to Old Scots, Irish poets resort to Old English?

I want to close with two poems that present very different accounts of the Irish–Scottish relationship: different versions but also different sides; betrayal but also shared suffering. The first poem is by James Joyce, and expresses the theme of betrayal that characterises much of his writing on Scotland. In 'Gas from a Burner', published in 1912, Joyce wrote:

> Poor sister Scotland! Her doom is fell
> She cannot find any more Stuarts to sell.
>
> (Levin 1977: 462–3)

The second poem, called 'Donegal', is by the Scottish Gaelic poet Derrick Thomson (Ruaraidh MacThomais), and puts matters in a different light. It is in Gaelic, and although it is called 'Donegal', its subject is the Gaelic language(s). The translation (in English, not Scots) closes with these lines:

> all it asks is to clamber, like the goats,
> on sharp rocky pinnacles, above the blue sea.
>
> Until the ragged children carry it away with them
> on the steamer to England,
> or to Glasgow, where it dies
> in its sister's arms –
> the royal language of Scotland and of Ireland
> become a sacrifice of atonement on the altar of
> riches.
>
> (Dunn 1992: 219)

A double sore heart – betrayal and sacrifice – but atonement too, as two countries marginalised by England express themselves in three languages, with one eye on England, the other on America – two countries that have been rooted out of Europe by the British state, that have avoided making eye-contact with one another, yet compatible and comparable in so many ways. Edna Longley advocates '[language] which crosses rather than takes sides' (1991: 654). Across the margins, close to the edge, lands of missing middles and double sore hearts, hampered and askew. Ireland, verses, Scotland. But one person's margin is another's metropolis. As Colin Nicholson points out:

> Scotland continues to experience, and must perforce struggle with, the imperatives of a homogenizing culture emanating from London and the south-east of England, still imperially powerful over the domestic territories of the British Isles. Such metropolitan systems of culture marginalise whatever divergences happen to exist on so-called 'peripheries'. But for those who live there these peripheries are centres. (1992; xii)

From the so-called centre, all peripheries might look the same, but from those putative peripheries, things may look – and sound – very different.

Language can take sides in different ways. Cairns Craig has pondered the paradox that Scottish literature has won its independence with a gusto lacking in the political sphere:

> Why then should Scottish literature have retained and indeed asserted its independence in a context where the Scottish people – unlike the Irish, for example – have seemed deeply resistant or apathetic about other forms of independence? ... In part it is that Scotland has, despite both internal and external pressures, never been integrated into the cultural values of the British state. The texture of Scottish life, in its religious, educational, legal, linguistic forms, remains distinct from that of England to an extent which is little recognized in England, let alone the outside world. (cited in Nicholson 1992: xii)

The habit of perceiving language as national, dialect as regional, and accent as social, is compounded in a colonial context, because class is inflected by race (and nation) and nations are subordinated as regions, provincialised and patronised. Educationalist Lindsay Paterson suggests that class is at the root of perceptions of language and art:

> Now, not much in Scottish culture happens without reference to England, and the implicit contrast running through all this is with English. The convention that has grown up along with this aggressive Scots is that an 'English' accent signifies social detachment ... But the linguistic contrast with English has not mainly been with England itself so much as with those Scottish social groups that can be claimed to have betrayed their country. (1996: 77)

Class is the key to understanding attitudes to colloquialism in a colonial context. Picking up on a point made by Raymond Williams in his subtle account of Synge and O'Casey, Declan Kiberd identifies a social strand in the language of Irish poetry:

> Irish eloquence is implicitly presented in many plays as a kind of consolation for poverty, and so O'Casey's slum-dwellers are seen to create in rolling speeches a kind of spaciousness that they can never find in their tenements. While collecting folklore in a Galway workhouse, Lady Gregory pronounced herself struck by the contrast between the destitution of the tellers and the splendour of their tales, but a more modern Irish generation has been less charmed by that disjunction. Current reservations about eloquence are dramatized with much subtlety in Brian Friel's *Translations*, where the hedge-schoolmaster, Hugh, explains his native culture to the visiting Englishman Yolland: 'Indeed,

Lieutenant. A rich language. A rich literature. You'll find, sir, that certain cultures expend on their vocabularies and syntax acquisitive energies and ostentations entirely lacking in their material lives. I suppose you could call us a spiritual people.' He claims that a 'syntax opulent with tomorrows' is 'our response to mud cabins and a diet of potatoes'. (1991: 1313)

This is a critical passage, because it captures a central tension in modern Irish writing and criticism. The old eloquence that threatened to turn into stage Irishness, the eloquence of dialect or 'poet's talking', has been supplanted by another eloquence, apparently invisible, in which writers adopt an anglicised mode that avoids engaging with an 'inferiorised' Irishness. Kiberd's allusion to 'a more modern Irish generation ... less charmed by [the] disjunction' between economic poverty and linguistic plenty is telling. For 'reservations about eloquence' are both an understandable reaction to the consoling and compensatory rhetoric that stands in for a fundamental lack – this is Williams's argument in his essay on Synge and O'Casey – but at the same time they arguably amount to a desire for upward mobility that glosses over social and linguistic realities. Speaking of Synge and his contemporaries, Williams wrote: 'What the writers found, in their own medium, was "richness", but the richness was a function of a more pressing poverty, and this was at times idealized, at times compounded'. Of O'Casey, Williams remarked: 'But the most interesting later work is where the interest always was: in the true nature of that endless fantasy of Irish talk' (1981: 148, 169). The latter part of the twentieth century witnessed a reaction against the 'Elizabethan richness' commended by Yeats. Irish poets would speak the Queen's English, but it would be the English of Elizabeth II.

Kiberd's own language is revealing. Speaking of the predicament of the Irish writer, caught between Irish and English modes, Kiberd remarks:

Many artists, most notably Synge, have sought to bridge that schism by injecting toxins of Gaelic syntax and imagery into their writing. In lesser writers, this can give rise to the factitious eloquence that is now so despised. A psychological mechanism of compensation, it can leave a certain type of Irish chauvinist congratulating himself on his poetic deviations from standard English, in order to console himself for his failure to create anything in the Irish language. (1991: 1314)

A 'factitious eloquence that is now so despised' – this is how Irish English is perceived after Synge and O'Casey, and never mind 'lesser writers'. 'Fear of affectation', Heaney's mother's fear, is there, but so too is its obverse, fear of lapsing into 'sub-standard' English. The other Irish chauvinist is the one who, having no facility for Irish, and despising Irish English as a demeaning form of English, chooses the high road and passes for English. Kiberd cites Michael Hartnett's 'A Farewell to English' as an exemplary account of the quandary of the contemporary Irish poet:

> Our commis-chefs attend and learn the trade,
> bemoan the scraps of Gaelic that they know:
> add to a simple Anglo-Saxon stock
> Cuchulainn's marrow-bones to marinate,
> a dash of Ó Rathaille simmered slow,
> a glass of University hic-haec-hoc:
> sniff and stand back and proudly offer you
> the celebrated Anglo-Irish stew.

(cited in Kiberd 1991: 1314)

While Scottish poets are proud of their Anglo-Scottish stew, it turns the stomachs of Irish poets. 'Anglo-Irish' and 'Anglo-Scottish' mean different things. The 'Anglo-Irish' tradition is bound up with a discredited dominant minority. In Scotland, Scots has emerged as a language of resistance and reinvention. Paradoxically – or perhaps not – Irish literature has enjoyed greater global success as the more anglicised form. Marilyn Reizbaum, who has done so much to establish an Irish–Scottish comparison, notes that: 'Other writers in Scotland [as well as Liz Lochhead] have used and are more and more using Scots, despite the example of Hugh MacDiarmid whose use of Scots has made his work seem inaccessible to or unworthy of an English-speaking audience' (1992: 184). Despite the example of MacDiarmid, his archaisms and inaccessibility, Scots survives as a poetic language. In Ireland, because of the example of Synge and O'Casey, Irish English founders. The language barrier is a class barrier, and a colonial one too. A double bind that ties the tongue, forks and forges it. Across the margins, language is always political, especially when it is poetic.

Notes

1   This chapter is based on a lecture delivered as part of a course called 'Border Crossings' while I was Gerard Manley Hopkins Professor of English at John Carroll University, Cleveland, Ohio, 24 September 1998. I wish to thank Jeanne Colleran and Maryclaire Moroney for the generous invitation that made this chapter possible.

2

'A warmer memory': speaking of Ireland[I]

COLIN GRAHAM

The colonized considers those venerable scholars relics and thinks of them as sleepwalkers who are living in an old dream. (Memmi 1990 [1957]: 172)

[He] says that in the course of his labours it would happen that inspiration failed him: he then would go downstairs and out of his house, and enter a public urinal whose odor was suffocating. He breathed deeply, and having thus 'approached as close as he could to the object of his horror', he returned to his work. I cannot help recalling the author's countenance, noble, emaciated, the nostrils quivering. (Bataille on Michelet, quoted in Barthes 1987 [1954]: 221)

The role of the intellectual voice in the construction of radical identities has been central to the post-colonial critique of Ireland.[2] Memmi's amusedly affectionate dismissal of 'venerable scholars' sleepwalking their way through a history that is constantly passing them by is an appealing way to circumvent the interminable question 'Can the subaltern speak?', which shadows, *in potentia*, all pronouncements on the post-colonial subject and, by analogy, all acts of speaking of Ireland too. Spivak's question and its possible declensions essentially deny that an academic voice can be elevated to a point of enlightenment above the shadows of history and, since Spivak's essay, post-colonial theory has had a short-hand way in which to express its awareness of the potentially crippling vacuity at its centre. Yet Irish criticism, post-colonial or otherwise, along with post-colonial criticism more generally, *has* gone on despite itself, with a Sisyphan doggedness, and continues to find a way of speaking 'of' Ireland. Memmi's analysis and Spivak's question pressurise intellectually radical discourse that avows to be from 'below', in two distinct ways. For Memmi, the conditions of colonialism and the post-colonial outstrip the capacities of the scholarly, so that the possibility of finding an adequate, conceptual and historical framework for the (post-)colonial is always archaised and shut off by the place in which that framework must be articulated. For Spivak, the critical voice (or any voice which speaks 'about' the colonised) immediately suffers the distancing institutionality which fractures the 'object' of discourse from the voice which speaks it and which it attempts to make its own, simultaneous 'subject'. So for both Memmi and Spivak, the very moment at which 'marginality' is articulated is the moment at which its purity founders.

In remembering the anecdote about Michelet, Bataille 'embodies' this dilemma; the impossibility of an authoritative margin. And Bataille thus ennobles the pathos of Michelet's solution – Michelet, constantly 'feeling' history as personal physiological trauma, tries to break through to 'the people', his object of study, by forcing himself through another physiological trauma which brings him face to face with the evidence of 'their' literal body politic. The quivering of Michelet's nostrils may be comically deflationary, in the first instance (like Memmi's intellectuals Michelet could be missing the substance of history, experiencing the nightmare of loss while dreaming delusions of grandeur), but his descent downstairs, his leaving of the sanctity of his own house and place of writing, and his self-degradation in primal excreta, function as a parable of the 'scholarly' when it lives off 'the people' as the basis of its existence. Michelet is alone, silent, inadequate, but ultimately valiant because he confronts and knows the abyss at the centre of his project. Above all, Michelet (in having this story known as well as enacting it) forces his writing about 'the people' to a crisis, which involves the elemental nature of his self-identity. In doing this Michelet certainly anticipates the gap between colonised people and post-colonial critique which has recently resurfaced; more profoundly he moves to the edge of that aporia, needing the object of his study to be the most sensate of realities, and insisting that it disturb his own calm. If Michelet cannot be *of* the people (and as we will see later he knew that he always failed to be), his sense of their corporeality as refracted through his own is as appropriately 'noble' and 'emaciated' as the dilemma which he lives out.

In his book on Michelet, Roland Barthes allows him to incant the indulgences of 'venerable scholars' who utter 'the people'. This essay uses Barthes' Michelet to initiate a discussion of the strategies of writing about Ireland in relation to the critical 'self' which becomes implicated in that 'Ireland'. I examine the role which the 'warmer memory' of 'the people' crucially undertakes in the processes of a criticism which takes to itself or asserts identity politics, and discuss the 'organic' necessities of the intellectual as they are reacted against and reconstructed in Joyce's Stephen Dedalus. Barthes' Michelet, my argument goes, exemplifies the fact that 'crossing marginality' is the constitutive paradox of the radical intellectual voice, and that taking that paradox to its basest, corporeal conclusion is one way in which it can be confronted and understood.

I

Michelet's view of history intrigues Barthes for many reasons (its critical sense of the bodily is only one example[3]). But above all it offers Barthes, pre-*Mythologies*, a challenge which Michelet also sets himself when he suggests that in history writing 'words must be heard which were never spoken' (quoted in Barthes 1987 [1954]: 102). In one way this is the purest of structuralist challenges; Barthes' Michelet is engaged in writing a history of France through a self-consciously doubled order of signs, in which historical events as signifiers act as a sign system in themselves, revealing history as other historians write and read it, but also point to a mythological second order of signs which delineates the words of an embedded and 'impossible language'. Michelet, as quoted by Barthes, writes:

> I was born of the people, I have the people in my heart. The monu-
> ments of its olden days have been my delight ... But the people's
> language, its language was inaccessible to me. I have not been able to
> make the people speak. (1987 [1954]: 199)

Michelet's failure as historian hinges on his acceptance of what Spivak, through Said, constantly reminds us of in 'Can the subaltern speak?': 'the critic's institutional responsibility' (1993: 75). And Michelet takes this 'responsibility' not in its meanest sense (that is, in being responsible to itself, to history, to objectivity, to disciplinary rigours), but in its weightiest connotation as predicatory foundation for the critical voice. Michelet's voice here is close to the 'baleful innocence'[4] that Spivak identifies when, in 'Can the subaltern speak?', she analyses Deleuze's conversation with Foucault. However, in the end, Michelet's baleful-ness, in its raw self-aware state, is entirely opposite to theirs. Contrast Michelet's abnegation in the urinal to Spivak's comment on Deleuze and Foucault: 'The banality of leftist intellectuals' lists of self-knowing, poli-tically canny subalterns stands revealed; representing them, the intellec-tuals represent themselves as transparent' (1993: 70). Michelet, painfully, cannot believe himself transparent and yet cannot break out of the

connective fabric of 'representation' which interweaves 'the choice of and
need for "heroes"' with re-presentation in the 'scene of writing'.[5] Writing
itself thus becomes for Michelet a bodily enterprise, just as the evidence
of the history he lives off takes on a repulsive-attractive corporeal form;
history for Michelet, as Barthes suggests, is to be 'consummated' and
'consumed' (1987 [1954]: 25). And yet Michelet's history, bound by the
strictures of representation, is riven by the movement to the material and
bodily, set against a realisation of the 'impossible language' needed to
conceive history. Both the textuality and the mystically unsayable nature
of this dilemma are embodied in Barthes' summary of Michelet's idea of
the 'historian's duties': 'The historian is in fact a civil magistrate in charge
of administering the estate of the dead' (1987 [1954]: 82). As civil *servant*
(of the people), as 'the magus who receives from the dead their actions'
and who is duty-bound to voice words 'never spoken' (82), Michelet's
own corporeality and selfhood are continually questioned in this self-
exiled existence between the paradoxically substantial ghosts which are
'the people' and the spectral realities which are historical facts.

The importance of Michelet's example lies in his ability (and in that
of Barthes' prompting critique) to make 'the people' site and receptor of
his energies while knowing their unbridgeable distance from himself.
Michelet, through Barthes, turns on their heads the transparency of the
subaltern and the self-knowing of the intellectual, so that 'the people',
source of his very existence, are at best for him an 'it', and so veering
towards being an Other, while the self 'Michelet' which writes is made
strange and decayed to itself. Moving towards the people and towards
him-self, Michelet vainly but heroically empties the heroism of history,
questions his own heroism, and keeps 'the people' from the text.

Michelet's example is no solution to the question of how the act of
representing 'the people' can be made transparent; what he stands as,
through Barthes, is a statement of the nature of the difficulties which
Spivak sees post-colonial and post-structuralist radicalism constantly
evading. Michelet frankly acknowledges the attraction of 'warmth' over
'light'; light being a 'critical idea [which] implies culture and brightness',
while warmth is 'a phenomenon of depth; it is the sign of the mass, of
the innumerable, of the people, of the barbarian' (Barthes 1987 [1954]:
184). And so it is that the 'voice of the people affords Michelet a warmer
memory that is more "linked together" than all the writings of the legis-
lators and witnesses' (Barthes 1987 [1954]: 82). The bifurcation of 'light'
and 'warmth' as poles of repulsion and attraction undoes that banality
which Spivak bemoans and puts in process a deconstruction of 'the

people' as intellectual piety.[6] The tension between scholasticism and the people can be figured in these terms, as they are for Michelet when in self-contemplation, and as they are in Joyce's Ithacan meeting of Stephen Dedalus and Leopold Bloom, as I suggest later. 'Light' and 'warmth' are definitively not opposites for Michelet; their phenomenological inter-relation and inter-reliance, and yet their inherent difference, give them a co-existence which conceptually is able to symbolise the tortured kind of self-sustenance which the intellectual voice finds itself reluctant, unable and unwilling to achieve. The 'warmth' of 'the people' for (Irish) criticism proves irresistible but may need to be forever unobtainable.

'The people' as Michelet always fails to find them are thus fetishised to some extent, and would be fully, if only he could find 'it', and so make 'it' into 'them'. 'The people' as 'it' plays hide and seek with Michelet so that he can never say for certain whether 'it' is now or will be soon a 'they'. All he has is the unrecapturable certainty of the past tense ('I was born of the people') and so he senses and remembers the 'warmth' of the people, but he never regains 'its' heat in his writing. The impossible language of the subaltern people will always attract him, by choice and by necessity; more than this, 'it' (as entity and as language) demands the absolute attention of his writing and in the end his whole self as intel-lectual. So Michelet's journey out his house is the closest that he can come to the double representation that he desires. That journey makes foundational and yet absent 'the people' and the form of language they demand but which cannot be attained.

Irish critical voices, I would argue, find themselves in varieties of Michelet's structural predicament. The 'hidden' Ireland of Irish criticism (or more generally, writing about Ireland) is very obviously conceived in many ways by many writers, but that variety of politics and of inter-pretative modes need not be flattened out to a homogeneity in order to see that the site of that 'warmth' which Michelet sought, whether 'found', disavowed or revised, is the 'impossible language' which under-lies each statement of definition of what Ireland is or might be. Michelet's self-critical journey mirrors, for example, Daniel Corkery's journey into his 'hidden Ireland', 'leaving the cities and towns behind', venturing 'among the bogs and hills, far into the mountains … [where] the native Irish … still lurked' (1967 [1924]: 19–20). But we need not take either the journey or the 'hiddenness' of Ireland so literally in order to see how Barthes' Michelet reveals the warmth which Irish criticism seeks by being Irish criticism. The remainder of this chapter attempts, firstly, to see how the impossibility of speaking 'Ireland' underlies critical writing

about Ireland, and secondly, how this aporetic 'Ireland' implicates itself
in the self of the critical voice which seeks it out. In Irish criticism, the
'crossing of margins' may initially seem to suggest a metaphoric critical
vocabulary based on a kind of cultural geography. However, such spatial
conceptualisations of radical critique also cover a fundamental critical
anxiety about the 'crossing' out of the category of the intellectual which
the intellectual voice must undertake as soon as it speaks of that cultural
geography. To extend the above example, we might ask what it is that
leads Corkery, 'upbraided', as he terms it, at the end of *The Hidden
Ireland*, to finish his book with these heartfelt words of his own
inadequacies in the face of 'the people', and to render *himself* in terms of
physical incapacity:

> Here, then, my tribute, humble, halting, inept, unlearned, to a body of
> men who for long were almost entirely forgotten and who as yet are
> only clumsily apprehended – their lives, their works, their genius. Of all
> our forgotten dead, of whom these words following have been written,
> those poets, it seems to me, most terribly upbraid us: 'To them has been
> meted out the second death – the lot feared beyond all else by men of
> honour. They have been buried by the false hands of strangers in the
> deep pit of contempt, reproach and forgetfulness – an unmerited grave
> of silence and shame'. (1967 [1924]: 295)[7]

II

In speaking of Ireland, in any critical or metadiscursive context, the
question of what the word 'Ireland' signifies is obviously semantically
and politically fraught to the extent that it is tempting to suggest that
Irish critical discourse, in its multiple manifestations, finds itself *de facto*
always returned to exactly that defining activity. Giving 'Ireland' a meaning which fills out the term comfortably is seemingly the underwriting
principle of Irish criticism's existence, with the aesthetic, the cultural,
the generic and the 'minor' all given a presence within critical writing on
Ireland by their contribution as slivers of 'Ireland' which are temporarily
imagined as hived off from the undisruptable, unseeable whole. Each
book and article on Joyce or on the Whiteboys, each individual account
of Irish memoir, each reclamation of Irishness from the diaspora, then
risks becoming subsumed in the perpetually deferred but always desired,
Casaubon-like quest for the settling of 'the Irish question', a question
which both begs a definition and a definitive answer; and that question
transcends the politics of Unionism or nationalism, the force of

revisionist historiography, the regional and the local, and indeed the course of historical change itself, being always sure of its position as the *raison d'être* of what is spoken about 'Ireland' and never in fear of alteration by these pronouncements. It needs to be made clear that this is not the same as saying that Ireland as a political entity has never changed; nor is it the same as saying that Irish nationalism has a fixed, archaic sense of what the Irish nation is. This underwriting 'Ireland' is constituted not primarily by politics and history *per se*, but by the structural necessities of (what is inadequately termed) 'identity' and by the predominance of proper noun and adjective, Ireland and Irish, as identifications of place, identity and, just as comprehensively, academic discipline and intellectual thought; this 'Ireland' inhabits a domain which is closer, as an analogy, to the inevitable ever-presence of historiography within the evidence of history than it is to historical 'facts' or interpretations themselves. It is always implied and implicated in criticism's voice rather than being given substance by any transparent relationship which criticism claims to have with its object. Hence to speak of Ireland is to project forward to a future project in which all facts, opinions and statements on Ireland find a home within the encompassment of what 'Ireland' is; this 'Ireland' is constituted through critical language as a 'transcendental signified' which 'would place a reassuring end to the reference from sign to sign' (Derrida 1976: 49). And so we should anticipate that the expectation of reassurance and resolution will pervade the Irish critical voice, its 'Ireland' always cast hopefully into a sense of an ending.

However, such an 'end' would be far from only reassuring, since this critically anticipated 'Ireland' also brings a danger. Its putative and ever-promised achievement carries with it the death of 'Ireland' as foundation; in its promise to 'place a reassuring end to the reference from sign to sign' it carries the fear of turning 'Ireland' into real 'presence'. Through its articulation 'Ireland' is *not* the effective end-point of a narrative, despite the constant futurity of a notional set of Irelands in the realm of the political. The transcendent 'Ireland', which accommodates all statements about Ireland, slips out of time before it can be entrapped, and thus avoids collapsing the trope of narration. Indeed it could be argued (as I suggest below with regard to Declan Kiberd and Emer Nolan in their critiques of Joyce) that narrative time is the way in which 'Ireland' escapes and puts off definition, ensuring its place as an absent presence now, and a promissory repletion later, when time itself is full and 'nostalgia' no longer has a role.

This notionally transcendent 'Ireland' is not, then, just another sign. No alternative transcendent lies in wait to take over; the possible alternatives (those which are foundational, for example, in liberal humanism *and* nationalism – the literary, the good, the just) have already been deployed in the perpetual process of definition and fixing, and so exist below the transcendent status of 'Ireland', having been in its service. Hence there must be a necessarily tremulous method of approaching 'Ireland' within Irish criticism; on the one hand seeking its definition as the key to all mythologies, as the *langue* of speaking about Ireland which binds together and explains the fact of speech in this discourse itself; on the other hand knowing that the act of defining 'Ireland' as *langue* begs a replacement which is unimaginable, given the exhaustion of resources deployed in order to get to that point of definition. For the critical voice, the 'self' which speaks in relation to 'Ireland' needs, expects and functions by the anticipation of continual deferral; only its own collapse into a vacuum is imaginable at any point beyond the ever held-off future moment of absolute fulfilment. Put simply, if 'Ireland' existed self-evidently, why would we need to examine it, contest it, invent it, state its anomalies, or write it?

That this underwriting 'Ireland' is a deferred transcendent, and thus always a symbol of futurity, could of course be traced in a genealogical way to the history of its formation. In a Foucauldian scheme one might be able to untangle the epistemic moment(s) at which 'Ireland' became the invisible listener to and ultimate receptor of all statements about itself. This would undoubtedly be a result of the context of European nationalism and British colonialism in which the structural functions of Irish nationality are again and again thrust into teleologies of progress and change, so that future transcendence is the refuge for 'Ireland', clearing the way for political Irelands to manifest themselves. (The work of Joep Leerssen (1996a, 1996b) represents a remarkable contribution towards such a project.) More clearly evident is that any post-colonial critique of Irish culture, for all its apparent and/or potential radicalism, runs the danger of all post-colonialism in regard to its understanding of time itself. As Anne McClintock points out, through the term 'post-colonial theory' the focus of critical analysis

> is ... shifted from the binary axis of *power* ... to the binary axis of *time*, an axis even less productive of political nuance ... [The] *singularity* of the term effects a re-centering of global history around the single rubric of European time. Colonialism returns at the moment of its disappearance. (1993: 292–3, original emphasis)

For Irish post-colonialism the effects of this narrativising of a theory, which has a supposed theoretical bent towards the synchronic examination of systems of colonialism, are doubly inflected through the particularities of the nation-narrative and its state of suspension post-Partition. Thus the paradoxical reintroduction of 'European time' lifts 'Ireland' as a form of address out of its sign system and propels it for its own preservation into a future which needs to be undetermined. The desire for a synchronous definition of what 'Ireland' is remains behind as trace evidence of this continual projection forward, while the linear temporality which enthrals radical politics mean that 'Ireland' makes promises which perplexingly are never kept.

III

The link between the twin strands I have been developing here can be established in another way by noting their shared trait of impossibility and their use of a necessary intractability; 'Ireland' as subject, as well as the critical voice which speaks of 'Ireland', both disappear into a place which lies beyond what can be known, so that the tantalising prospect of a new 'Bloomusalem' remains eternally fresh. Hence Michelet and his relationship with 'the people' is useful since it embodies both a subject and an academic voice which needs and constitutes this dependency as perpetually unfulfilled.

Barthes' Michelet represents a paragon of the academic quest for its national subject; raising that search to the level of trauma certainly clarifies that the 'culture' sought can function as much more than a material superstructure, and that it has a predicatory role for critical discourse which is projected into an ever-deferred future. The drama of Michelet's descent from his study is also personal, in the most fundamental of ways. It is Michelet who feels the need for 'the people' (to an extent it is Michelet who labels and identifies 'the people'), just as it is Michelet who is jarred by the 'impossible language' which keeps the people 'inaccessible' (Barthes 1987 [1954]: 188); Michelet 'sees himself as feeble, unhealthy' (Moriarty 1991: 187), and, in the urinal, his abjection is a dramatised ontological crisis in which Michelet's 'self' competes for priority with the idea of 'the people' which induces his crisis. In inculcating a pathos of the critical voice as disjunctive from yet seeking for its subject, Michelet acknowledges the risk of a bathetic self-engrossment that is its own end. We may not expect others to follow his extraordinary example, but keeping Michelet in mind helps in thinking about how the

critical voice in its own right is constituted by its construction of
'Ireland', and how, as in Michelet, the primacy of 'the people', or
'Ireland', may fade into the critical voice's fascinated instabilities as it
searches for the fantasy of teleological fulfilment. Beyond this, we might
also begin to ask what happens to the known instabilities and incapacities
of the intellectual voice once, at least superficially, the 'post-national',
'post-identity', postmodern world seemingly lessens the need for a radicalism which speaks 'for' anyone collectively. What Michelet through
Barthes seems to reveal is a particular instance of the necessity for the
intellectual to cross its own margins; when the ideological insistence on
margins begins to lessen, the role of the radical institutionalised critical
voice is thrown back upon itself. When Ireland, for example, is
reconceived in a 'Council of the Isles' context, will the radical intellectual
be left behind, assuming it is speaking 'for', but listening increasingly to
itself? The remainder of this essay is an attempt to understand the
structure of that intellectual voice, as a beginning to thinking about how
it might suffer change.

Michelet's search for atonement in the urinal has an obvious
counterpart in Irish writing in the 'Ithaca' chapter of *Ulysses*, when
Stephen and Bloom urinate together. Equally the Stephen of *Stephen
Hero, A Portrait of the Artist as a Young Man*, and *Ulysses* has in many
ways become the archetype of a fledging Irish intellectual, the 'under-
graduate artist-hero' (Deane 1990: 31) in dispute with himself on the
question of his relation to 'the people'. In his diary entries at the end of *A
Portrait*, Stephen famously and bitingly recounts Mulrennan's return
from the west of Ireland where 'he met an old man there in a mountain
cabin' (Joyce 1992 [1916]: 274). Stephen's 'fear [of the peasant's] ...
redrimmed horny eyes' and his anticipated 'struggle' to the death with
the old man pass quickly into a reconsideration which is a form of
distanciation: '... Till what? Till he yield to me? No. I mean him no
harm' (274). As David Cairns and Shaun Richards note, Joyce's attempt
to achieve an unobtrusive concern for the peasant, to reassess and
diminish the pressing claims of Stephen's connection with the peasant, is
'untypical' of the period (1988: 85). Moreover, Len Platt points to the
distinct way in which Joyce negotiates the ever-present demands of
addressing a 'real' Ireland in opposition to Synge and Yeats, whose
contact with the peasantry is too often unproblematically physical and
has a 'reality [which] throbs with significance, which the text simply and
humbly transcribes' (1998: 199). Stephen's existence as character and as
representation of the young intellectual is the initial act of distancing

which enables Joyce to escape the necessity for 'struggle' (which, arguably, Yeats and Synge escape through a revivalist form of mythologis-
ation). Stephen's passingly anticipated, chaotic confrontation with the
peasant is a direct inversion of Michelet's panic at the loss of contact
with the people, and reiterates 'the people' as a structural foundation
before the revolution of a contingent forgetting of them.

As Declan Kiberd says of this part of Stephen's narrative, '[this] is
not just a caustic parody of Synge's peasants, but a terrified recognition
that Joyce's liberation from Ireland was more apparent than real' (1995:
333). Kiberd sees here an anticipation of the 'guilty compromise' of 'post-
colonial exile' which means, on the part of the writer, 'a refusal of a more
direct engagement' (333), and this is certainly one way of expressing the
dynamic of 'the people' for the post-colonial intellectual. Stephen's diary
entry for 14 April is also part of a sequence which is illuminated further
by looking at the preceding and successive days – the previous day's entry
recounts the much discussed revelation that the word 'tundish' is
'English and good old blunt English too' (Joyce 1992 [1916]: 274), while
on 15 April Stephen writes of his last meeting with EC, a meeting which,
like that *imagined* the day before with the peasant, ends with an effort at
achieved distance ('in fact ... O, give it up, old chap! Sleep it off!' [275]).
The three entries replay *encounters* of varying hostility (with the Dean of
Studies and his Englishness, the peasant and the acute version of Irishness which he represents, EC and the tremor which her sexuality brings
to Stephen) and are thus linked by the repulsion-attraction form of
personalised contact, merging the physically abject with the politically
righteous, which Michelet desires and which Stephen is, in all three
cases, pulled towards before finding forms of rejection which are suitably
temperate.

If, as is often the case, Stephen is elided into 'Joyce', then there is
work to be done by the radical Irish critic in reclaiming through Joyce's
writing a voicing of either 'Ireland' or 'the people', and not only because,
as Vincent Cheng, points out, Joyce's relation to Ireland has traditionally
gone relatively unprivileged because the 'Academy ... has chosen to construct a sanitized "Joyce" whose contributions are now to be measured
only by the standards of canonical High Modernism' (1995: 3). Stephen's
rejection of something that is at least Dublin if not Ireland, followed by
his (and Joyce's) return to that rejected entity in *Ulysses* and *Finnegans
Wake*, seems to offer a possibility of redemption for an Irish criticism of
Joyce. Kiberd, for example, finds Ireland emerging triumphant in a form
of orality which is a 'tradition' set in motion alongside the 'bookishness'

also found in *Ulysses*, with the balance 'tilted finally towards the older tradition' (1995: 355). Emer Nolan suggests of *Finnegans Wake* that

> [when] ALP-as-river joins the sea, something specific is lost in an oceanic chaos. As with her, so with Ireland. Both have entered the devil's era of modernity, liberated into difference, lost to identity. This is not a simple transition. Joyce both celebrates and mourns it; his readers have so far tended only to join in the celebration (1995: 181).

Taken together, the rising again of oral tradition out of 'bookishness' and the mourning of lost identity looks to be a reinstatement, through Joyce, of the forms of nationalism he himself ironises.[8] Nolan and Kiberd, in their different ways, insist on Joyce's reintroduction and resolution of the post-colonial problematic of 'the people' as precept for intellectual speech. Seamus Deane's remark on a post-Burkean Irish trope which sees Ireland as having 'no narrative but the narrative of nostalgia' embodies, in charged forms, both Kiberd's 'tradition' 'renovated' (another of Deane's words) and Nolan's deeply ethical pleading for a 'mourning' of lost 'identity' and the realisation that incoherence is the price of the 'devil's era of modernity'.

Deane says, further, that '[nostalgia] was the dynamic that impelled the search for the future' (1997: 2).[9] Certainly, critical futures are implied by Nolan and Kiberd; in Nolan's complaint that Joyce's 'readers have so far tended' to read his nationalism in one way, and in Kiberd's suggestion that *Ulysses* 'would only be given its full expression in the act of being read aloud' (1995: 355) (presumably also anticipating *Finnegans Wake*), both critics position their analyses as entailing future projects. These futures importantly cast Joyce's Ireland from an unsatisfactorily indeterminate present into a futurity which can allow for a resolution which can be decided upon *then*; and that future is dependent on a wash back to what is figured as a 'past', a 'tradition', a state before 'loss'. In other words, underwriting these complex critical repositionings of Joyce and Ireland is a state in which Joyce and Ireland are synchronous with each other, but only because history coincides with itself so that the organicism of the intellectual is transformed into transparency, and in which the past we have never known meets itself again in the future.

The lesson which Michelet so painfully learns is, however, a very different one, and might be borne in mind as we construct our future critical Irelands out of our putative Irish pasts. The 'lost' organicism of the intellectual is too swiftly conceptualised in temporal terms, which mutate easily into historical terms. Both Stephen and Michelet see their distance from 'the people' as an occurrence of biography; therefore a slippage to personal narrative, then to cultural narrative, is an enticing mindset for imagining the 'recovery' of this loss. But as Anne McClintock (quoted on p. 38) reminds us, the post-colonial compels criticism, against its own better judgement, to see linear temporalities first and synchronous structures second. Stephen's biography in *A Portrait*, along with his return to Ireland in *Ulysses*, tantalises with the elements necessary for Deane's nostalgic futures, but, I would argue, Michelet's example usefully reveals to us that the failure to meet 'the people' in the intellectual voice, the failure to make the subaltern speak, is not a temporally 'new' phenomenon at any stage, but is a consistent fate of the intellectual voice. Thus pasts are nostalgised and futures imagined, and mourning and prediction (and more grandly, prophecy) become compelling modes of academic speech.

IV

Joyce as ever can be seen to anticipate this. Bloom is no 'redrimmed horny' eyed peasant, but in his Everyman role he becomes Stephen's counter-part and his substitute father. Stephen and Bloom are, archetypally in early Joyce criticism, 'two souls in search of the spiritual salvation that they can never find' (Roberts 1970: 612). As Anthony Burgess puts it, in 'Ithaca' even the act of making cocoa reminds us 'of the unconscious groping towards each other that Bloom and Stephen have, usually off their guard, in the margins of thought, exhibited all day' (1982: 171). For Stephen, Bloom can be what Mulrennan's old man of the West cannot be. In 'Ithaca' the ordinariness of the corporeal becomes an act of celebration rather than abjection, constituting a response to Michelet's crisis and his privation.

In a critique of Fredric Jameson's account of *Ulysses*, Thomas Hofheinz lambastes Jameson's continual positioning of the collective as primary over the individual (the 'theoretical compulsion to subsume individual human lives within ideal collectivities' (1995: 15)[10]). While Jameson's position is somewhat caricatured as a result, the point is well made:

> Jameson's assertion that the cocoa-making [in 'Ithaca'] is 'inauthentic' because the kettle is mass-produced and somehow not an organic part of its user's 'destiny' depends upon a bizarre assumption that such domestically familiar objects are not meaningful to those individuals who cherish them. (1995: 14)

Developing Hofheinz's point, I want to argue that in 'Ithaca' can be found a moment of ordinariness (among many possible others) which addresses the profound tension between the collective and the personal, the national and the 'human', the political and the everyday, and which also reveals Joyce's text to be returning to that fundamental notion of 'the people' as precept for the intellectual voice in a revising if open-ended (and eventually gendered) way. And in his defence of cocoa-making, Hofheinz is strangely correct, since it is in the ordinariness of the bodily, not in a 'struggle' with a cultural demon, that Stephen, the figure of the intellectual, finds himself as close as possible to 'the people' in a new way ('the people' having been redefined and so brought closer). Here also the self-excoriation which Michelet forces himself to endure is circumvented, as are the stringencies of grand narrative, and the pain and mourning of continual cultural deferral are turned to shadows.

Suzette A. Henke, in *James Joyce and the Politics of Desire*, writes: '"Ithaca" concludes the man's epic (his)story' (1990: 122). My contention about the chapter is similar, in that the aspects of 'Ithaca' on which I focus show Joyce's text to be coincidental with the fundamentals of the Micheletian dilemma, in which history and heroism are brought into contact with the voice that speaks both. The rich duality of the Bloom–Stephen relationship (father–son, Everyman–intellectual) plays out the desire for 'contact' which Stephen retracts from in three different ways in the diary entries towards the end of *A Portrait* because the crises which result are self-perpetuating. 'Ithaca' reveals these '(his)stories' to be imbued with a masculine fear of 'contact' which is simultaneously a fear of being washed over by 'history' ('history' demanding the presence of the people and so functioning as the reminder that the intellectual self should efface itself to the point of transparency and to the end of alterity). Hence I am suggesting that reading 'Ithaca' provides some kind of release from the bonds which Michelet confronts, by particularising, parodying and accepting the structural deficiencies of the intellectual voice.

Stepping outside 7 Eccles Street, Stephen Dedalus and Leopold Bloom contemplate the stars, their wonder continually compromised by the 'catechismal' (or impersonal) technique of the Ithacan narrative.[11] Bloom's meditations 'of evolution increasingly vaster' (Joyce 1989 [1922]: 573) lead him through the celestial and the mathematical and the contemplation of alien life 'Martian, Mercurial, Veneral, Jovian, Saturnian, Neptunian or Uranian' (574), and eventually to a typical Bloomian recognition that 'an apogean humanity of beings created in varying forms ... would probably there as here remain inalterably and inalienably attached to vanities, to vanities of vanities and to all that is vanity' (574). Bloom's often touchingly instinctive inclusivity here reaches an 'apogee' in that it extends even beyond the human to the literally 'alien', the ultimate of alterities, and collapses all into the humility of 'vanity'. Bloom then considers the stars, as a 'logical conclusion' (the term which the cate-chismal questioning voice uses at this point), a 'Utopia', 'a mobility of illusory forms immobilised in space, remobilised in air' (575), and ends his 'logical' contemplation with the realisation that the heavenly bodies are 'a past which possibly had ceased to exist as a present before its probable spectators had entered actual present existence' (575).

Bloom is, in other words, able to analytically recognise the 'present' as always viewing the past, recapturing it as itself, and, I would suggest, it is this (as a capacity for such realisation and in the particular analysis of 'time') which allows the relationship between Stephen and Bloom to move on to a reorganisation of the recurrent trope of the intellectual's distance from *his* subject and his own (male) subjectivity. Bloom has, to put it a different way, an ability to understand time as past, present and (Utopian) future, but not necessarily to need them placed in that order, and in this his potential liberation from the absolutes of linearity allow his sense of the 'moment' and of synchronicity a freedom for which Stephen is still 'struggling'.

Bloom's passage from the rationalised discourse of astronomy, inter-laced with his contemplation of humanity's 'vanity' and inability to place even the night sky in a telos, is the bridge which facilitates the bringing together of Stephen and Molly (which has been signalled earlier, for example, in the cabman's shelter, when Bloom shows Stephen a mildly erotic photograph of Molly [533]). This is effected firstly through the 'esthetic value' which poets have attached to the heavens (a reminder of Stephen's pretensions), and then through the 'science' of 'selenographical charts', since this in turn allows for a question asking about the 'special affinities ... between the moon and woman' (576). Stephen and Bloom now both gaze up at Molly's window, and Bloom having elucidated 'the mystery of an invisible attractive person, his wife Marion (Molly) Bloom', Stephen and Bloom are left silently to contemplate each other. The moment of contact is described thus:

Both then were silent?
Silent, each contemplating the other in both mirrors of the reciprocal flesh of theirhisnothis fellowfaces. (577)

Thinking of Molly turns both *men* to a contemplation of each other and of what Emmanuel Levinas calls 'the face of the Other as … the original site of the sensible' (Hand 1996: 82). After an undefined period of inactivity in which Michelet's 'light' and 'warmth' are integrated in Stephen and Bloom's joint illumination by the feminised moon/Molly's lamp, the 'sensible' 'flesh' of this masculinised moment of silence is turned to the most male of endings when Stephen and Bloom, at 'Stephen's suggestion, at Bloom's instigation' (577), piss together.

Clearly, in terms of my argument, this incidental moment in 'Ithaca' can be set beside Michelet as a replaying and a revision of that desire for intellectual self-abjection. Stephen, unlike Michelet, has Bloom by his side and an absoluteness of isolation is no longer possible. The suspended looking into 'theirhisnothis fellowfaces' is not only for Stephen (and Bloom) a form of companionship, and, despite the gendered nature of the events, it is not solely a male bonding exercise. As Levinas suggests: 'The Other becomes my neighbour precisely through the way his face summons me, calls for me, begs for me, and in doing so recalls my responsibility, and calls me into question' (Hand 1996: 83). The 'fellow-faces' are defined at this point by each other alone,[12] and the ethical charge which they create in seeing each other's faces is, as Levinas suggests, both the end of an enclosed sense of self and a recall of responsibility which is forced to 'face' the Other, not just imagine it distantly. The alterity found in the 'face to face' calls Stephen to a responsibility for the Other which he (if we take 'Stephen' as a continuous character in Joyce's fiction) has not been able to find previously within the Dean's paternalistic colonialism, the peasant's challenge of essential Irishness, or EC's romance. And in a sense we have moved here beyond Michelet's trauma of the loss of 'the people' as subject. As Levinas suggests: 'It is as if the other established a relationship or a relationship were established whose whole intensity consists in not presupposing the idea of community' (Hand 1996: 83–4). Stephen and Bloom have, in other words, fleetingly surpassed that sometimes stifling foundational need to speak to the future nation, seeing in the difference of each other a 'deeper' version of ethical responsibility than even that 'depth' which the 'the people' gives. As Richard Kearney says, Joyce 'preferred to deconstruct rather than reconstruct the myth of a Unity of Culture'; and we can go further than Kearney, since when Joyce finds 'where *I* becomes *other*' it is not only that he overturns 'the classic myth of narrative as a one-dimensional communication of some fixed predetermined meaning'; the I becoming other is the point at which Joyce gets underneath the 'Unity of Culture', showing its attested status as only-possible-first-principle to be a self-perpetuating sense of its own 'destiny' which has an alternative and an alterity (Kearney 1988: 32, 34).[13] What Paul Ricouer calls 'the aporia of anchoring', the central trauma of the self, is deployed by Joyce as an antidote to the 'identification with heroic figures [which] clearly displays … otherness assumed as one's own'; for Stephen and Bloom the time which is described as 'theirhisnothis' turns a captured otherness into a confronted alterity and dissipates the trait of 'loyalty' to 'causes' which results from the *idem* and *ipse* natures of the self being made to 'overlap', to 'accord with one another'. Of this process, which conflates sameness and selfhood, Ricouer writes: '[an] element of loyalty is thus incorporated into character and makes it turn toward fidelity, hence toward maintaining the self' (1992: 52, 121). Joyce's Stephen struggles with the necessity of 'loyalty' as part of the maintenance of the self, and in 'Ithaca', in a qualified, gendered, almost comic way, he glimpses in the face of Bloom a form of otherness which demands no outside 'loyalty' but fulfils his desire and lost hope for responsibility.

It is thus in the paring away of '(his)story', in the recognition of 'vanity', and despite the incessant demands of logical and temporal linearity, that Stephen finds literal bodily relief following ethical contact. The fraught distance, which is necessarily embedded in the intellectual's idea of 'the people', is temporarily forgotten. This, of course, must end. The time has already ended, once the pissing begins, and as they piss, Bloom and Stephen are reasserted in their difference – Bloom's thoughts remain bodily (he contemplates, among other things, 'tumescence', 'irritability', 'sanitariness' [577]), and Stephen is reclaimed by the intellectual and by history (he is parodied as his thoughts wander to the sanctity of Christ's foreskin). However, just before this, staring at each other, Bloom and Stephen have found themselves not 'presupposing the idea of community' and the idea of 'the people', but under the thrall of an 'anarchic responsibility, which summons me from a nowhere into a present time' (Hand 1996: 84), much as the light from the stars which Bloom observes arrives in the present from an unimaginable time and distance.

This Ithacan moment is not new in Joyce. In his recent essay on Joyce and Scotland, Willy Maley notes how politically informed Joyce criticism has ignored the historicity of Scotland as an example for Joyce (this saying as much about Irish criticism as it does about Joyce's ignorance of Scotland). Maley sifts a series a references to Scotland in Joyce, including the point in 'The Dead' when Gabriel, still recently stung by Miss Ivors' accusation of West Britonism, talks distractedly to

Mrs Malins about Glasgow. The repeated banality of the phrases
'beautiful house' and 'nice friends', and 'good crossing' and 'beautiful
crossing' to describe Mrs Malins' journey, on one level registers the
grating ordinariness which she irritatingly represents in Gabriel's mind
as he tries 'to banish ... all memory of the unpleasant incident with Miss
Ivors' (quoted in Maley 2000b: 210). But that word 'crossing' is also a
way of reprimanding Gabriel, just as Miss Ivors has done. Mrs Malins'
crossing to him, in Dublin, is in contrast to his inability to 'cross' to her
decent ordinariness. So while the prevailing discourse here of is one sea-
crossings, of inter-British Isles movement, Gabriel's self-regarding dis-
missiveness reminds the reader of the 'fellowfaces' who may seem initially erased by the intellectual, but who will always return as a summons
to ethics.

To summarise this chapter, it is necessary to go back to the beginning. Michelet sets out for us, through Barthes' reading of him, how 'the
people' troubles academic discourse on culture and how it becomes a
foundational pretext for speaking about that culture at all. My suggestion is that in the Irish context, and partly in relation to the particular
forms of political and historical factors which have been in play, Ireland
has become an always 'putative', future 'Ireland' demanding a double
form of deference: insisting on being bowed down to, while at the same
time pressing itself into a continual futurity which can never facilitate
full definition. Corkery's feeling of being 'upbraided' by the Ireland he
tries to describe replicates Michelet's disappointed desire to meet, touch
and ventriloquise 'the people' without the self-consciousness of knowing
that such articulation is happening. The example of Stephen in Joyce's
works shows that, firstly, in *A Portrait*, Stephen is unwilling to accept the
duty to 'the people' with which Michelet berates himself. Then, in
'Ithaca', Stephen, face to face with Bloom, replaces that rejection of 'the
people' with a form of alterity that questions his ontology at a level
beyond Michelet's intellectual dilemma. For Stephen, Bloom is 'the face
of the Other' which demands what Levinas calls 'the right to be' (Hand
1996: 86), and which in so doing questions Stephen's own justification
for being. This is why Barthes' Michelet constitutes so important a
model; he both reveals the barrier to be surpassed, and at the same time
his insistence on the ethics which throw the intellectual self into doubt is
a lesson in how to move on. For the Irish critical voice, the recognition
can be that 'Ireland' calls that voice home beguilingly and encom-
passingly. We may not want to change this destiny for our critique,
which may be fated to fall forever into unsatisfied forms of definition,

and become servile to the idea of 'the people'.[14] But we need to know its existence, its power to turn us into Memmi's 'sleepwalkers', and that, despite placing itself as a presupposition, it is not the only place in which the ethics of the critical voice can find their justification.

Notes

1 A version of this chapter will appear in my book *Deconstructing Ireland: Identity, Theory, Culture* (2001).
2 On this subject see Kirkland (1999), to whose essay I am indebted.
3 Michael Moriarty notes that the 'phenomenological stress on the lived experience of a physical individual in contact with the material world is central to Barthes' ... *Michelet* of 1954' (1991: 187).
4 Discussing Deleuze's 'genuflection' to 'the worker's struggle' Spivak writes: 'The invocation of the worker's struggle is baleful in its very innocence' (1993: 67).
5 See Spivak's discussion of *Vertretung* and *Darstellung* (1993: 74, and *passim*).
6 Spivak writes: 'The subaltern cannot speak. There is no virtue in global laundry lists with "woman" as a pious item' (1993: 104).
7 The quotation with which Corkery ends is from Alice Stopford Green, *The Making of Ireland and Its Undoing* (1909).
8 This has certainly been the most contentious of issues in the Irish reclamation of Joyce in recent years, and Nolan's study is one of the most sustained and clear advocations of the argument. Cheng, in *Joyce, Race and Empire*, for all that he submits to L. P. Curtis's scheme of *Punch*-inspired and evidenced racism, in the end argues for a Joyce set against 'the pitfalls and limits of certain very alluring but limited nationalist visions ... [by which] one is doomed to failure by reproducing the same binary hierarchies inherited from one's oppressors' (1995: 218). On this topic see also Maley (1998).
9 I am indebted here to Claire Connolly's discussion (2000) of Deane's *Strange Country*.
10 Hofheinz is writing specifically of Jameson's essay '*Ulysses* in History' (1982), and more generally of Jameson's *The Political Unconscious: Narrative as a Socially Symbolic Act* (1982b).
11 Thus the technique is standardly described in Joyce criticism; see, for example, Gifford and Seidman 1989: 566.
12 Though see Vicki Mahaffey's reading of the same incident, which suggests that this pragmatic joining of Stephen and Bloom is symbolised as 'waste' through their urination. Mahaffey does however note that an 'example of mutual recognition through difference is the moment when Bloom and Stephen regard each other as both familiar and strange, when they see in each other the outlines of the "*unheimlich*"' (1999: 259, 264).
13 Kearney's analysis sees Joyce's project as one revolving, in a double sense, on the word.
14 The 'servility' of the intellectual to Irish nationalism is famously summarised by Padraig Pearse: 'Patriotism is at once a faith and a service ... and it is not sufficient to say "I believe" unless one can also say "I serve"'. Pearse's words here are quoted (with slight variation) concerning Joyce's views of nationalism by Seamus Deane (1987: 94–5) and Richard Kearney (1988: 32).

3

'Where do you belong?': De-scribing Imperial identity from alien to migrant

PETER CHILDS

Introduction: writing the post-colonial nation

'England,' said Christophine who was watching me, 'you think there is such a place?' … 'You do not believe there is a country called England?' She blinked and answered quickly, 'I don't *know*, I know what I see with my eyes and I never see it.' (Jean Rhys, *Wide Sargasso Sea*, 1996, 92)

Understanding the novel as a formative influence on the imagining of national collectivity, Timothy Brennan argues that 'it is especially in Third World fiction after the Second World War that the fictional uses of "nation" and "nationalism" are most pronounced.' He goes on to say that, following the war, English social identity underwent a transformation based on its earlier imperial encounters. Colonialism in reverse created 'a new sense of what it means to be "English"' (1990: 46–7). However, Brennan does not consider what changes have been wrought on that society, what reinventions of tradition have manufactured new Englands of the mind, alongside the pronouncements of newly forged nationalist identities in 'Third World' fiction. By contrast, Patrick Wright does this in some detail in *On Living in an Old Country*, where he makes an important if familiar point that is necessary to balance the vogue for Benedict Anderson's conception of the nation as 'imagined community' (1991). Wright, considering post-war England, concludes that

> [people] live in different worlds even though they share the same locality: *there is no single community or quarter*. What is pleasantly 'old' for one person is decayed and broken for another. Just as a person with money has a different experience of shopping in the area than someone with almost none, a white homeowner is likely to have a different experience of the police … than a black person – homeowner or not. (1985: 237, original emphasis).

Perhaps more than any other, the nation that has been colonised in reverse exists at the intersection of these two viewpoints about the differentiated, conceptualised community – a new sense of not Englishness but Englishnesses: multiple imagined communities within and not across nations.

Similarly, Homi K. Bhabha argues that, contrary to the rhetoric of national selfhood that proclaims the homogeneity of a 'people', the nation 'is *internally* marked by the discourses of minorities, the heterogeneous histories of contending peoples, antagonistic authorities and tense locations of cultural difference' (1994: 148, original emphasis). There is thus a tension between statements that refer to a past, pre-formed nation and to a (differently constituted) present nation. In post-colonial space, where a large plurality of communities are imagined within the nation, the cultural threat of difference shifts from the nation's exteriorities to its interiorities because the unified people invoked by the narrative differ from the diverse people addressed by it: 'the wandering peoples who will not be contained within the *Heim* of the national culture … but are themselves the marks of a shifting boundary that alienates the frontiers of the modern nation' (Bhabha 1994: 164). Taking his cue from Anderson, Bhabha has also claimed to identify in cultural representations and narratives the nation's discursive position between polarised terms such as private/public, progression/regression, belonging/alienation, custom/power, order/licence, justice/injustice. For Bhabha, it is at the intersection of each of these pairs of conflictual articulations, not in their resolution, that the nation inheres. Arguing that the nation is also revealed in its margins, he proposes that a nation is less defined by its distinctions from an 'other' that is outside it than by narratives at the inward and outward facing boundaries between cultures and texts.

To take a further example, Edward Said has maintained in *Culture and Imperialism* (1993) that the imposition of national identity is implicit in the domestic novel in its boundaries, exclusions, and silences – the Imperial interstices of English society that Said's contrapuntal reading can reveal by turning the narrative inside out, temporarily centralising its margins. Such emphases on borders, heterogeneity, and reading against the grain require analyses of national identity which move away from binaries of domestic and foreign, native and immigrant, belonging and alienation, and instead consider the people, cultures and discourses that cross or collapse these categories.

In his analysis of a black Atlantic culture, Paul Gilroy proposes diaspora as an alternative way of understanding modernity and cultural identities (the term 'diaspora' was taken up by historians of Africa and slavery in the 1950s, although Gilroy says that its genealogy as a concept in black cultural history is obscure). He maintains that diasporic identities work at 'other levels than those marked by national boundaries' (1993: 218). Similarly, Stuart Hall argues that the contemporary signifi-cance of diaspora in the Caribbean can be apprehended through Lacan's theory of enunciation and its implications for identity. If the speaking and spoken subject do not coincide then 'identity' is therefore not an essence but a positioning in discourse, and that positioning, or represen-tation, will itself be conditioned by the position spoken from. Hall adds to this Derrida's theory of meaning, which is always deferred as it forever disseminates along endless chains of signifiers: meaning is constantly *moving*. While not quite suggesting that everyone is now a migrant, Hall does believe that the post-structuralist theory of linguistic identity offers a new paradigm for viewing human identity as always moving, never arrived at, and therefore in some ways related to diaspora rather than a discourse of homelands and rootedness. Hall compares this with a tradi-tional view of identity in the West, which sees it as self-evident and self-defining. A single, homogenous selfhood is replaced by a recognition of a disseminated heterogeneity and diversity: 'Diaspora identities are those which are constantly producing and reproducing themselves anew, through transformation and difference' (1993: 400). Given this re-evaluation of identity, Hall argues that diasporic culture is instrumental in post-colonial formations wherever there is recognition of displacement, hybridity, colonial history, and creolised language. Consequently, Gilroy can conclude that

> Black Britain defines itself crucially as part of a diaspora. Its unique cultures draw inspiration from those developed by black populations elsewhere. In particular, the culture and politics of black America and the Caribbean have become raw materials for creative processes which redefine what it means to be black, adapting it to distinctively British experiences and meanings. (1987: 154)

Gilroy sees this model of identity opposed and preferable to those of national, 'racial' and ethnic absolutism (1987: 154–7). But in what langu-age is such a change in self-definition conducted and what is at stake in a shift from a discourse that sees polarised identities (dis)located in either rootedness or rootlessness, belonging or alienation, to one that sees them characterised by relocations through oscillation, travel, diaspora and migration? This is a question I will discuss in the rest of this essay with reference to prose writings concerned with India(ns) and England since Independence in 1947.

No direction home

> The whole point that made it impossible to give way, even to argue, was that we *couldn't* go Home. We couldn't become English, because we were half-Indian. We couldn't become Indian, because we were half-English. We could only stay where we were and be what we were. (Patrick Taylor, a Eurasian character in *Bhowani Junction*, by John Masters, 1983, 27–8, original emphasis)

The British frequently felt alienated in India, psychically distanced from those they were surrounded by, physically distanced from those they were emotionally close to. Their 'home' and 'people' were elsewhere, they did not 'belong' on the sub-continent, in the hostile climate and unfamiliar terrain under *The Alien Sky*, in the title of one of Paul Scott's early novels. They frequently clung all the more forcefully therefore to ideas of a national identity, whose characteristics were, unsurprisingly, defined and intensified by perceived differences from an Indian identity. Yet, Indian otherness in relation to a fully formed English national identity was, up until recent reconsiderations in Indo-Anglian fiction, described in terms of rootlessness, fragmentation and alienation. Which is to say that under the Raj the English were partly comforted in their psychical and physical alienation by metaphysical assertions on the historical and national homelessness of Indians. A common opinion has also been that, post-Independence, the British sense of Imperial and economic failure was projected on to migrating peoples, as aliens, immigrants, foreigners. What is clear in both instances, despite the contrary positions of the English in India and in England, is a straightforward contrast between those with homes, roots, nations, and those who are rootless, homeless, and alien – an opposition which has found a place near the centre of discussions of English and Indian difference.

Rabindranath Tagore once noted that there is no word in any Indian language equivalent to 'nation' but that this concept arrived in India with the British. In contrast, Sir Arthur Quiller-Couch, in his study of patriotism and literature, argues that English patriotism 'intensifies upon that which, untranslatable to the foreigner, is comprised for us in a single easy word – Home'; a term which means not only 'family house' but 'place of belonging' and 'nation' (1918: 306). With the imposition of English rule and culture, in addition to the arrival of the concept of the 'nation', enshrined in the colonies as 'Home', Indian nationalist identity arose in response to British colonialism and therefore, to a considerable extent, to British nationalism, which always bolstered its hold in India by claiming to unify a fragmented country. It is the protracted reiteration of India as a self-alienated, divided country that has most frequently marked perceptions of an Indo-British national difference and also characterised British action in India (policies of division are well documented, from the British fetishisation of Hindu–Muslim differences in the eighteenth century to the splitting of Bengal at the beginning of the twentieth century). This process did not end with Independence and, according to Ashis Bannerjee, 'Partition seems to have driven very deep into the Indian political psyche the threat of further dismemberment' (1989: 284). Bannerjee also argues that successfully laying the blame for Partition at the feet of the English 'Divide and Rule' policy was a major triumph for the Nationalists, who pitted the idea of India's 'unity in diversity' against it. This was a particular feat of unification considering that Tagore had concluded, along with the British, that the greatest barriers to nationalism in India on top of a religious divide were the divisions and inequalities of caste within Hindu society (Tagore 1976: 66–7).

According to O. P. Bhatnagar, British colonialism created in India 'a psycho-pathological complex of racial, cultural, and moral crisis' (1985: 27). Bhatnagar ascribes this simply to the importation and imposition of Western ideas, institutions, and values. He argues that the colonial encounter provoked a response

> of caricature, sarcasm and satire, exposing both who refused to change as in *The Private Life of an Indian Prince* by Mulk Raj Anand, and who changed to be an underdog as in G. V. Desani's *All About H. Hatterr*. Caricatures of anglicized men and women have become a favourite with several post-independence Indian English novelists … showing the cultural inadequacy of the change. (1985: 35)

Yet, many of those Westernised Indians were also the most powerful individuals on the sub-continent. Nehru wrote in *The Discovery of India* that:

> India was in my blood and there was much in her that instinctively thrilled me. And yet, I approached her almost as an alien critic, full of dislike for the present as well as for many of the relics of the past I saw. To some extent I came to her via the West and looked at her as a friendly Westerner might have done. (1946: 38)

The aggregate of these examples suggests that to an appreciable extent the perception of the representative Indian as at best self-divided and at

worst a homeless and rootless outsider was established in a wide range of
discourses, as here at the centre of Indian government at Independence,
by the displacement of British colonial alienation.

Neither here nor there: alienation

In terms of the Indo-British relationship, the half-century since
Independence has been a period of sundering, as India and Pakistan
have been prised away from Britain, but also one of suturing, as Indo-
Anglian or Indian English identities have been uneasily embraced or at
least acknowledged. India has always figured in Englishness as one kind
of defining difference to some degree, long before discourses of English
national identity surfaced themselves. From this perspective, when
national images of Englishness did gain wide currency in the nineteenth
century, the importance of India to English identity lay in its status as
imperial possession, as an immense proof of an increasingly problematic
national accomplishment in the world.

Just as many commentators argue that the English founded and
found themselves as an imperial nation in India, for Paul Scott it is in
India that the English 'came to the end of themselves' (1976a [1973]: 3).
Throughout *The Raj Quartet*, and particularly in the second volume *The
Day of the Scorpion*, there is a repeated image of the British protected by
their carapace – by their imperial history, their traditions and certainties
represented by their white skins. Scott portrays this as a circle of
Englishness, both containing and protecting the Anglo-Indians, and he
has several of the characters either transgress or die within its circum-
ference (usually figured as a circle of light or fire). By contrast, in Scott's
final novel, *Staying On*, Lucy Smalley, last representative of Scott's
colonials in the 1970s, feels her 'own white skin' is 'increasingly incapable
of containing me, let alone of acting as defensive armour' (1978: 111). For
Scott, this is the difference that developed between the 1940s and 1970s:
a loss of the sense of imperial history containing English identity like a
skin or protecting it like a shell. This gradual collapse of a similarly
slowly established Englishness located in an imperial identity, which for
Scott stems from the inter-war years and especially the rise of Gandhi's
'Quit India' campaign, is evident in many ways post-war. For example,
in 1951 nearly sixty per cent of the UK population was unable to name a
single British colony (Lawrence 1982: 69–70). On the other hand, a
second point which is not incompatible with the first is that R. K.
Narayan recorded on his visit to the UK in the 1950s that '[most] people

in England, especially those living outside London, were unaware that India was no longer a colony' (1990: 32) – and this at a time when Enoch Powell was planning India's re-conquest in order to resurrect England's greatness (Nairn 1981: 265).

In the 1960s India acquired a significant role in Euroamerican discourse only as the West's immaterial opposite. From the legacy of Huxley, Hesse and Isherwood, the British, from the Beatles to Iris Murdoch (for example, *Bruno's Dream*, 1969), sought enlightenment in India just as many of their ancestors claimed to export it there. But to most British people, the sun had set on not just the Empire but the Commonwealth too. At the end of the decade, the editorial of a special sixtieth anniversary edition of *The Round Table* lamented that

> [the] fading of the vision of Empire-Commonwealth as an instrument of British world power has brought with it the progressive attenuation of interest in the Commonwealth within Britain herself. *Aut Caesar, aut nihil.* To many people in Britain the Commonwealth now seems a useless, indeed an inconvenient pretence. It is no longer a source of wealth and power ... As for the British, the urban society of the rich, white northern hemisphere appears more elegant, more amusing, above all, for the time being, more profitable than those far-away lands of which we remember less and less. The creeping indifference of Britain herself to the world community, which she founded, is perhaps the greatest danger that the Commonwealth has to face. (Howard and Jackson 1970: 379)

This is similar to the sentiment conveyed by Scott's *The Raj Quartet*, which laments the indifference of the English 'at home' to their own Empire even in the 1940s. In the final volume, *A Division of the Spoils*, a major new character, an historian called Guy Perron, is introduced. His Aunt Charlotte comes to represent for Perron the indifference of the British to their Empire. Her refusal to accept any part of the responsibility for 'the one-quarter million deaths in the Punjab and elsewhere ... confirmed my impression of her historical significance (and mine), of the overwhelming importance of the part that had been played in British-Indian affairs by the indifference and the ignorance of the English at home' (1976b: 222). At the end of the Second World War, Perron's Aunt Charlotte thinks Britain should quit India, but only because all Britain's resources are needed to fund post-war rebuilding and the Welfare State. In a letter to his publisher in 1973, Scott emphasised that this was central to the entire *Quartet*:

The overall argument of the sequence is that the greatest contribution
to the tragi-comedy of Anglo-India was the total indifference to and
ignorance of Indian affairs of the people at home, who finally decided
to hand India back in as many pieces as was necessary so long as it was
got rid of. (1990)

In 1960, ten writers, including Doris Lessing and J. P. Donleavy, contributed to a book entitled *Alienation*, which offered a series of personal
views of England from people born elsewhere. One entry was by Victor
Anant, an Indian who saw himself as one of 'Macaulay's bastards'. His
essay is called 'The three faces of an Indian', and begins:

It is characteristic of people born, historically speaking, on a borderline
and reared in a no-man's land of values to live lazily; and lazy living, in
plainer words, means living by opportunism, treachery, cowardice,
hypocrisy, and wit. There is no effort implied in such a way of life, no
awareness of a need to make a deliberate choice. It is a fact of nature –
just as, in politics, the notorious unreliability of border areas may
primarily be a result of their geographical situation.
    I know this from direct reflection on my own situation. I am one of
these people. (1960: 79)

Anant believes this because he has decided after seven years of living in
London that people like himself are 'homeless orphans': 'We are looked
upon as children of conflict, born in transit, that we will eternally remain
torn within ourselves but that we can be taught to recognize our duality
... playing the role of cultural schizophrenic' (89). Anant sees Britain
and India as two nations, like other nation-pairs, who are incompatible
until the production of what he calls 'the third face', a face not in-
between but different from either of the other two.

Anant goes on to say that 'people like me are heirs to two sets of
customs, are shaped, in our daily lives, by dual codes of behaviour' (80).
At one stage he makes a remark similar to Timothy Brennan's earlier
point about the emphasis on 'the nation' in post-war 'Third World
fiction'.[1] But Anant makes his point in relation to pre-Independence
fiction, about which he writes that it

stands only as a record of a phase in Indian history. Because that period
is significant the writing is also significant; but because of the very
nature of their preoccupations those writers all seem to be posing one
problem of a nation, not the many problems of an individual. Not one
Indian – or a type of Indian – but a whole community was the hero. (81)

This sounds like a criticism of socialist realism but its chief concern
seems to be with the lack of alternative narratives in Indian fiction in

English. The story was always (although Anant makes an exception of Narayan) concerned with national liberation.

Post-Independence writers, up to 1960, had for Anant a 'curiously self-analytical tremor'. There were themes in their work of individual aspiration, self-mockery, nostalgia for Indo-Britain, and self-propaganda, 'but the most important significant trend in this new range of articulateness is the *distance* now created between the individual Indian and India. Alienation has arrived in Bombay, Madras and Calcutta' (1960: 84, original emphasis).

Anant's awareness of being an heir to two sets of customs is a feeling that also impinges on other 'Indian' writers growing up in Britain. Meera Syal describes how her semi-autobiographical character Anita came to this realisation that she had no home that she had ever visited:

> Papa's singing always unleashed these emotions which were unfamiliar and instinctive at the same time, in a language I could not recognise but felt I could speak in my sleep, in my dreams, evocative of a country I had never visited but which sounded like the only home I had ever known. The songs made me realise that there was a corner of me that would be forever not England. (1996: 11)

In a further example of her alienation from a national identity, Syal's Anita talks of her separation from cultural roots:

> I always came bottom in history; I did not want to be taught what a mess my relatives had made of India since the British left them (their fault of course, nothing to do with me), and longed to ask them why, after so many years of hating the 'goras', had they packed up their cases and followed them back here. (1996: 211–12)[2]

Perhaps the best-known writer on cultural alienation of this kind in the 1960s is the Trinidadian of Indian descent V. S. Naipaul. Naipaul's displaced individuals epitomise the highpoint of Indian homelessness in the face of English modes of identity. Homi Bhabha even talks of his forays into theory beginning at the moment he realised that the metaphor of the home in the West, both in terms of belonging and of the 'house of fiction', would not accommodate his reading of diaspora and homelessness in Naipaul's *A House for Mr Biswas* (1961): 'here you had a novel where the realism, if you like, was unable to contain the anguish of displacement and movement as poor Mr. Biswas was looking for his house.' Naipaul also exemplifies Bhabha's comment on key aspects of post-colonial identity, which had been overlooked up to the eighties by theory in its discussion of interpellation. He explains that '[the] colonial subject was actually very aware of his or her inauthenticity ... a form of inauthenticity which was clearly seen to be culturally, politically, and socially constructed and which then turns into a kind of inward experience, through which most of political and social life is negotiated' (Bhabha 1991: 57). Of equal importance to his fiction, Naipaul's *An Area of Darkness* (1964) set an agenda that was addressed by much subsequent writing on India in a way that no book had achieved since *A Passage to India*. In it he decides that: 'With one part of myself I felt the coming together of England and India as a violation; with the other I saw it as ridiculous, resulting in a comic mixture of costumes and the widespread use of an imperfectly understood language' (1968: 189–90). Stepping over the borderline between England and India in the 1960s created for Naipaul both tragedy and comedy. The people it created for Naipaul were *The Mimic Men* (1967) who did not 'belong', like his protagonist Ralph Singh: 'where you are born is a funny thing ... You get to know the trees and the plants. You will never know any other trees and plants like that ... You go away. You ask, "What is that tree?" Somebody will tell you ... But it isn't the same' (171).

For Naipaul, India had disappeared from English identity by the 1960s: 'after less than twenty years India has faded out of the British consciousness: the Raj was an expression of the English involvement with themselves rather than with the country they ruled' (1968: 200–1). But Indians had reintroduced themselves to Britain since the 1950s, preparing the ground for a burst of Indo-Anglian cultural activity from the 1980s onwards, and prompting what Salman Rushdie calls a 'raj revival' by the British in the wake of 'Mrs Torture's' election – a nostalgia for the Empire that has been most notable in the literary establishment's reception of certain novels and then films which portrayed a tragicomic mixture of 'costume' dramas against the backdrop of an 'imperfectly understood' culture. The repeated phase of alienation was playing itself out as farce, and Anglo-Indians themselves began to explore new identities based less on displacement, homelessness, and exile than on migration and relocation.

Travelling home: migration

But most of the time, people will ask me – will ask anyone like me – are you Indian? Pakistani? English? ... We are increasingly becoming a world of migrants, made up of bits and fragments from here, there. We are here and we have never really left anywhere we have been. (Salman Rushdie, quoted in Marzorati 1989: 100)

Writing in 1990, Viney Kirpal divides the Indian novel in English into the three generations I am also outlining in this essay: those who emerged pre-independence in the 1930s, those who up-rooted themselves in Independence/independence in the 1960s and those who engaged with a post-colonial world in the 1980s (xiii–xxiii). Though somewhat overly focused on decades, Kirpal is able to sketch a coherent overview. The emergent writers of the 1930s, Raja Rao, Mulk Raj Anand, and R. K. Narayan, blazed a trail in terms of Indian identity, Indian uses of the English language, and the relation of the two to colonialism and nationalism. As we have seen, much of the writing of the 1960s concerned itself with East–West divisions, with dislocations, separations and alienations. The turning point for the 1980s was *Midnight's Children*, but Kirpal argues that the defining features of novels of that decade are, again, parallels between the individual and the nation's history; protagonists who are tense and sceptical; language that is taut, energetic and concise as well as humorous; and characters that are cosmopolitan and not regionalised.

Also since the 1960s, not least because far more Indian writing in English has been written since then, the idea of Indian identity has figured more prominently in narratives of Englishness as the troubled margins of the nation have increasingly been located not just at its geo-cultural edges but internally, as I discussed in the introduction. In Indian English writing, Englishness has become a subject for explicit discussion, review and satire in terms of imperialism (as in Gita Mehta's *Raj* or Shashi Tharoor's *The Great Indian Novel*) or in terms of the aftermath of imperialism (as in Ruth Prawer Jhabvala's novels). There is a greater prominence for Indian English fiction in debates over the novel than ever before, especially through such well-publicised work as Vikram Seth's *A Suitable Boy* and Arundhati Roy's *The God of Small Things*. Accompanying this is the redefinition of anglicised or westernised Indian identity post-Independence (in several of Desai's novels, Upamanyu Chatterjee's *English, August* or Rukun Advani's *Beethoven Among the Cows*). In British writing there is the growing English analysis of key colonial events from the 'mutiny' in 1857 (J. G. Farrell's *The Siege of Krishnapur*) through to Partition in 1947 (Paul Scott's *The Raj Quartet*). Many novels of national crisis chart the shift more forcibly in terms of a post-imperial malaise, as do a number of post-war plays which feature characters left over from the raj, such as Osborne's *Look Back in Anger* and David Edgar's *Destiny*. But, nearly all recent 'British' novels about India are retrospective: Farrell, Scott, Masters, Kaye and others write historical fiction. By contrast, far more novels by Indian than English novelists have been written about Partition (Coswajee 1982; Dhawan 1982; Kirpal 1990). More importantly for my discussion there is the ever-growing number of texts that articulate or examine new Indian English or migrant ethnicities in the UK (for example, by Rushdie, Amit Chaudhuri, Sunetra Gupta, Hanif Kureishi, Ravinder Randhawa and Shyama Perera).

These texts have articulated new positions on questions of national and international identity, opposing the New Right's attempt in Britain to delimit the possibilities for versions of Englishness by opposing ideas of one 'true' identity and another which departs from it, and instead predicating identity on valorised qualities of newness and migrancy, of not origin but originality, redefining 'this and that' away from 'self' and 'other' and towards the welcome recognition of movements between 'here' and 'there'.

Discussion of alienation is founded upon a discourse of belonging. The alien is displaced from a 'home' which is either elsewhere or, in the title of Kamala Markandaya's 1972 novel, 'nowhere'. Her protagonist, Srinivas, is *The Nowhere Man* because he does not 'belong' in Britain, where he has little family, few friends, and a house but not a 'home'. Which is to say that the discourse of alienation itself rests on ideas of locations and roots, not relocations and movements. To be alien is not to belong, and similarly to be a migrant is not to have a 'home'. Yet migration, on the one hand, implies a movement between two or more 'homes', and on the other hand suggests that identity inheres not in rootedness, in an arguably parochial idea of continuity-in-stasis, but in travelling. In other words, the image of the alien is created by the questions asked in framing identity: 'where do you belong?', 'where do you come from?', 'where is your home?' These are questions about (places in) the past, not the future; they are questions about where individuals and their families originate, not where they are headed. This is not to deny the cultural investment individuals have in the first kind of question but to insist that the second kind is also, if not more, important. In contrast to Markandaya's 'Nowhere' man, Hanif Kureishi's Karim Amir in *The Buddha of Suburbia* is 'from the south London suburbs ... and going somewhere' (1990: 3), a balance of past and future, 'home' and 'somewhere' else, which locates identity in one place but then relocates it in the movement to another.

I am therefore arguing for a revised concept of identity emerging in Indo-Anglian fiction along lines suggested by Stuart Hall and Paul Gilroy. 'We are all migrants', as Hall almost says, or a 'world of migrants' as Rushdie has it. A new ethnicity needs to work through ideas of identity based on home, belonging and origins to ones based on travel, change, and not the past but the present and the future. Hall calls these identities 'diasporic', focusing on the large-scale movements of peoples, which I am calling 'migrant', focusing on the translocated individual protagonists of Indo-Anglian writings. Not 'immigrant', which suggests the individual should not be here, or 'emigrant', which suggests that the individual felt he or she should not be 'there', but 'migrant' – someone who is not standing still but someone who has travelled and who is 'going somewhere'. Saladin, Rushdie's demonised migrant in *The Satanic Verses*, is told: 'Your soul, my dear sir, is the same. Only in its migration it has adopted this presently varying form' (1988: 277). The migrant, whether bird or human, does not simply belong in one place and not another but moves between both places, or, more correctly, along a line from one place to another. Particular locations represent the endpoint of identities, which are characterised not by stasis but movement.

Migration oversteps the *Borderline* (1981), Kureishi's early play about South Asians in Britain. *The Buddha of Suburbia* also concerns transgression in its two parts, about the suburb and the city, as Karim sets off on his picaresque travels from one to the other. Yet this not a comment solely on Indo-Anglian identity – it applies to all the characters in the novel. Almost everyone travels, either between countries (Haroon, Shinko, Changez, Charlie) or to the city (Jamila, Eva and Haroon with Karim and Charlie in tow). In these migrations, there is not a sense of rootlessness but of having moved on, of having not transcended but travelled away from and of wanting to continue 'somewhere else'; such that the identities which interest the reader are those that morph and evolve not those that remain constant or 'rooted'. Kureishi's primary characters are not nowhere figures who have lost one home and found only alienation in another, but migrants who develop, accumulate and grow away from the racism, stereotypes, and traditions that hem in their lives in the first half of the novel. Their addition to the places to which they relocate does not mean dilution but increase, just as the bilingualist who is so often denigrated out of hand for having a comparative understanding of the host language can instead or also be venerated for an understanding of linguistic difference and semantic plurality.[3] It is usually when identity or expression is owned and guarded, dressed up as correct or incorrect, that alienation results. This is the language of home, belonging, origin, purity and their opposites of alienation and contamination, which refuse alternative emphases on newness, travel, and miscegenation. It has in this regard been salutary to observe the rise in Indian travel writing on England since the 1980s, after Nirad Chaudhuri's pioneering account in *A Passage to England* (1959) of his alienation ('I had not been there even a week when I realised how impossible it was for either the East or the West to resemble each other in any significant trait' [25]). The new accounts range from Prafulla Mohanti's experience of the contrasts between Indian village life and British urban racism in *Through Brown Eyes* (1985) to Firdaus Kanga's tempered Anglophilia, from Bombay to Finchley, in *Heaven on Wheels* (1991).

The need for a realignment of identity from an axis of belonging/ alienation to a continuum of translocated migrancy is evident in the discourse of essentialised national identities. Like all metaphysical identities, Englishness is *essentially* only a vacant term; to acknowledge its history and negotiate its political uses, its vacancy needs to be continually restated and its space contested. This can best happen through a constant revision of the traditional view of national identity in relation to the current population, since Englishness is manufactured and maintained in the vacillation between the two. In short, both new mythology and cultural displacement confound any 'authentic' sense of a 'national' identity and point to its redundancy (Bhabha 1990a). The nation, as a perpetually vacant yet ideologically saturated (id)entity, is reinhabited at its every contact with whatever cultures are (over)lapping its borders, revising the established and redirecting the ongoing narrative of Englishness (Gilroy 1993: 217–19). Against this, Krishan Kumar sees the contemporary 'Englishness' of the New Right stepping from the ruins of 'Britishness' in the 1970s and 1980s brought about by the three-cornered assertions of Celtic nationalism (1995: 89). The new voices of Englishness were Margaret Thatcher, Norman Tebbit, and Enoch Powell, who asserted their nationalism not just against those in other countries but against the 'foreigners' within, and in doing so replicated in a post-colonial Britain the racist effects of nationalism under colonialism.[4] This is itself a notable transition turning xenophobia inwards to a focal point within the nation's borders.

While national identities are frequently both overcoded and circumscribed in terms of 'racial' and physical markers, it is only since the phenomenon that Louise Bennett's poem calls 'Colonisation in reverse' (Markham 1989: 62–3) that the possibility of Black Englishnesses has been widely discussed, not least by and in relation to second-generation Asians in Britain, in terms of New ethnicities and multiple identities. Kureishi, who in this at least resembles his hero Karim, is a case in point:

born in England of an English mother and a father who came to the UK from Bombay in 1947. In *The Buddha of Suburbia*, the theme of hybridity is constant: the first page tells us 'I am an Englishman born and bred, almost … Perhaps it is the odd mixture of continents and blood, of here and there, of belonging and not, that makes me restless and easily bored' (1990: 3). Questions of place and hybridity pervade the book, which in several ways concerns Karim Amir's oscillation between these poles of 'here and there'. The novel deals with identity primarily in terms of relocation, as does Kureishi's earlier autobiographical essay 'The rainbow sign', which is structured in a tripartite movement from 'One: England', through 'Two: Pakistan', back to 'Three: England' (Kureishi 1989).[5] This has two significances I want to mention here. On the one hand, the essay signals the move away from unitary subject positions, and on the other it locates identity in terms of an oscillation, a movement back and forth between widely divergent cultures as well as places. As Homi K. Bhabha says, there is a

> need to think beyond narratives of originary and initial subjectivities and to focus on those moments or processes that are produced in the articulation of cultural differences. These 'in-between' spaces provide the terrain for elaborating strategies of selfhood – singular or communal – that initiate new signs of identity. (1994: 1–2)

Kureishi's novel operates in this in-between space but it charts a specific trajectory across it. Karim's path takes him from the 'not white/not quite' beginning of that 'almost' to a recognition of a new ethnicity, a variant of black Englishness, towards the end of the book – an identity not 'rooted' in a country but in a newness born in travel, anchored by the new shoots nourished by relocation. In parallel, the sexual and racial prejudices of English society are shown to accommodate the resurgence of the political New Right, which surfaces at the book's close as Karim and others celebrate their personal successes in a restaurant on the night of the 1979 general election. In keeping with Hall's idea of a new ethnicity perpetuated through diaspora, the primary model Kureishi uses to indicate cultural shift is that of migrancy – from India to England, from the suburbs to the city, from England to the United States and back. But at the same time, the counter-forces of reactionary nationalism are shown to be resisting any revision to the monologic narrative of Englishness, just as the New Right also emerges to counter the new forces that the novel has described, from radical music, squats, sexual freedom, drugs and miscegenation, to socialism and, of course, migrancy.

To take a final example, Rushdie is himself a first-generation migrant who considers himself to have only 'imaginary homelands' (1992: 17), to have been borne across and 'translated' like the hero of his novel *Shame* (1983). Paul Gilroy writes that, since the 'Rushdie Affair' of 1989:

> Whatever view of Rushdie one holds, his fate offers another small, but significant, omen of the extent to which the almost metaphysical values of England and Englishness are currently being contested through their connection to 'race' and ethnicity. His experiences are also a reminder of the difficulties involved in attempts to construct a more pluralistic, post-colonial sense of British culture and national identity. (1993: 10–11)[6]

The difficulties arise because of a need in those who consider themselves rooted and belonging to protect an authentic, unalienated identity which perceives itself (and its home and wealth) to be in danger from newness, from the migrant who is unfamiliar. But the moment of importance for Indian diasporic identities in England did not occur with 'The Rushdie Affair' over *The Satanic Verses* in 1989 but with *Midnight's Children* and the urban riots in 1981. Syed Manzu Islam writes: 'If "15 August 1947" is the name of the event in the historical time of the Indian postcolonial nation state, then it is equivalent to the time of "London, 1981" – the historical time of the migrant as subject of the British national state' (1999: 129). If Partition was the final colonial act of alienation enforced by the English in India, then its legacy, so evident in 1960s writing, began to be extirpated by the migrant's assertion of new British ethnicities on the streets and in the publishing houses of London from 1981 onwards. The journey is itself not only temporal, but one of millions of postcolonial migrants world-wide, and of the concept of national identity itself, from Anant's England of 'Alienation' to Rushdie's 'world of migrants'.

Notes

1 Brennan is of course indebted to Fredric Jameson's point in his controversial essay on 'third world literature' (1986) to which Aijaz Ahmad (1987) took such exception.
2 'Gora' was a word applied to the British tommies and means 'whitey'. The *Hobson-Jobson* dictionary says it applies to any European who is not a sahib (Yule and Burnell 1996: 388).
3 For a discussion of this see Tzvetan Todorov's essay 'Dialogism and schizophrenia' in his book *An Other Tongue* (1994), 203–14.
4 Tom Nairn amongst others has argued that racism derives from nationalism. Nairn is salutary because he argues it in terms of Englishness in his influential book *The Break-up of Britain* (1981).

5 Interestingly, the essay's reprinting in the volume entitled *Patriotism* edited by
   Raphael Samuel (1989), under the title 'London and Karachi', organises its
   headings around these cities and not their countries, thus honing the specificity
   of the earlier publication.
6 See also Talal Asad's article on 'the Rushdie Affair' (1990) in which, *contra*
   Gilroy's and Bhabha's position, he suggests that distinct cultural traditions need
   to be acknowledged, for both logical and political reasons.

4

Gender and nation: debatable lands and passable boundaries

AILEEN CHRISTIANSON

'Debatable lands' and 'passable boundaries': both concepts are emblematic of the kind of inevitably shifting, multi-dimensional perspectives that are found in any consideration of nation and gender.[1] Homi K. Bhabha writes of the 'ambivalent margin of the nation-space' and 'the ambivalent, antagonistic perspective of nation as narration' (1990a: 4). These 'ambivalent margins' are contained in the Scottish metaphor of the Debatable Land. Originally the term was for that area 'holdin to be Debateable Lands betwixt the twa nations of Scotland and England', and very specifically defined as 'now forming the Parishes of Canonbie in Scotland and Kirk Andrews on Esk in England' (Carlyle 1868: appendix 33, 1). It became first a term for the Scottish/English borders as a whole, which were fought over and consequently neither static nor entirely definable. Its subsequent manifestation is as a metaphor for any borderline state or idea.[2] Women's writing in particular is often assessed in terms of borders and margins that provide those tropes of liminality used to point up a fluidity and an ambiguity identified with the position of women in society. Maggie Humm, for example, adopts such terms in ways that echo the Scots concept of debatable land:

> The border is not only a question of place which assumes some one dimensional literary plane without hierarchy or class but of *difference*, since in looking at literary borders we find asymmetry, absence and marginalisation ... Border women are not decentred fragmented individuals but writers who have begun to cohere a core identity by entering the transitional space between self and other. The border is the trope of difference and potential conflict, between races, between cultures and between sexual preferences. (1991: 6)

Nation, region, gender, class and sexuality: they all produce their own boundaries and we pass back and forth across them throughout our lives, all of them constructed by our circumstances and our societies' expectations. These multi-dimensional perspectives are in a perpetual state of flux, with oppositions and alliances in constantly shifting relationships, both within ourselves and with others. Edward Said writes in *Culture and Imperialism* of the great many languages, histories and forms that circulate '[in] the cultural discourses of decolonization' (1993: 280). It is this same kind of plurality, circularity and interconnection that occurs in the conflicting discourses of nation, region, gender, sexuality and class. These discourses also provide the problematic 'contours' in what Said refers to as our 'imagined or ideal community' (280). His notion of literature and culture 'as hybrid … and encumbered, or entangled and overlapping with what used to be regarded as extraneous elements' (384) also applies to society's conflicting demands on our loyalty, creating particular and, at times, clashing demands on our commitment. The question is how conjunctions and disjunctions between the marginality of our femaleness and of our nation are to be figured. This idea of a double marginality was expressed by Joy Hendry in her image 'The double knot in the peeny' (1987a), invented to describe 'the double disadvantage suffered by Scottish women writers in being firstly Scottish and secondly female' (1987b: 291). Suzanne Hagemann writes that 'beyond their historically specific situation, woman and Scots are paradigms of marginality' (1997: 323) but this seems too mechanistic a separation of women and Scots, positioning them in a binary relationship, as though Scots are all male; it imposes too formulaic a narrative structure on the national history, risking exactly that kind of rigidity which excludes gender from the nation's narrative.

If nationalism is a post-rationalist or enlightenment substitute for religion, with fake-historical roots to legitimise it, as Benedict Anderson argues (1991: 11), then given the patriarchal, male-centred nature of Christianity and most other world religions, and the oppressive nature of their relation to women, it is inevitable that the construction of the idea of the 'nation' should have been equally male-centred and patriarchal, manifesting itself in the traditions of warrior nations, warrior clan systems, with women as bearers of warriors or symbolic female figures of nationhood – the equivalent nationalist muses to the traditionally female poetic muse. The Irish poet Eavan Boland problematises this within the Irish context:

Within a poetry inflected by its national tradition, women have often been double-exposed, like a flawed photograph, over the image and identity of the nation. The nationalization of the feminine, the feminization of the national, had become a powerful and customary inscription in the poetry of that very nineteenth-century Ireland. 'Kathleen ni Houlihan!' exclaimed McNeice. 'Why/must a country like a ship or a car, be always/female?' (1996: 196)

Anderson, despite seeing nationhood as a socio-cultural concept, a given, like gender: 'everyone can, should, will "have" a nationality, as he or she "has" a gender' (1991: 5), nowhere examines the role of gender in nationhood. His national movements are run by men, for men; historically accurate perhaps, but his lack of examination is unimaginative in relation to half of the populations of his imagined communities.[3] His view that 'the nation is always conceived as a deep, horizontal comradeship' (7) shows that 'he ignores the significance of gender in his anlayses. The very term horizontal comradeship, although theoretically gender-neutral, brings with it connotations of masculine solidarity' (McDowell 1999: 195). His five pages of bibliography cited only seven or eight articles or books by women. Is this because women were not attracted by the study of the 'nation' because of the patriarchal nature of the states embodying nations? Perhaps we imagine a different community, one in which we are not represented by Britannia, the 'motherland', or Kathleen ni Houlihan. Ellen Galford's cantankerous Pictish Queen, 'Albanna, She Wolf of the North', rising up from Arthur's Seat in our hour of need under Thatcherite rule, described in her novel *Queendom Come* (1990: 7, 11), is much closer to an imagined possible saviour for women than Robert the Bruce or William Wallace.[4] Boland has articulated the problems for Irish women writers, in particular, of 'fictive queens and national sybils' (1996:135). When she began writing, 'the word *woman* and the word *poet* were almost magnetically opposed' (xi, original emphases) and she wrote *Object Lessons: The Life of the Woman and the Poet in Our Time* 'to probe the virulence and necessity of the idea of a nation' which intersected 'with a specific poetic inheritance', in turn cutting across her 'as a woman and a poet' (125). She had found that

> the Irish nation as an existing construct in Irish poetry was not available to me ... all too often, when I was searching for such an inclusion, what I found was a rhetoric of imagery which alienated me: a fusion of the national and the feminine which seemed to simplify both. (127–8)

Problems created by systems of representation for the nation are only one aspect of the issue of identification. Region, gender, nation, sexuality, class (as well as work and family) also produce particular and conflicting demands on our loyalties, creating a shifting sense of priorities and commitment. It is not so much that class, region or gender intersect with nation, as that they interrogate and problematise it. There is no need to be an international Marxist or Catholic or feminist believing that loyalty to class, religion or gender is supra-national, to be conscious that particular group identities can resist a central national identity. It is clear that women have always had different kinds of split demands and pulls of loyalty, stemming in part from the original passing of ownership of the woman's body from fathers to husbands, loyalties split between outside and inside the family, between parents and partner (of whatever sex), between children and husband/father. These kinds of shifting demands ensure that a commitment to monolithic concepts like 'nationality' is problematic, especially when legal nationality is seen as stemming from the father, not the mother. If the national ideal is constructed around primarily male concerns or ideologies, then commitment to those wide general concepts is likely to be difficult, tinged by scepticism, ironic dismissal, or feelings of exclusion or incompletion. 'Scottish' is tempered or altered by 'woman'. And if Scottish is the 'other' to English, with England used as the dominant reference point, and woman the 'other' to man, Scotswomen have felt a double otherness, a double marginality, or 'double democratic deficit' as the political scientists name it (Brown 2001: 204). We experience ourselves 'only fragmentarily, in the little-structured margins of a dominant ideology, as waste, or excess' (Irigaray 1985: 30). The dominant ideology for us has been both Anglocentric and male (the latter clearly having its own complicated inherent conflicts and contradictions).

But experiencing ourselves 'fragmentarily, in the … margins of the dominant ideology' can be given a positive reading. Janice Galloway, one of the most thoughtful about her craft and radical in style of contemporary Scottish fiction writers, points out that the 'structures and *normal* practices of both politics and the law make it difficult for women to speak as women directly because there's little accommodation for a female way of seeing' (Leigh March 1999a: 85, original emphasis). But she sees women's 'traditional attraction to fiction' as having 'a go at reconstructing the structures':

> Simply for a woman to write as a woman, to be as honest about it as
> possible, is a statement; not falling into the conventions of assuming
> guy stuff is 'real' stuff and we're a frill, a fuck or a boring bit that does
> housework or raises your kids round the edge. That stuff is not round

the edge! It's the fucking middle of everything. Deliberately pointing up that otherness, where what passes for normal has no bearing on you or ignores you – that fascinates me. (1999: 86)

Our experiences overlap, in the same way that Said describes literary experiences as 'overlapping with one another and interdependent … despite national boundaries and coercively legislated national autonomies, history and geography are transfigured in new maps, in new and far less stable entities, in new types of connections' (1993: 384). Said's 'global, contrapuntal analysis' (1993: 386), rejecting 'conceptions of history that stress linear development' (384), is exactly the approach that can also be used *within* the nation to ensure inclusion of disparate and clashing elements, using 'all sorts of spatial or geographical and rhetorical practices – inflections, limits, constraints, intrusions, inclusions, prohibitions – all of them tending to elucidate a complex and uneven topography' (Said 1993: 386). His 'atonal ensemble' (386), like our 'debatable lands', is a metaphor for the shifting inclusiveness necessary to encompass the confusing demands on our loyalty of nation, region, gender, sexuality and class. The complexity and unevenness of the topography is fruitful. So there is a lure in fragmentation and the margins for some of us; there are possibilities for ambiguity and for the power of the marginal, the dispossessed, the peripheral, to assert our right to existence, to be heard, to be experienced positively. No one on the margins wants to acknowledge being central and those truly of the centre rarely acknowledge the power of the margins. Our dialogue is not with them but with each other.[5]

If Scotland's sense of nationhood has a civic rather than an ethnic base, with our surviving national institutions such as the law and education, and the mixed ethnic origins of Scots, then it is not surprising that women may feel excluded from a full sense of being part of *this* imagined nation. Only in the last twenty-five years or less have women been able to participate fully in the civic institutions that constitute our nationness. And there is a persistent maleness in Scottish civic life that is problematic. Even now, there are very few women in top education posts, despite a majority of women in the lower echelons; the first woman High Court judge and the first Solicitor General were not appointed until 1996 and 2001 respectively; there have been no female Lord Advocates nor women Moderators of the General Assembly of the Church of Scotland or, even less likely, women priests in the Roman Catholic Church. Finally, to use the word 'emasculate' to refer to what central government did to local government after 1979 is not to use a gender-specific or biased word but to choose a fitting description, given the overwhelmingly male bias of central government at Westminster (particularly under Margaret Thatcher, but continued under John Major and Tony Blair) and of senior local government officials, leaders and elected MPs. The higher proportion of women MSPs in the Scottish Parliament and high profile posts for women in the Scottish Executive since May 1999 may (it is to be hoped if not necessarily believed) indicate some kind of positive change in Scotland.

As long as this maleness is central to the political/national structures, the acceptance of maleness as 'universal-male', with female categorised as 'particular-female', continues. Nan Shepherd (the modernist north-east Scottish novelist) reverses and undercuts the universal/particular, male/female conflict in her intensely complex novel, *The Weatherhouse* (1996b [1930]), exposing the universal as less important, less truly honest, than the particular. She explores a version of the male-universal/female-particular dichotomy when the central male character, Garry, is shown pursuing 'splendid generalities' (84) at the expense of the specific. In his persecution of a particular woman, he denies his motives are personal: 'It was not as a person that he wanted Louie punished, but as the embodiment of a disgrace' (72). But Garry's certainty in 'splendid generalities' is interrogated by the women in the novel, providing a critical opposition to any assumption by the reader of a male-universal connection. Shepherd's fiction has been long neglected by virtue of her specificity in north-east, rural, female subject matter. In contrast to this neglect, there is a view that sees fiction about working-class men as having a national (with an implicit universal) application. Cairns Craig extends this to Scottish writers (and, when he was writing in the 1980s, these were implicitly male[6]) in his introduction to the twentieth-century volume of *The History of Scottish Literature* with the assertion:

> To the extent that much of Scottish middle-class society models itself on English values, distinctively Scottish culture has more affinity with the working classes than English culture, is more imbued with a continuing sense of a living 'folk' culture … Scottish writers are both more working class and more philosophical than in England. (1987: 3)

Drew Milne sees Craig's introduction as drawing attention to 'the defining locus of contemporary Scottish writing' as being in 'the dialectical relation between urban vernacular and the politics of the city' (1994: 400). In an essay interrogating the concept of the 'hard man' ('terminal form of masculinity') as representative of Scottishness or Scottish maleness, Christopher Whyte perceives a 'hegemonic shift' where 'urban fiction in Scotland has increasingly and explicitly assumed the burden of national representation ... Once urban fiction was assigned a central position, its class and gender placements took on national implications' (1998: 278):

> The task of embodying and transmitting Scottishness is, as it were, devolved to the unemployed, the socially underprivileged, in both actual and representational contexts. Even a writer like James Kelman, despite his libertarian and egalitarian views, can be seen as participating in a 'representational pact' of this kind with consumers of his fiction. (275)

This 'representational pact' allows James Kelman's intensely personal and particular explorations of individual working-class West of Scotland men to be seen as both representing Scottishness and containing a 'commitment to celebrating the realities of contemporary and essentially urban Scotland' (Gifford 1992: 9).[7] But this same pact means that Elspeth Barker's *O Caledonia* (1992 [1991]) has been explicitly rejected as having any national application – because the heroine is middle class and diametrically opposed in her femaleness to anything that Kelman's heroes might represent. A heroine shown growing into 'the dim, blood-boultered altar of womanhood' (1992: 130) is too gendered for some. 'I don't recognise Scotland here', said Douglas Gifford of *O Caledonia*, 'the family may be chill Calvinists, but their attitude – upper class and estate-remote – isn't at all representative of Glasgow, Edinburgh, or Scottish culture of the time', and he criticises it for 'hardly being part of a diagnosis of what's wrong with Caledonia' (1992: 11). But why should the intensely imagined girlhood in the North East of a heroine who is murdered in a castle age sixteen be any less emblematic of nationhood than a man who wakes up blind in a prison cell in the West of Scotland (Kelman 1995: 9)? His essential 'maleness' is not any more intrinsically a comment on the 'Scottish' condition than her femaleness. It has been interpreted into that by the assumptions of his critics/readers. Politically working-class, male, Glaswegian writers are constructed as more 'authentic' than middle-class, female writers in exile – cut off from the authenticity of 'folk' roots by their class, their gender and their exile. But for those of us brought up as women in Scotland, *O Caledonia* contains an authenticity of response to the condition of Scottish womanness that Kelman cannot offer.[8]

Within Scotland's boundaries there are regional communities demanding a loyalty and recognition as strong as a nationalist commitment with the same shifting perspective of commitment between nation and region as there is between gender and nation. As Cairns Craig writes: 'Scottish novels may construct their narratives as paradigms of a

national consciousness, but they generally do so by locating their narrative within strictly demarcated regional boundaries' (1998: 221). This justification for the interpretation of the regional novel in Scottish literature
as 'national' can be extrapolated onto the construction of individual
fictional characters as 'paradigms of a national consciousness'. But where
this extrapolation becomes problematic is when one region, class, or
gender (for example, Glasgow, working-class, male) is used for the
representation of the 'whole' nation to the exclusion of others. This
hegemonic hold of the idea of the lowland Scottish working-class male
(Whyte's 'hegemonic shift') on perceptions of 'Scottishness' contrasts
with the lack of power that this grouping has in 'real' life. The urge to
universalise from the gendered particular is problematic, leaving, as it
does, half of the nation unrepresented in the imagined world being put
forward as 'Scottish'.

Scottish women's twentieth-century fiction, whether centred fully
on women or equally on women and men, ensures at least that, in
reading it, we start from a position of imagined identity with women. It
starts from the position that women are central rather than peripheral or
marginal, even when social constrictions are being examined and the
limitations of gender roles explored. Galloway links women's writing
with Scottish writing in this:

> And to reprioritise, to speak as though your norms are the ones that
> matter, is what's happened to Scottish writing as well recently. Scottish
> writers have started writing as though their language and national
> priorities signify, whereas for years we took on the fiction they didn't.
> The Let's Imagine We Matter thing is important. *What if I don't accept
> that I'm marginal, add-on territory* – it's the same root for me. (Leigh
> March 1999a: 86, original emphasis)

Just as previously the male was always seen and used as of central
importance in constructions of 'Scotland', now the female can be interpreted in the same extrapolated way to define Scottishness, though this
kind of identification often carries uneasiness and ambiguities, 'as
elliptical and ambiguous as the world outside' (1999a: 86).[9]

If we examine a range of writing from late twentieth-century
women we find concern with gender identification and representation.
However, if we return to women writers of the 1920s and 1930s, we find
them exploring a greater restriction of possibilities for women within
social or political life.[10] Nancy Brysson Morrison's *The Gowk Storm* (1988
[1933]) explores the growing up of three sisters in an isolated Perthshire
manse, imprisoned culturally and, at times, literally by the weather. The

most rebellious daughter dies after exposure to an unforgiving storm.
She is like the cow whose byre is heightened to improve its winter living
conditions, an 'uneven' window knocked in the wall:

> A white cow glimmered through the darkness that smelt of milk and
> hay. Its chain clanked as it turned its heavy head to look at us. Through
> a tiny uneven window, light struggled faintly and lit up a spider's web
> spanning encrusted beams ... 'Ay, ay ... he thocht it wouldna be so dull-
> like for the coo so she could get a keek oot in the winter'. (1988 [1933]:
> 41–2)

But the cow is still chained, still imprisoned, a paradigm for the position
of women in Scottish society in the 1920s and 1930s who could see out
from 'uneven' windows, but could not escape from cultural and social
limitations.

But what this earlier twentieth-century Scottish women's fiction also
mapped out was the infinite possibilities of the imagination: through
education, through reading, through landscape. Landscape in Scotland
incorporates light and infinity. In Shepherd's *The Weatherhouse* (like
Willa Muir's title, *Imagined Corners*, echoing Donne's 'At the round
earth's imagined corners'), it 'was a country that liberated. More than
half the world was sky. The coastline vanished at one of the four corners
of the earth, Ellen lost herself in its immensity' (1996b [1930]: 9–10). The
imagery of light and infinity permeates the novel, 'the blue sea trembled
on the boundaries of space' (112), infecting those characters (female and
male) who experience it with the sense of invisible edges to the world, of
possibilities reaching out into infinity, in contrast to the constrictions of
their daily life.

It is as though for these women, the constrictions of earthly life are
released by the light and landscape into the edge of time and endless
uncharted possibilities, possibilities that were more fractured or con-
strained in life, providing another version of Irigaray's internalised '(Re)-
discovering herself, for a woman ... *never being simply one*' with a 'sort of
expanding universe to which no limits could be fixed and which would
not be incoherence nonetheless' (1985: 30–1, original emphasis). Shepherd
is most explicit about this conjunction of landscape, light, and Scotland
in her first novel, *The Quarry Wood* (1996a [1928]). The protagonist
Martha, from a north-east crofting family, passionately pursues knowledge as a child, goes to Aberdeen University and then returns to her
home area in the hills of Aberdeenshire to become a teacher. As a child,
she is told a half-remembered 'bit screed' by her father:

> 'On the sooth o' Scotland there's England, on the north the Arory-bory

– Burnett's lassie, the reid-heided ane – Alice; on the east – fat's east
o't? … I some think it was the sun – the risin' sun. Ay, fairly. That's fat
it was. Noo, the wast. Fat's wast o' Scotland, Matty' … Geordie could
get no further with the boundaries of Scotland … They stood on
Scotland and there was nothing north of them but light. It was Dussie
who wondered what bounded Scotland when the Aurora was not there
… 'Yon's the wordie, Mattie – fat the meenister was readin' aboot.
Eternity. That's fat's wast o' Scotland. I mind it noo' … Eternity did
not seem to be on any of her maps: but neither was the Aurora. She
accepted that negligence of the map-makers as she accepted so much
else in life. She had enough to occupy her meanwhile in discovering
what life held, without concerning herself with what it lacked. (1996a
[1928]: 19–20)

Shepherd shows here the disjunctions between the maps available for
women, 'the negligence of map-makers', and the pragmatic capacity of
women to get on with the exploration of the reality of 'discovering what
life held'. Martha, setting out on her voyage of the intellect, education
and love, accepts the oddity of the boundaries of Scotland which are
shown as mysteriously and infinitely expansive through light and
eternity. Only to the south is travel in the imagination limited by the real
border with England.[11] Similarly, in *O Caledonia*, a more recent novel,
also set partly in the north-east of Scotland and imbued with the
characteristics of both the literature and the landscape of that area, we
find that 'for Janet it was the view ahead which held all the enchantment
she had ever yearned for; in the distance the hills lapped against each
other to the far limits of the visible world' (Barker 1992 [1991]: 33–4).
Barker's novel in its yearning for intellectual freedom and its exploration
of the limitations of 1940s' femininity seems positioned much more with
the earlier Scottish women writers than her contemporaries.

One of those contemporaries, Janice Galloway, charts different
boundaries from Shepherd and Barker in her first novel, *The Trick is to
Keep Breathing* (1991 [1989]). In its first-person portrayal of a breakdown
there are internal, conflicting senses of existence and non-existence and
absence. Joy, the narrator, scours the written word in a search for self:

It's important to write things down. The written word is important.
The forms of the letters: significances between the loops and dashes.
You scour them looking for the truth. I read *The Prophet*, Gide, Kafka,
Ivor Cutler. *Gone with the Wind*, *Fat is a Feminist Issue*, Norman Mac-
Caig and Byron, *Lanark*, Muriel Spark, *How to cope with your Nerves/
Loneliness/Anxiety*, Antonia White and Adrian Mole. *The Frances Gay
Friendship Book* and James Kelman. ee cummings. *Unexplained Mysteries*

and *Life after Dark*. I read magazines, newspapers, billboards, government health warnings, advertising leaflets, saucebottles, cans of beans,
Scottish Folk Tales and The Bible. They reveal glimpses of things just
beyond the reach of understanding but never the whole truth. I fall into
a recurring loop every morning after. (195–6)

This passage provides emblematic juxtapositions which show the extent
our selves, written and lived, are constructed from heterogeneous cultural
influences, clamouring and clashing discourses found in the cultural
artefacts of late twentieth-century Scottish women's lives. Galloway's
'glimpses of things just beyond the reach of understanding' are the
internal landscape's confused equivalent to the 'far limits of the visible
world' (Barker 1992: 34) in the external landscapes of Scotland. Galloway's internal dialogues make Joy's head 'the site of a multiplicity of
competing voices, a dialogue of dialect no longer distributed between
different characters in the narrative but interiorised in an inner dialectic'
(Craig 1998: 238). The 'inner dialectic' is unresolved; the loops of the
words, the forms of the letters, provide a trap instead of a map with
Galloway showing the instability and inaccessibility of meaning in the
written word. Joy's uncertainty and ambiguity comes not from madness
but from a reasoned response to a conflicting and conflicted world.[12]

Contemporary Scottish women writers may now write from an
assumption of rights and possibilities for change but they also still write
out of the inequalities of women's positions, 'writing to *make visible*'
(Leigh March 1999: 92, original emphasis), writing themselves into a
culture that has been dominated by male cultural icons. As Kathleen
Jamie has said in relation to Robert Burns:

> I don't think we need a national bard. I think folk call him that out of
> laziness, because they can't be bothered to read what's been written
> since. It's a monolithic attitude, where every era seems to have enshrined
> one male. A vibrant culture, as we have, is in the hands of many, many
> people. (quoted in Dunkerley, 1996)[13]

Hugh MacDiarmid, the writer who bestrode the Scottish literary renaissance (in many ways defining it), had an iconographic function similar to
Burns in Scottish intellectual and literary life after the Second World
War. The female equivalent to the MacDiarmid monolith seemed to be
Muriel Spark: prolific, isolated, providing a slippery, eliptical and philo-
sophically cunning counterpart, both of them admired or revered, but
neither apparently directly the beginning of a vibrant new tradition. Spark
has previously been treated by and large as a unique writer, subsumed into
the 'English' canon by non-Scottish readers. Her themes and preoccu-

pations, however, place her firmly within the Scottish tradition and her inheritors have appeared in the 1990s; Elspeth Barker, Shena Mackay, Candia McWilliam, A. L. Kennedy and Janice Galloway all carry elements of Spark within their themes and style. Spark's writing has a cold, observant eye – a 'people-watcher, a behaviourist', as she describes herself (1992: 25) – detached from the life around her, amused and unengaged, containing both the coldness of the excluded and a cool observation of the masculinised world of Scottish life and culture. It is symptomatic that the woman writer who has had most obvious influence on contemporary women writers has chosen exile and that her work should be so open to critical interpretations which ignore or are ignorant of the obvious Scottish dimensions of her work.

The universalised male centre such as MacDiarmid (or Burns) beloved of traditional (male) Scottish culture, is limiting. The Alasdair Gray model, on the other hand, leaping into multi-life in 1981 with *Lanark*, proved much more fruitful. His ironic and humorous questioning of maleness, West of Scotlandness, his fragmented creations, all proved inspirational for younger Scottish writers even though his second work, *1982 Janine* (1984), was more problematic for women readers in its conscious use of pornography to make political points about the disempowered Scottish male. The protagonist Jock is feminised and weakened (the two being seen as equivalent) by his role as the oppressed Scottish male. He carries for his author and some critics (for example, Craig 1999: 183–92) the assumption that the male out of power is equivalent to the woman oppressed in the sex industry (Janine is a fantasy pornographic plaything of Jock's), absolving the male of complicity in the violence of pornography.[14]

As Gray was stirring up writing, the women's movement was stirring up Scottish society. Post-1979 and the failure of the campaign for a devolved Scottish Assembly, the work of issue-based women's groups such as Rape Crisis Centres, Scottish Women's Aid and the Scottish Abortion Campaign ensured that campaigning for change in women's legal and social positions was grounded in the difference of Scots Law and developed separately from groups in England. Though starting from an identical analysis of male abuse of power, our awareness of English ignorance of our different campaigning needs meant that some of us developed a specifically Scottish perspective to feminism. International feminism often means a homogenising in the direction of the imperial centres; for example, Anglocentric for Scottish feminists, and US-centric for Canadian feminists. The 1980s were a time of political constriction after the Tory victory under Thatcher in 1979, but for feminism in Scotland they were also a time of consolidation and advance; rape in marriage was established as a crime (before England), incestuous rape was exposed as something not happening on the periphery, be it peripheral Edinburgh council estates or the Western Isles, but something being done violently to children (mainly, though not exclusively, girls) in the best and worst of families. Domestic violence was acknowledged as not a 'domestic' problem, but a problem of male violence against women, of abuse of power. The campaign of Zero Tolerance of violence against women of the 1990s in Scotland, based on a Canadian model, was built on the work of 1980s' feminists.[15]

It is against this background of specific social change accomplished by women, and of cultural energy, represented by Gray's and Kelman's fiction, and by the writing of Tom Leonard (for example, *Intimate Voices*, 1984) and the work of poet and dramatist Liz Lochhead, that the newer writers in the 1990s (such as Galloway, A. L. Kennedy, Jackie Kay or Laura Hird) emerge and move in fresh directions. The map has been redrawn so that they write from a confident assumption that being female and being Scottish are culturally positive; writing out of the same kind of natural assumption of place in the culture previously available to male writers. Galloway, with her intensely individualised, West of Scotland women's stories, explicitly draws attention to her feminism and her femaleness. A. L. Kennedy, less overtly political, perhaps, writes that she has 'a problem. I am a woman, I am heterosexual, I am more Scottish than anything else and I write. But I don't know how these things interrelate' (1995: 100) and insists that 'the great thing about books' is that they are 'not nation-specific, not race-specific, not religion-specific' but 'about humanity' (Leigh March 1999b: 108). Jackie Kay's works, from the poetic drama of *The Adoption Papers* (1991) to the novel *Trumpet* (1998), centre on complicated questions of gender, sexuality and race in a way new to Scottish writing. Laura Hird represents younger voices, her stance equivalent to those male writers she appeared with in *Children of Albion Rovers* (Williamson 1996) and the writers interviewed in *Repetitive Beat Generation* (Redhead 2000), drawing the harshness of young Edinburgh lives, writing of the complicity of women in our position, and looking on middle age as a foreign country.[16] In Benedict Anderson's phrase, their 'fiction seeps quietly and continuously into reality' (1991: 36). Their writing is essential for the part it plays in contributing to an imagined wholeness in the nation, ensuring that Scotland's 'narrative of "identity"' (Anderson 1991: 205) includes women. Their work ensures exploration of shifting allegiances and passsable boundaries in counterpoint to the limiting containment of that earlier static male cultural mode which was the stultifying norm.

It used to be said that nineteenth-century fiction looked for closure, and twentieth-century literature resisted it (although when we looked again, post-postmodernism, it was clear that much nineteenth-century fiction carried its own anxieties in the metaphors and subtexts embedded in its apparent order). But the resistance to, the *impossibility* of, closure is carried into the twenty-first century. So Margaret, at the end of A. L. Kennedy's *Looking for the Possible Dance*, walks out into an urban landscape through a door which is as suggestive of light and infinity as the edges of the north-east world:

> from a distance its doorways seem white, more like curtains of white than ways through walls and into light. Margaret walks to one door and sinks into brilliant air, becoming first a moving shadow, then a curve, a dancing line. (1993: 250)

This ending – now criticised by Kennedy as 'the illusion of arriving at the end of a story but actually you just arrive at the end of a railway line' (Leigh March 1999b: 100) – shimmers with possibilities. It is in this openness that Scottish women's writing presents its multiple and heterogeneous relation to gender and nation.

There is a constant leap of imagination required of women reading literature by men, with male-centred concerns. As Boland writes: 'teenage dreams of action and heroism are filled with exciting and impossible transpositions of sexuality ... If I wanted to feel the power of nation as well as its defeat, then I would take on the properties of hero' (1996: 65). In twentieth-century writing the same kind of imaginative travel is necessary to where gender interacts with nation so that nation cannot be narrated as exclusively male or, indeed, exclusively female. Any exploration must be tentative, flexible, non-linear as the only certainty carried by 'debatable lands' is that of uncertainty, of border crossings, dispute, debate, contiguity and interaction, equivalent, perhaps, to Bhabha's 'inscription and articulation of culture's *hybridity*. To that end we should remember that it is the "inter" – the cutting edge of translation and negotiation, the *in-between* space – that carries the burden of meaning of culture' (1994: 38, original emphases). Lands of thought that are interrogated and fought over, these debatable lands are Said's 'complex and uneven topography' (1993: 386), as much about women's space within the nation as about the boundaries of Scotland.

Notes

1 This chapter is based in part on an earlier essay, 'Imagined Corners to Debatable Land: Passable Boundaries' (Christianson 1996).

2 In 1850, Dinah Mulock Craik applied it to that other liminal geographical space in Scotland, the northern side of the rift valley that delimits highlands from lowlands, describing an 'old Scotswoman – who, coming from the debatable ground between Highlands and Lowlands, had united to the rigid piety of the latter much wild Gaelic superstition' (27). See also Anderson 1992: 34–5.

3 The nation is '*imagined* because the members of even the smallest nation will never know most of their fellow-members, meet them, or even hear of them, yet in the minds of each lives the image of their communion' (Anderson 1991: 6, original emphasis).

4 The historical figures with their acquired heroic and nationalist meanings are intended, rather than their Hollywood manifestations in *Braveheart* (1995), though the two may well interconnect as male symbols, as in the adoption of the face painted with the Saltire by fans of football (that centralising trope not of nationhood but of maleness).

5 For example, there are many connections between Scotland and Ireland to do with religion and emigration in different centuries, Catholics into Scotland and Protestants into Ireland.

6 For an influential analysis of 'the male monopoly on Scottish culture' see Anderson and Norquay 1984. See also the subsequent correspondence in *Cencrastus*, 16: 46, and 17: 43–4 (Spring and Summer, 1984).

7 Janice Galloway, sometimes coupled with Kelman as a fellow West of Scotland, working-class writer (for example Gifford 1992: 9), takes a complicated view of Kelman as 'writing not so much about as *through* Glasgow. His landscapes are very often alien hostile places, more states of mind (albeit states of mind influenced by physical landscape) than anything else. They needn't be Glasgow, and less and less are they becoming Glasgow. He's moved much more into the territory of abstract writing. I never really think of Jim as Scottish at all, which strikes outsiders as funny … Most of those who choose to get bogged down with the language are making a political choice – *I won't read through this filter, I choose to make it illegitimate*. I think Jim's writing through an existential tradition, using traditionally illegitimised language perhaps, but it's the existential stuff that shapes his meaning. That's the most profound thing about Jim's work, not the Scottishness' (Leigh March 1999a: 87, original emphases). She refers in particular to the fuss in the English press when Kelman won the 1994 Booker prize for *How Late It Was How Late*. For a description of this, see Taylor (one of the judges and a Scottish journalist) 1994. Critical (as opposed to journalistic) approaches to Kelman have not been simplistic, most critics seeing him both as an existential and a class- rather than nation-identified writer; for example, see Milne (1994) and Nicoll (2000).

8 Janet's experiences do not just resonate for middle-class women; Dorothy McMillan finds 'sufficient intersections' with her own memories of a council house upbringing (1995: 94). See also Christianson (2000).

9 For a consideration of the difficulties of interpreting nation and gender in Galloway's work in particular, see Norquay (2000).

10 I include in my consideration of gender and nation those women writers of the first half of the twentieth century whose works disappeared from our literary

maps, giving those maps a misleading and incomplete slant. I also include them because on their re-publication in the 1980s they became 'new' writers, slotting into a historical place in modernist Scottish writing but also representing new and exciting work in the freshness of readers' responses. But they also provide a warning. The disappearance and reappearance of women in history and in writing – the surges of activity in the last two hundred years, the reinvention of commitment and analysis of women's position, is echoed in the writing of women, each generation forgetting and losing the work of the generation before last. Might this cycle recur in Scotland and elsewhere (in Australia, Canada, Ireland or the US, for example)?

11 See also Carter 2000: 52–3.

12 What Joy is *not* is symbolic of 'Scotland'. Joy's 'I looked. I was still there. A black hole among the green stars. Empty space. I had nothing inside me … Nothing at all' (1991 [1989]: 146), is interpreted by Craig as 'the image not only of a woman negated by a patriarchal society but of a society aware of itself only as an absence, a society living, in the 1980s, in the aftermath of its failure to be reborn' (1999: 199). That is, Joy = Scotland, woman exemplifying nation; Craig thus invokes and continues that problematic dynamic of nation symbolised as female, incorporating Galloway and other contemporary women writers into his grand masculine narrative, one which acknowledges the region in nation, but blurs or even ignores the complexities of gender's place in the nation's narratives.

13 For some of the problems presented by MacDiarmid for women, see Anderson and Norquay (1984) and Christianson (1993).

14 A. L. Kennedy says of Kelman and Gray: 'I've probably got more sympathy with Alasdair because he does weird stuff' (Leigh March 1999b: 101). For critical readings of Gray, see Lumsden (1993) and Whyte (1998).

15 A major source for detailed information about Scottish rape crisis campaigns is the Edinburgh Rape Crisis Centre's reports, first (1981), second (tenth anniversary, 1988) and third (fifteenth anniversary, 1993) (all Edinburgh: Edinburgh Rape Crisis Collective), and subsequent annual ones. See also Christianson and Greenan (2001). Short histories of many other women's groups in Scotland in the eighties are in Henderson and Mackay (1990).

16 The woman of 'the elderly couple' in Hird's 'Tillicoutry/Anywhere' is in her fifties (1997: 143). For further consideration of contemporary Scottish women writers, see individual chapters in Christianson and Lumsden (2000).

5

The Union and Jack:
British masculinities, pomophobia,
and the post-nation

BERTHOLD SCHOENE

Starting with a general theoretical investigation into nationalist imageries of masculine and feminine embodiment, this essay offers a tentative outline of some of the most problematic shifts in the conceptualisation and literary representation of man, self and nation in Britain throughout the twentieth century. The second part of the essay comprises a close reading of John Osborne's *Look Back in Anger* (1993 [1956]), which is to illustrate the syndromic inextricability of masculinist and nationalist discourses within a patriarchal context and, moreover, to disclose the representational symptoms of these discourses' critical decline as interpellative models of successful self-identification in post-imperial Britain. Finally, shifting its focus to a discussion of masculine modes of self-representation in contemporary Scottish men's writing, the essay highlights the utopian potentialities of subnational emancipation; at the same time, it questions the ultimate political viability of any devolutionary attempt to move beyond masculinist notions of man, self and nation. Although I develop no direct correspondence here, given the role that the ideology of 'Englishness' has historically played throughout these islands, I suggest that this critique of gender and national identity could be usefully adapted all across the Atlantic archipelago.

The Union and Jack

In striking contrast to Virginia Woolf's cosmopolitan assertion in *Three Guineas* that 'as a woman I have no country ... As a woman my country is the whole world' (1993 [1938]: 234), Antony Easthope writes in *What a Man's Gotta Do* that 'if I am masculine I am at one with the nation' (1986: 57). Both propositions clearly identify nationalism as a profoundly gendered discourse that interpellates men as 'insiders' while at the same time excluding and quite literally 'alienating' women. However, unlike Woolf, who appears to blame men's congenital bellicosity – 'a sex instinct' (1993 [1938]: 234) – for their deleterious susceptibility to patriotism, and patriotically motivated warfare in particular, Easthope's enquiry works to expose the insidious dynamics of patriarchal conditioning that not only ensure, but in fact insist, that there be for men, as Woolf puts it, 'some glory, some necessity, some satisfaction in fighting which [women] have never felt or enjoyed' (1993 [1938]: 121).

As a conjunctive reading of Easthope's and Woolf's essays demonstrates, both men and women find themselves caught up in processes of normative self-formation that, in strategic fulfillment of a patriarchally propagated complementarity of the sexes, render women innocent bystanders while casting men in the role of their dutifully heroic protectors. Thus, even Woolf's most resolutely feminist endeavour to identify for women a possible position of resistance within patriarchal society seems ultimately at risk of reinscribing the passive, virtuous role traditionally allocated to the female: men's seemingly incorrigible 'badness' comes to be contrasted with women's (equally incorrigible) angelic 'goodness'. What Woolf seems unable to recognise is the compelling functionality of femininity and masculinity within patriarchal and nationalist discourse. Traditional gender formations facilitate the orchestration of an allegedly harmonious, systemic interplay of complementary polarities, whose ultimate objective is the construction and continuous reconsolidation of communal cohesion. Metaphorically speaking, the soldierly masculinity of all men is summoned to form an impenetrable armour shielding the domestic body of all women's soft and vulnerable femininity within. Such a patriarchal rhetoric of nationalist containment evidently bears its own contradictions and ideological inconsistencies. What the writings of a dissenting woman intellectual like Woolf reveal, for example, is that what ostensibly stands at the very core of the nation's interests – that is, 'woman', in the broadest possible sense of the term – also always constitutes, at least potentially, an inimical site of emergent discontent, threatening to undermine the nation state's traditionalist pose of indivisible oneness.

As George Mosse writes in *The Image of Man*, 'women who left their prescribed roles ... joined the counter-types as the enemies against whom manliness sharpened its image' (1996: 12). By successfully evading the grasp of traditional gender imperatives, women become 'unwomanly' and thus enemies of the patriarchally organised nation state, which champions conservative masculinist values: homeostasis, integrity and homogeneity, indivisibility and heroic self-effacement, clear-cut, definitive boundaries as well as a committed and irrevocable subjection to what Craig Calhoun has designated as 'the rhetoric of nation' (1997: 4; see also Easthope 1986: 57). As I intend to demonstrate, nations traditionally represent deeply paranoid formations of the people that paradoxically thrive on both at once a strict oppositional segregation of the sexes and an adamant disavowal of their intrinsic heterogeneity, or self-and-otherness. In the modernist era of the early twentieth century this fundamental deconstructive disunity at the heart of nationalist discourse – albeit 'repressed and disguised by the veneer of national unity' (Plain 1996: 20) and thus prone to strengthen the alleged bond of complementarity between the nation's men and women – gives rise to the gender-specifically disparate experience of nationhood which Woolf addresses so passionately in *Three Guineas*:

> If you [i.e. men] insist upon fighting to protect me, or 'our' country, let it be understood, soberly and rationally between us, that you are fighting to gratify a sex instinct which I cannot share; to produce benefits which I have not shared and probably will not share; but not to gratify my instincts, or to protect either myself or my country. (1993 [1938]: 234)

But if women's relationship to the nation is so clearly fraught with irresolvable contradictions, a sense of negativity and exclusion, would it be fair to assume that men's experience of national belonging is entirely unproblematic, that is, privileged and beneficial rather than oppressive or exploitative? As Mosse points out, men have traditionally been called upon not only to defend (if necessary with their lives), but moreover to epitomise the territorial and historical solidity and self-containment of the nation, its supposedly inalienable claim to political sovereignty as well as its homeostatic resilience to historical change. However, what Mosse fails to address are the tragic implications that such a conscriptive masculine embodiment of the nation must inevitably entail for the well-being of the individual male. Summoned to project and uphold an appearance of invincible strength in order to deter other nations from attempting to attack or invade their territory, men must subscribe, not only with their bodies but with their whole being, to the formation of a hard national shell, that is, a stiff, parametric boundary between the enemy without and, as we shall see, the potentially even unrulier enemy within. This collective masculine fortification of the nation's boundaries requires a total disembodiment of the individual male, a self-effacing, evacuative surrender of his individual interiority to the tumescent inscription of supra-individual, communal causes. Symptomatically, so Kaja Silverman argues,

> when the male subject is brought into a traumatic encounter with lack, as in the situation of war, he often experiences it as the impairment of his anatomical masculinity. What is really at issue, though, is a psychic disintegration – the disintegration, that is, of a bound and armored ego, predicated upon the illusion of coherence and control. (1992: 62)

As an indispensable part of the rhetoric of the patriarchally organised nation state, the individual male's private persona is required to perform a vanishing act by allowing itself to be assimilated without trace into a collective masculinist show of communal uniformity, designed to camouflage the nation's otherwise helplessly exposed feminine body within. Thus, the rhetoric of nation clearly ties in with what in *Male Matters* Calvin Thomas refers to as 'the long-standing patriarchal ideology in which embodiment and femininity are equated, in which male bodies do not matter [and remain ultimately invisible], in which only women are supposed to have bodies, in which only women's bodies are seen' (1996: 15). Men are led to mistake the corporeality of others – wives, mothers and children – for a manifestation of their own bodiliness which, in turn, freezes into an effectively disembodied, territorialist utterance of internal homogeneity and cohesion. This ideologically motivated split of the nation into a feminine body protectively contained and held together by a fixed set of masculine demarcations exerts an impossible pressure on the individual male, a pressure that must ultimately prove quite literally 'insufferable' since it prohibits men from legitimately experiencing trauma and pain as a result of bodily violation. Because the body is traditionally designated as female, and men are expected to obfuscate their bodily vulnerability through an exterior display of bravery and courage, openly to admit to an experience of violation would, for a 'real' man, be equivalent to committing a grossly unmanly act of confessional self-emasculation.

The body – and, with it, everything traditionally construed as or associated with the feminine – poses a continuous subversive threat of emasculation to the heroic athletics of patriarchal masculinity. Within nationalist discourse this means that what is ideally to be cherished, loved and – if necessary – to be defended with one's life simultaneously represents an incorporation of the unmanly to be loathed and categorically abjected. Hence, rather than facilitating harmonious relations between the sexes, nationalism reveals itself as a deeply domophobic and misogynous discourse informed by irreconcilable conflictual tensions between the masculine and the feminine, that is, between the systemically controlled and the ultimately uncontrollable. It seems important in this context that not only is it the soldierly duty of all men to protect the nation from external menace, they must also keep a vigilant eye on the tremulous, intrinsically recalcitrant body of the nation itself, its (or should we say 'her'?) inveterate susceptibility to sudden socio-political shifts and fluxes, as well as its treacherous tendency to spawn rebellious or revolutionary counterdiscourses of the nation that threaten to undermine or spill across the homeostatic fixtures of the given status quo. As Homi K. Bhabha explains in *The Location of Culture*, such 'counter-narratives of the nation ... continually evoke and erase its totalizing boundaries – both actual and conceptual – [and] disturb those ideological manoeuvres through which "imagined communities" are given essentialist identities' (1994: 149).

In 'Narratives of nationalism: being "British"', Iain Chambers distinguishes between two different concepts of nationhood which, within the framework of the present argument, could easily be described as grounded in mutually incompatible 'masculine' and 'feminine' principles of communal assemblage, the masculine principle stressing traditionalist unity, whereas the feminine principle comprehends nationality as a propagation of diversity thriving on never-ending processes of communal configuration and reconfiguration. Chambers writes:

> Here we face the possibility of two perspectives and two versions of 'Britishness'. One is Anglo-centric, frequently conservative, backward-looking, and increasingly located in a frozen and largely stereotyped idea of national culture. The other is ex-centric, open-ended, and multi-ethnic. The first is based on a homogeneous 'unity' in which history, tradition, and individual biographies and roles, including ethnic and sexual ones, are fundamentally fixed and embalmed in the national epic, in the mere fact of being 'British'. The other perspective suggests an overlapping network of histories and traditions, a heterogeneous complexity in which positions and identities, including that of the 'national', cannot be taken for granted, are not interminably fixed but are in flux. (1993: 153–4)

According to Gillian Beer, the gradually increasing dismantling of traditionalist narratives of the nation throughout the twentieth century is not only to do with counterdiscursive agitation but also, perhaps more pertinently, with technological progress. In 'The island and the aeroplane:

the case of Virginia Woolf', first published in Bhabha's influential collection *Nation and Narration*, Beer demonstrates how, with the arrival of the aeroplane, it became ever more difficult to perpetuate the myth of Britain, and of England in particular, as an invincible, safely detached and autonomous fortress-island. Boundaries, especially those that used to safely encapsulate the national bodies of island states, began to blur out of focus. The new bird's-eye perspective gradually replaced Britain's vision of itself as a self-contained, insular unit with one that accentuated its global – or at least its neighbourly – interconnectedness, its panoramic diversity as well as its embeddedness within contexts larger than that of the nation. Paraphrasing Gertrude Stein, Beer speaks of 'the formal reordering of the earth when seen from the aeroplane – a reordering which does away with centrality and very largely with borders'; as she continues to explain, '[it] is an ordering at the opposite extreme from that of the island, in which centrality is emphasized and the enclosure of land within surrounding shores is the controlling meaning' (1990: 265).

Postmodern technologies have considerably accelerated this process of decentralisation in all areas of both public and private life. However, what frequently tends to go under in the general salutation of growing globalisation is a close analysis of the manifold anxieties that motivate reactionary responses to such a seemingly unstoppable destabilisation of the old 'insular' order, as well as the patent gender-specificity of these anxieties, both in terms of individual subjectivity and communal or national self-formation. The cultural conditions of both modernity and postmodernity have effected – as well as in their own turn been affected by – an existential shattering or dispersal of the self as we used to know it. As Thomas Byers notes in 'Terminating the postmodern: masculinity and pomophobia', the multifarious epistemological quandaries incurred by postmodernity in particular 'pose threats to the continued existence of the reified subject of bourgeois humanism' (1995: 6), causing 'the traditional subject, *particularly the masculine subject*, [to find itself] in the throes of an identity crisis' (7, my emphasis). A violent masculinist backlash seems pre-programmed, triggered by what Byers describes as 'pomophobia', that is, traditional masculinity's existential fear and rejection of all kinds of postmodern destabilisation and, most importantly perhaps, the liquid(is)ation of hitherto fixed epistemic boundaries through postmodernity's radical demolition of all totalising systems of cultural identification. Ever more vociferously cornered by the manifold processes of minoritarian 'coming out' that characterise our postmodern era of pluralist diversification, white, western, middle and upper-class, heterosexual masculinity of the patriarchal mould is about to become obsolete and reduced to a hopelessly outmoded anachronism. It seems that only if men – as a minority as yet oblivious of its own minoritarian status – could be made to 'come out' as well and embrace a counter-discursive, decidedly post-patriarchal identity, would they be able to begin to partake in the newly reassembling communal forum of a turbulently, often tumultuously, reconfiguring symbolic sphere that bears the promise of reconstituting contemporary society.

However, as Byers demonstrates, instead of catalysing a radical overhaul and reconceptualisation of traditional modes of both individual and communal identification, the postmodern demise of 'man' is just as likely to instigate a pomophobic reaction, manifesting itself in paranoid reassertions of the ancient binarist categories of the self and its other(s). As Byers continues to explain, the acute omnipresence of paranoia in postmodern culture must primarily be understood as 'an extreme concern with the defense of the (illusory) unity, integrity, and significance of the subject' (1995: 12). Perhaps, paranoia, as the expression of a fundamental epistemic rupture brought about by a wide range of different postmodern destabilisations, can also help to explain the apparently schizophrenic disposition of twentieth-century western culture as a whole. Whereas modernist and postmodernist writers, artists and intellectuals appear to cultivate an aesthetics of self-abolition and self-dispersal, twentieth-century politics has been marked, often latently but sometimes cataclysmically, by reactionary, hyperbolic reassertions of the self. Responding to the threat of a total dissipation of traditionalist boundaries that used to clearly demarcate the presence of both the masculine self and the patriarchal nation state, both man and nation seem inclined to reassert themselves hyperbolically, that is, by means of a deliberate pomophobic reinforcement of their allegedly original (yet in fact nostalgic and entirely imaginary) definitive contours and monumental stature. Fascism and ethnic cleansing are the inevitable result, propagating a relentless reinscription of terrifyingly atavistic, masculinist formations of subjectivity and nationhood, formations whose powerful artifice has, according to Byers's poignant description, always been desperately 'pumped up by ideological steroids' (1995: 27). Both post-modernist fascism (as in Germany of the 1930s and 1940s) and post-postmodernist fascism (as in Yugoslavia of the 1990s) are thus perhaps best understood as violent paranoid reactions to the increasing epistemic dissolution of traditional notions of identity as facilitated by both traditional masculine subjectivity and patriarchal nationalism. The impending demise of the hegemonic self is held at bay by attempts to re-establish an imagined old order of perfect self-sameness, purity and communal homogeneity. In short, the abolition of the self is deferred, however precariously, by abolishing – uprooting, raping and killing – the other.

In *Male Matters* Calvin Thomas probes this apparently inextricable correlation between two mutually incompatible manifestations of modernity with an urgent list of provocative questions. 'Is modernity as self-hyperbole a repression of modernity as self-abolition?', he asks.

> That is, are those philosophical, political, and aesthetic responses to and projects of modernity that gather themselves into self-hyperbole a repression of the experience of modernity as self-shattering? Is this hyperbolic gathering of modernity into a totalizing project staked not only on the repression of self-abolition but on the active abolition of the other? And is the acceptance or even celebration of the self-shattering experience of modernity the necessarily unorganizing rallying cry for the impossible communities of the postmodern? (1996: 24–5)

But pomophobia does not always of necessity manifest itself in crass, catastrophically violent, fascistic reassertions of the ancient self/other binary. Its presence may be latent in a culture as, I find, it is in Britain, particularly in English culture but perhaps also, so I would like to argue, in Scottish culture. Since the collapse of the Empire, the British nation has been suffering from a severe cultural identity crisis, considerably exacerbated by the fact that it now sees its socio-economic status, cultural prestige and national identity challenged by immigrant populations from the ex-colonies, who have begun to ascend the social ladder to ever greater equality and sameness. To compound matters further, so John Osmond argues in *The Divided Kingdom*, unlike the separate Ulster, Scots and Welsh identities, British identity is not 'based on territory, traditional culture and a republican sense of "the people"', but on 'hopelessly old-fashioned and *ad hoc* structures', such as the monarchy, the military, bourgeois class values and 'the tired procedures of Lords and Commons at Westminster' (1988: 192, 221). Britain's loss of Empire, its relative economic decline and reluctant entry into the European Community, as well as the ever more vociferous emergence of separatist Scottish, Welsh and Ulster identities, have fractured British identity by exposing it as grounded in the thin air of a now outdated imperial rhetoric. From as early as 1956 – significantly the year of the Suez Crisis, commonly regarded as the political event that ended Britain's imperial career as a world power – one can find reflections of this national identity crisis in English literature, most spectacularly perhaps in John Osborne's play *Look Back in Anger*, which shows a young Englishman, Jimmy Porter, fight his pomophobic fear of imminent self-dispersal by aiming to shatter and assimilate the self of his closest other, that of his wife Alison.

The Union and Jimmy

In more than just one respect, Osborne's Jimmy Porter epitomises a crisis in self-authentication that seems endemic to post-war British culture in its entirety. The play is an index of the postmodern decentring of the traditional masculine subject, accelerated by the collapse of the Empire and the incipience of a diversity of minoritarian liberation movements. *Look Back in Anger* presents us with a young anti-hero about to realise that man's centre-stage role in society has become precarious and questionable, destabilised by a general loss of certainty, faith and commitment, corrupted by a history of unjust, exploitative rule both at home and in the colonies, compromised by political apathy and opportunism, and contested by various subordinate identities beginning to voice and pursue their hitherto unacknowledged desires. Since, so Jimmy declares, 'there aren't any good, brave causes left' (1993 [1956]: 83), all the grand conflictual tensions between himself and the world at large release themselves in hurtful, often excruciatingly petty rhetorical tirades against Alison, his wife. However, *Look Back in Anger* is only secondarily concerned with the asphyxiation of young manly zest within the claustrophobic confines of an allegedly female-governed domesticity. The primary issue at stake is the hegemony of imperial English masculinity.

Deploring a political climate in which 'nobody thinks, nobody cares', Jimmy expresses his desire for 'something strong, something simple, something English', adding that he 'can understand how [Alison's] Daddy must have felt when he came back from India, after all those years away' (13). The grand imperial design is 'unsettled' and, irrespective of their class or generation, Englishmen are united in their nostalgic mourning of 'the England [Colonel Redfern, Alison's father] left in 1914' (66). As Jimmy confesses, 'if you've got no world of your own, it's rather pleasant to regret the passing of someone else's' (13). Jimmy's rhetoric is transfused with references to the Empire, alluding to Alison's domestic chores as 'the White Woman's Burden' while calling Cliff, the Porters' lodger and friend – notably a Welshman – 'a savage' in constant need of Jimmy's magnanimous supervision: 'What do you think you're going to do when I'm not around to look after you? Well, what are you going to do? Tell me?' (12). Clearly not satisfied with sprawling in the central limelight, Jimmy expands his presence until he is in a position to occupy the whole stage at all times, imposing his psychological territorialism upon Alison and Cliff by means of endless oration, obnoxious pipe smoke and, whilst offstage, bouts of noisy trumpeting. Jimmy's hegemonic sense of self depends for its affirmation entirely on the responses he is able to elicit from others. Should his audience suddenly disperse instead of clustering attentively around him, and for once begin to concentrate on an exploration of their own interiority rather than eternally answering to the urgency of his allegedly superior needs, Jimmy's leadership would crumble and his claim to heroic status evaporate. As Osborne's stage directions indicate, Jimmy's frantic last-minute attempts at consolidating his position cannot pre-empt his imminent dematerialisation: 'He has lost [Alison and Cliff], and he knows it, but he won't leave it' (10).

It seems tempting to read Jimmy's angry young male struggle for an anachronistic kind of masculine dominance, already lost to devolutionary processes of ever greater societal diversification, as symptomatic of the break-up of the British Empire in the 1950s. Both patriarchal masculinity and European imperialism rely for their superiority on the unconditional subservience of a clearly defined margin of others. As colonies all over the globe took the end of World War II as an opportunity to opt for national independence, in *Look Back in Anger* we witness the first stirrings of organised self-assertion amongst women, gay men and – in Cliff's case – the minoritarian Anglo-Celtic subnations of Great Britain. Cliff eventually decides to move out and get married. Alison leaves her husband, if only temporarily. Her friend Helena is introduced as a woman with a 'sense of matriarchal authority [that] makes most men who meet her anxious, not only to please but to impress' (36). Not enough, earlier in the play we hear Jimmy express jealous admiration for Alison's gay friend Webster and his 'Michelangelo Brigade' for having, unlike him, a cause worth fighting for. Naturally, all these subversive destabilisations of the old order must provoke some kind of pomophobic backlash from Jimmy who, despite his self-professed role as a working-class rebel, appears to identify first and foremost as a heterosexual English male and hence as a standard representative of the patriarchal norm.

Deprived of its manifold imperial opportunities for exotic self-expansion and self-aggrandisement, the British nation of the 1950s found itself at a loss for viable means and strategies to accommodate the young male energies its own glamorous idealisation of a certain kind of heroic masculinity had fostered. Conscriptive army service turned out to be but a poor and hopelessly inadequate substitute for the loss of real-life challenges like the war-effort or the adventures opened up by the imperial enterprise. At the same time, attempts at domesticating the British male by redefining the masculine role as that of a breadwinner, considerate partner in marriage, responsible father and DIY expert only resulted in the Angry Young Male backlash (Segal 1990: 1–25), of which Jimmy Porter stands as a paradigmatic example. For the first time ever, British patriarchy found itself uncomfortably confined within its own insular parameters, parameters that could no longer hold the imperial Englishman's traditional self-image of hegemonic superiority. The ever more assertive emancipation of a wide range of minoritarian differences from within postmodern Britain's multicultural make-up has effectively brought about a gradual minoritisation of the hitherto uncontested normative standard of imperial masculinity whose cultural self-representations – traditionally taken for granted and deemed entirely unproblematic – are now in great need of radical re-envisioning.

What I would like to explore in the concluding part of this chapter is the notion that such a devolutionary overhaul and counterdiscursive remoulding of traditional conceptions of British manhood can only derive from what used to constitute the margins of imperial Britishness, not only the categorically ostracised position of the feminine but also, more importantly perhaps, the negative exteriority of a wide range of nationally, ethnically or sexually deviant 'countertypes' of British masculinity. My main focus will be on the 'countertype' of Scottish masculinity which, due to its recent re-emergence from a historical location of subnational marginality, appears to offer itself as a particularly pertinent and rewarding case study.

The Union and Jock

No doubt the most conspicuous difference between English and Scottish masculinities resides in the fact that, with reference to R. W. Connell's definition of four different realisations of patriarchal masculinity, Scottish masculinity would not normally be described as a 'hegemonic', but rather as a 'marginalised' or 'subordinate', if perhaps all too frequently 'complicitous', kind of masculinity (1995: 76–81). Within this context it seems worthwhile to have a closer look at the prominent motif of the double, or *doppelgänger*, which, since James Hogg's *Confessions of a Justified Sinner* (1824) and Robert Louis Stevenson's *Dr Jekyll and Mr Hyde* (1999 [1886]), has enjoyed such great popularity in both creative and critical Scottish writing, and Scottish men's writing especially. Would it be legitimate to read the *doppelgänger* motif as a gender-specific obsession with difference, not so much with what Adrienne Scullion has described as 'society's fear of the *unheimlich* aspects of the feminine' (1995: 201) as, more specifically, the Scottish male's fear of his own intrinsic self-and-otherness, or 'effeminacy'? Notably, within the imperial framework of English-Scottish relations, the Scottish male is always already feminised as a disempowered native (br)other. His condition is one of subordinate marginalisation which, whilst sensitising him to the plights of the systemically oppressed (women, for example), makes it all the more important for him to rigorously detach himself from the feminine, both within and outside of himself, in order not to compromise his already badly shaken sense of masculine self-containment even further. The result is a psychic split expressing itself in precarious and highly conflictual assertions of the integrity of a self that finds itself continuously embattled and destabilised by its own irrepressible alterity.

Scottish masculinity represents a case of highly ambivalent cross-interpellation. It occupies no fixed position of indisputable social hegemony but is caught up in continuous oscillation between the diametrically opposed sites of (post)colonial marginality on the one hand and patriarchal dominance on the other. This simultaneous inferiority and superiority make an uneasy blend, highlighting Scottish men's complicity with a system of oppression (that of patriarchy) while, at the same time, necessitating their commitment to counterdiscursive resistance (against English domination and remote control). Due to the Scottish male's position of subordinate marginality, it seems tempting to speculate that, unlike his English counterpart, he would not be prone to lash out against his others in a fit of pomophobic angst but instead enter into a coalition with them, a coalition that would greatly benefit from postmodernity's manifold devolutionary processes of destabilisation. In fact, in many respects the Scottish male's counterdiscursive marginality would seem to render him a perfect representative of Julia Kristeva's idea of 'woman' as a *sujet en procès*, or subject-in-the-making, which would effectively place him 'on the side of the explosion of social codes: with revolutionary moments' (1981: 166).

Indeed, as I have illustrated in *Writing Men*, there are a number of contemporary British men writers who, in recent years, have become highly self-conscious of the gender-specificity of their writing, and among them are many Scottish writers, for example Iain Banks, Alasdair Gray and even, if perhaps less successfully, Irvine Welsh. Inspired by feminist strategies of emancipation, these writers have begun to re-assess their given status as representatives of a standard norm whose systemic hegemony is safeguarded by a pomophobic oppression of alterity in all its significatory manifestations. Significantly, to resist and unlearn the sexist practices of masculine self-fashioning, these men writers often deliberately assume a position of societal marginality – traditionally occupied by women and other subordinate identities – from which they are able to 'come out' of patriarchy's interpellative frame and rehabilitate their gender in new, less one-dimensionally specific configurations. It is in this respect that heterosexual men might perhaps benefit from allowing themselves to be inspired not only by feminist but also gay male strategies of emancipation. Intriguingly, as a comparison of writings by gay and pro-feminist straight male authors reveals, the utopian position of marginality, circuitously arrived at by straight male protagonists, is fundamentally little different from the gay male heroes' original point of departure.

In *Male Subjectivity at the Margins* Kaja Silverman has dedicated a whole book to an analysis of these 'marginal male subjectivities ... which absent themselves from the line of paternal succession, and ... in one way or another occupy the domain of femininity' (1992: 389). Propounding 'the theoretical articulation of some non-phallic masculinities [as] an urgent feminist issue', Silverman's study foregrounds subordinate masculinities

> which not only acknowledge but embrace castration, alterity, and specularity. Although these attributes represent the unavoidable tropes of all subjectivity, they generally feature prominently only within the conscious existence of the female subject. Conventional masculinity is largely predicated upon their denial. Saying 'no' to power necessarily implies achieving some kind of reconciliation with these structuring terms, and hence with femininity. It means, in other words, the collapse of that system of fortification whereby sexual difference is secured, a system dependent upon projection, disavowal and fetishism. (3)

The question to be asked now is whether contemporary Scottish masculinity could possibly be described as a devolutionary kind of masculinity that has embraced its feminine marginality and is saying 'no' to power. In 'Not(e) from the margin', an essay written in 1995 in response to an English woman colleague's suggestion that 'nationalism is always bad news for women', Christopher Whyte suggests that indeed, due to its status as a minoritarian counterdiscourse, Scottishness 'could, conceivably if not actually, be more receptive and more nurturing to women, gay men and other "marginal" groups than larger, more dominant cultures.' The generally highly conflictual and problematical tensions between nationalism and minoritarian counternarratives of national belonging are likely to dissolve, so Whyte argues, in a country whose rhetoric of nation constitutes in itself such a minoritarian counter-narrative. Thus, Whyte continues, 'a Scottish woman might, under certain circumstances, feel closer to a Scottish man than to an English woman' (1995b: 34). However, in an essay written only three years later, Whyte adopts an entirely different and far less optimistic stance, con-cluding that, 'in a context such as Scotland's, where national self-determination continues to be a burning issue, gender antagonisms may be aggravated rather than resolved' (1998: 284). Analysing various repre-sentations of masculinity in contemporary Scottish fiction and looking at the works of Alasdair Gray, Alan Warner and Irvine Welsh in particular, Whyte identifies the Scottish *hard man*'s alleged marginality as a pathetic pose motivated by pretentious pseudo-feminist affectations rather than any genuine desire to facilitate a radical overhaul of traditional power structures within Scottish society, let alone enter into a counterdiscursive coalition with women and/or gay men. In fact, rather than exploring and negotiating their own feminine quandary of subnational castration, alterity and specularity, Scottish men writers seem prone to merely appropriate and thus upstage the marginality of women.

Symptomatically, 'the figure of the reclining male, a hero who is incapacitated in some way and may even be hospitalised' (Whyte 1998: 279), makes a recurrent appearance in contemporary Scottish men's writing, for instance in Iain Banks's *The Bridge* (1986), Alasdair Gray's *1982 Janine* (1984) and Irvine Welsh's *Marabou Stork Nightmares* (1996). Whereas Whyte recognises these heroes' supineness as a (stereo)typically feminine position, deployed to signal the men's apparent 'incapab[ility] of adopting an upright, "erect" pose', he also feels obliged to comment on what he regards as the deeply fraudulent artifice of such a meta-phorical device. 'The damage that reduced [the male protagonists] to this state is', so Whyte points out, 'as often as not self-inflicted' (1998: 280), meaning that their putative marginality is more often than not the result of a petulant temper tantrum in response to being denied access to a position of authority, autonomy and power to which they deem them-selves rightfully entitled. In no way is it comparable to the burden of actual real-life discrimination and societal ostracism borne by 'unwomanly' women and gay men. In light of Scotland's recently accomplished devo-lution, Whyte's concern that Scottishness may now begin to undergo a hyperbolic reassertion of itself as a monologic master discourse at risk of recklessly shattering its erstwhile alliance with other, alternative counter-narratives of the nation is surely to be taken very seriously.

In conclusion, I would like to return to Kaja Silverman's suggestion that men's embrace of marginality, their collective resolution to say 'no' to power and reject what Calvin Thomas so pertinently designates as 'the phallicized ego' (1996: 21), could put an end to 'the murderous logic of traditional male subjectivity' (Silverman 1992: 389), its unwholesome obsession with the erection of definitive boundaries, be they individual or communal, and its uncritical promotion of the self 'to the status of an ethical ideal' that, due to its hyperbolic elevation, becomes, as Leo Bersani has asserted, 'a sanction for violence' (1987: 222). Finding itself at the beginning of a new era, Scotland has been given the chance to resist a re-erection of the hyperbolic self and its patriarchally organised nation state. By taking on board Iain Chambers' position that 'the "nation" as a cultural and linguistic unit is not a closed history, something that has already been achieved, but is an open, malleable framework in the making' (1993: 160), Scotland could develop into what Catherine Hall calls a 'post-nation', that is, 'a society that has discarded the notion of a homogeneous nation state with singular forms of belonging' (1996: 67). Such a post-nation would take its inspiration from what Silverman envisages as a 'libidinal politics' of desire and radical self-and-otherness. The aim would be to once and for all demolish the nation as a disembodied system of paranoid fortification and to put in its place the living body of the nation's wide diversity of different people(s) who continue to express and (re-)identify themselves in ceaseless processes of dialogic and fundamentally counterdiscursive intercommunication.

There are at least two – admittedly utopianist – epistemic prelimin-aries whose fulfillment would be absolutely crucial for the successful facilitation of a post-national state with which both men and women could wholeheartedly identify – intellectually as well as, more impor-tantly perhaps, libidinally – and which would incorporate rather than merely accommodate the nation's vast repertoire of different narratives of national belonging. First, the people would have to communally unlearn the concept of 'otherness', especially in terms of the hoary mind/body dualism that burdens women with the symbolic embodiment of the nation whilst requiring men to disembody themselves and disappear into a representational façade of the nation's inflexibly demarcated bound-aries. Secondly, the people would have to say a collective 'no' to power, which would necessitate a radical reconceptualisation of the very concept of identity, not in terms of a superiority/inferiority or sameness/difference binary, but in terms of what, with reference to the work of Leo Bersani, Calvin Thomas discusses as 'the value of powerlessness, and of meaning-lessness, of nonidentity or dis-identification, in both women and men' (1996: 35). To my knowledge there is so far only one male-authored Scottish novel that comes close to illustrating both these utopianist preliminaries, and that is Iain Banks's *The Wasp Factory* (1990 [1984]), which features a boy protagonist (Frank) who turns out to be 'really' a girl and who in the novel's concluding vision comes to embrace her 'effeminate' brother Eric, whose performative artifice of an insufferable masculine heroism has cracked and disintegrated under patriarchal pressure.

Albeit only in vaguely allegorical terms, Banks's *The Wasp Factory* addresses the issue of Scottish postmodernity, that is, contemporary Scotland's communal struggle for national (re)identification. Signifi-cantly, Frank (as an exemplary representative of Scottish masculinity) must eventually abandon his pomophobic project of phallic self-fashion-ing. The hitherto unchallenged lord of the island becomes a Kristevan *sujet en procès*, eager to resume his quest for self-authentication but now required to do so from a position of feminine marginality rather than phallocentric independence. Stripped of its spurious self-consistency and fraudulent traditionalism, the new Scotland is left to re-inscribe itself in a dialogic exploration of its own – as well as its (br)other's – alterity. Importantly, Banks's vision of subversive change is not apocalyptic but epiphanic, deconstructive rather than purely annihilative. 'Poor Eric came home to see his brother', the novel concludes, 'only to find (Zap! Pow! Dams burst! Bombs go off! Wasps fry: ttssss!) he's got a sister' (1990 [1984]: 184). The apparent cataclysm is parenthetically contained within the notion of a revelational homecoming. Although the old order has undergone an explosive decentralisation, it is not radically destroyed but transformed into a welcoming refuge for the uprooted and temp-orarily insane.

Initially, in their confusion, both Frank and Eric set fire to the picture-book icons of the Scottish pastoral (rabbits, dogs, sheep). Miraculously, however, despite the fact that it sits on a basement full of cordite, hoarded by the boys' grandfather, the family estate of the Cauldhames emerges unscathed from this panoramic conflagration. The old Scotland is not totally erased by the angry insurrection of 'an evil demon we have lurking, a symbol for all our family misdeeds' (1990 [1984]: 53). Rather, like the traditional gender formations that have sus-tained it so far, it appears to find itself at the beginning of a regenerative period of post-national change.

PART II
Cultural negotiations

6

Paper margins: the 'outside' in poetry in the 1980s and 1990s

LINDEN PEACH

Poetry emanating from what a few decades ago would have been deemed 'the margins' has become the major focus of publishing houses, journals and criticism, the latter evident in two recent collections of essays: *Poetry in the British Isles: Non-Metropolitan Perspectives* (Ludwig and Fietz 1995) and *Contemporary British Poetry: Essays in Theory and Criticism* (Acheson and Huk 1996). I say 'were deemed' because, as Terry Eagleton has observed, the marginal has become 'somehow central' (1989/90: 4), an observation cited by the editors of *The New Poetry* (Hulse, Kennedy and Morley 1993: 18) and by Romana Huk in *Contemporary British Poetry* (Acheson and Huk 1996: 3). It is not the intention of this chapter, however, to survey the richness and diversity of poetry from what Eagleton sees as the new centre. Such a project would require a book in itself and then would probably fail for lack of space. Instead, I want to probe Eagleton's assumption in the light of some of the trends in poetry and poetry criticism in the 1980s and 1990s, while suggesting, however inadequately given the space available, the variety of work that became available in these decades.

It hardly needs pointing out that the poetry scene has changed since the publication of *British Poetry Since 1970*, in which Blake Morrison stereotyped the published poet as writing from a 'nostalgic liberal humanism' with 'strong respect for "traditional" forms, even strict metre and rhyme' (Jones and Schmidt 1980: 142). Morrison said as much two years later in the introduction to *The Penguin Book of Contemporary British Poetry* (1982: 11). But, as Robert Hampson and Peter Barry point out, if such a transformation had taken place by then, it was not reflected in the 'narrowness of poetic taste evidenced in the anthology's selection of poets and poems' (1993: 4). By the end of the decade, when it was clearer how the nature of published poetry had changed, *The New British Poetry* (Allnutt *et al.*, 1988) drew attention to what Morrison and Motion had overlooked with, for example, substantial representation of black British, feminist and experimental poetry. Publishing houses outside London, for example Bloodaxe Books in Newcastle-upon-Tyne, Carcanet in Manchester, Seren Books in South Wales and Blackstaff in Northern Ireland, have proved major players in bringing about this change, as have numerous poetry and literary magazines, various Arts Council initiatives, and locally organised poetry workshops and events. Even a cursory familiarity with published poetry in the last two decades – one has only to look at the two key anthologies of the 1990s from Newcastle-upon-Tyne: *The New Poetry* (Hulse, Kennedy and Morley 1993) and *New Blood* (Astley 1999) – would appear to confirm Eagleton's observation; in, for example, the strong presence of work by women as well as men from a range of different cultural communities including ethnic minorities and regional and working-class constituencies, through the proliferation of lesbian and gay writing, and the rich diversity of poetry emanating from Welsh, Scottish and Irish authors. But the poetry scene has been transformed in these decades not only in terms of the sensibilities, politics and form of emergent works but, as Romana Huk argues, 'the way in which the late twentieth century has become represented by critics, academics, and (as a consequence) publishers' (Acheson and Huk 1996: 3). Yet if recent criticism and current trends in publishing are to be credited with making the margins the new centre, that very criticism has itself been said to threaten 'to impoverish our understanding of poetry' (Day 1997: 1). But while Gary Day laments how the political has become the dominant idiom in poetry criticism, he never really defines whose 'understanding of poetry' he has in mind. A phrase like 'our understanding' is so shot through with value judgements and political implications that its insouciant employment, as here, must suggest that even in the 1990s the relationship between cultural politics and aesthetic issues is still a very pertinent subject.

We must be similarly cautious about Eagleton's argument that the marginal (which margins? from whose perspective?) has become central-ised (according to what criteria?). The extent to which his observation is entirely reflective of the poetry scene is questionable even a decade later. Not all the 'marginal' or formerly marginal communities have freed themselves to the same extent from involvement with a centre-margin paradigm. Within the margins there are further margins. The latter point is well reflected in the selection of poets in the significant anthology of the mid–1990s *The New Poetry*, even though its editors quote Eagleton triumphantly. While six poets from Scotland – Robert Crawford, Tom Leonard, Liz Lochhead, W. N. Herbert, Jackie Kay, Frank Kuppner – are included, only two poets from Wales, despite the volume and diversity of contemporary, Welsh English-language poetry, have been selected: Tony Curtis and Duncan Bush. And there are even further layers of marginalisation within the margins suggested here; only two of the poets representing Scotland are women while no Welsh woman poet is included. Although Nuala Ní Dhomhnaill's work in Irish is represented, with translations into English, it has obviously not been thought as politically sensitive to exclude work by a Welsh poet working in Welsh. Of course, any selection for an anthology cannot please everyone, and is bound to be open to criticism. But the relative representation of Welsh and Scottish writers, together with issues of gender and geographical balance within the selections, suggests that we are confronting issues about the different ways in which different margins may be regarded at different times and from different perspectives.

I wrote of 'familiarity with *published* poetry' above deliberately, wondering how many readers would balk at the word 'published'. The marginalisation of 'performance' poetry generally is an issue to which I will return later with reference, among others, to black British artists, for whom performance poetry has been an important (although only one) mode in the 1980s and 1990s. But the point might also be made here that of the sixty or so black British poets writing, recording or performing in Britain, only a handful, whether writing for the page or for the stage, are brought to the attention of students of literature or discussed in critical essays. Moreover, African and West Indian British poets generally enjoy a greater visibility than Asian British poets, despite notable exceptions such as Debjani Chatterjee.

Renewed focus on the periphery is usually linked in political terms to some sense of liberation, most obviously freedom from centralising forces and from the self-serving interests of the metropolis. But it is also a process of 'defamiliarisation'. As the poet and critic Jeremy Hooker points out, 'a bland centralism takes much for granted, as if the places where we or other people live are thoroughly known, and essentially much the same as the centre's image of itself' (Hooker 1982: 11). The impetus in the 1980s behind this approach to the 'margins' among academics across a range of disciplines was the rise in Europe and America of what came to be called 'new' or 'postmodern' geography, primarily concerned with re-theorising the relationship between history, geography and social life (see, for example, Keith and Pike 1993; Norquay and Smyth 1997; Rose 1993; Soja 1989). But in poetry criticism it was also an example of how academics and scholars began to give a higher profile to the socio-geographical aspects of emergent writers, and how significant young poets began to develop, and represent, this feature of their writing. When Scottish poet Stewart Cohen writes of Ayrshire, Simon Armitage depicts aspects of the North of England, Ciaran Carson explores Belfast, or Christine Evans conceptualises North Wales, they are not writing only from a sense of discovering themselves at an empowering margin where the centralising forces of the centre may be resisted, although ultimately that may be the effect of some of their work. At its best, their work is rooted in a sophisticated awareness of the interrelated social life, geography and history of what Jeremy Hooker in the mid–1980s called a 'circumambient environment':

> A place is a totality, a place is all that has created it through the process of time, it is the history, the geology, the circumambient environment, and in addition to that, it is the connection within a single compass of all those living forces. (Butler 1985: 203)

Thus, it is not that the metaphors and figures in, for example, Ciaran Carson's *The Irish For No* (1987), a key work from Northern Ireland in the late 1980s, are dense with social and cultural history but that the cartography of Belfast in which they are located is densely inscribed with sociocultural meanings. This particular circumambient environment is one that is constantly changing, not only through bombings and burnings but inscription and reinscription, through a past that is brought into a present which is constantly disintegrating. His tonal and syntactically complex writing documents and resists a system of signification which, as Neil Corcoran observes, is also a 'system of subjugation' (1992: 224). But since in postmodern Belfast the body itself is always liable to be commodified within this system of subjugation, the ultimate sites of resistance in *The Irish For No* are the discontinuities and intermittences of personal and cultural meaning in which the body is situated and represented.

Postmodern geography's emphasis upon the body as it is represented in the various spaces through which it moves has provided a new impetus for criticism to respond positively to poetry in which spatialised social and cultural differences are explored through the complexity of lived experience. The attention afforded the socio-spatial geography in Carson's work is an obvious example, but the way lesbian and gay poetry defamiliarises conventional ways of regarding space, particularly traditional distinctions between 'private' and 'public', also comes readily to mind. Not surprisingly, it is an important motif in the work of the black Scottish poet Jackie Kay who was herself brought up by white parents. In *The Adoption Papers* (1991) – which tells the story of a black girl's adoption from three different perspectives, the mother, the birth mother and the daughter herself – and many of the poems in *Other Lovers* (1992) – which contrasts relationships in a variety of temporal, emotional and physical contexts – Kay writes incisively about relationships which in private and public have been complicated by issues of race, memory, family and inheritance. Conventional temporal and place logic is collapsed in order to locate the body within more subtle private and public registers. While the relationship between the personal and the social is not gainsaid, the sense of obligation and responsibility derives from personal rather than public or cultural paradigms. Thus, Kay's work raises a number of issues in relation to Eagleton's assumption that the margins have become centralised: the role that poetry has, can have, in this new public space; the nature of political meaning ascribed to particular poetics; the extent to which poetry can be confined within aesthetic, geographical or socio-cultural boundaries; and the relationship between poetic freedom and, in the broad sense, 'political' or 'public' responsibility. But for Kay and for others of her generation who use the personal to breach the boundaries of public space, these issues are all based on terms that are reconfigured within their work.

Recent re-theorising of power relationships is extremely sceptical of the paradigm into which Tony Harrison, for example, sometimes lapses, in which subordinate groups are perceived as being silenced altogether and unable to express alternative views stemming from their different structural positions in society. As Emily Martin has observed, modern forms of power 'do not just deny, prohibit, repress, and restrict', they 'produce', for example, discourses and knowledge (1992: 409). Such models of resistance have been employed explicitly or implicitly in drawing a range of writers from Scotland, Wales and ethnic communities into the spotlight. But the poets from these nations and communities that have attracted most academic attention in the 1990s have been those whose work, although recognisably 'Scottish', 'Welsh' and/or black, is not tied too closely to a constraining sense of place (Bell 1991; Craig 1996a; Wynn Thomas 1995a). This is not to say, however, that while they take a broad perspective that appears to break away from geographical boundaries, they are not concerned with culturally specific and politically determined meanings. The most overlooked feature of the Scottish poet Robert Crawford's work is that he is not simply investigating Scottish history from a variety of perspectives but exploring how modern forms of power produce discourses and knowledge. As is clear from *The Scottish Assembly* (1990), one of the most significant volumes of poetry by a Scottish writer in the early 1990s, what is produced is often subversive, not necessarily in any directly antagonistic way, but through exposing the constructed nature of the dominant discourses. This point is well illustrated by 'Alba Einstein', which imagines a cultural industry developing around confirmation of Einstein's Scottish origins:

> Scots publishers hurled awa
> MacDiarmid like an overbaked potato, and swooped
> On the memorabilia: *Einstein Used My Fruitshop*,
> *Einstein in Old Postcards*, *Einstein's Bearsden Relatives*.
> Hot on their heels came the A. E. Fun Park,
> Quantum Court, Glen Einstein Highland Malt.
>
> (1990: 53)

A lot of the poetry discussed in academic journals and poetry magazines such as *Bête Noire* and *Verse* may be linked to a point stressed by Michel Foucault, that 'resistance is never in a position of exteriority in relation to power' (1982: 209). For me this is the point from which Carol Ann Duffy's well-known 'Standing Female Nude' (1985: 46), a key poem of the 1980s, starts out. On a cursory reading, the poem would appear to be an explication of how power silences subordinate groups. The artist's model, the speaker of the monologue, is literally told by the artist, 'Don't talk'; and his work objectifies her as a commodity to be bought, sold and possessed, as the socio-economic system does herself. However, her resistance is not only in the conclusion of the poem when the portrait is completed – 'I say/Twelve francs and get my shawl./It does not look like me.' – but in the discourses which her relation to the dominant power structures produce. In this sense, her portrait is never completed. The artistic representation, analogous to the bourgeoisie and the larger socio-economic system, does not silence her, but produces ironic, mocking counter discourses: 'The bourgeoisie will coo/at such an image of a river-whore. They call it Art'. Here the relationship between the male, clothed artist and the female, naked model is the product of two discourses which ostensibly interleave to sustain male power, but is potentially undermined by the counter discourses which the latter produces. These counter discourses are the product, as here, of resistance or of what is excluded when boundaries are drawn by those in power, a recurring theme in *Mean Time* (1993) and *The World's Wife* (1999). They are a way of resisting not only authority structures but how language constructs the individual's subjectivity.

Of course, issues of language and agency are inevitable themes in poetry emanating from what are, or were once, the margins. Here there would seem to be a basis for discussing the margins homogeneously. But we must be careful to remember that the structure of power in one periphery is not necessarily the same as in another. This is a point frequently made in the work of Mike Jenkins, a South Wales poet whose work is particularly appropriate to an essay on poetry and the margins. Although associated with Wales (which has itself been too often approached in terms of a centre-periphery paradigm), Jenkins has lived most of his adult life in a marginalised area within Wales: Merthyr, the oldest industrial town in Britain but now a by-word for post-industrial decline and social poverty. It is no coincidence that Jenkins's concern with the interconnections of language and power has become more pronounced as he has become more interested in giving voice to adolescents from the deprived Gurnos housing estate who attend the school in which he teaches. The use of non-standard English in poetry associated with the margins is often approached within rather limited parameters, relying on arguments that standard English 'cannot render the experiences of those on the margin, as if one idiom is expressive while another is not' (Day 1997: 4). Poets as diverse as the British Guyanese writer David Dabydeen, the black British performance poet Linton Kwesi Johnson, the Scottish writer Tom Leonard and the Welsh author Mike Jenkins use dialect for many complex reasons, one of which is to explore the production of counter discourses. 'Gurnos Boy' (from *A Dissident Voice* (1990), reprinted, with revisions, in *Graffiti Narratives*, 1994) is one of Jenkins's most successful poems about the estate. Like Duffy's artist's model, the boy handles many of the discourses that try to determine his individual subjectivity with a bitter, street-wise irony:

> This place is gettin famous f murderers,
> we produce em like Oovers washin-machines.
> If this Government push me much further
> I'll afta cut the posh people clean
> in theyr big ouses with burglar larms.

> (1994: 17–18)

The language in which black British writers work usually originates with their sense of themselves, of their history and of the diaspora to which they belong. This is certainly the case in two major works first published in the 1980s. David Dabydeen, who is able to work effectively across poetry, fiction and literary criticism with a similar aplomb, employs Creole dialect, in *Slave Song* (1984) and *Creole Odyssey* (1988), because it provides access to a particular culture, particular experiences and specific histories:

> Black men cover wid estate ash
> E ead haad an dry like calabash,
> Dut in e nose-hole, in e ear-hole,
> Dut in e soul, in e battie-hole.
>
> All
> day
> sun
> bun
> tongue
> bun
>
> all
> day
> troat
> cut
> haat
> hut
> wuk na dun, na dun, na dun!
> Hack! Hack! Hack! Hack!
> Cutlass slip an cut me cack!
>
> (1988: 31)

At one level, Dabydeen encapsulates the monotony and the brutality of slavery, here specifically cutting cane. But he also demonstrates a different social and textual affiliation for black people, in his case Guyanese, from that assumed by white British people who have a different history in terms of empire and slavery. The indentured worker of the cane plantations is not a voice that has often been as fully articulated as here. It does not directly challenge the dominant white discourses but indirectly exposes the fictitious nature of the constructs, of the social and textual narratives, that have given the British centre cohesion against the various margins on which it has been constructed. It calls into question the conventional disposition of space and time, suggesting the possibility of complex reconfigurations of difference and identity, exclusion and inclusion, centre and margin, outsider and insider.

No reconceptualising of the periphery has been as complex and far-reaching in its implications as the emergent emphasis in the 1990s upon 'internal difference' in Homi K. Bhabha's notion of 'dissemiNation', by which he means the way in which nations are 'internally marked by cultural difference, the heterogeneous histories of contending peoples, antagonistic authorities and tense cultural differences' (1990a: 299). Internal, sometimes antagonistic, differences within the periphery itself have often proved a more important and potent source of creativity for poetry than relationships with the centre, as is evident in the Scottish poet W. N. Herbert's *Forked Tongue* (1994) and *The Looters* (1989) by Robert Minhinnick, another poet associated with post-industrial South Wales, but this time Glamorgan's Heritage Coast on which he lives. In an essay on his own work, Minhinnick has observed:

> Wales is a country of strong creative frictions, at least I feel they should be creative, especially for writers. The rural and the industrial, traditional industry and new technology, the English and the Welsh languages, a past representing an emphatic and unique cultural identity and a present in which that identity might become irreversibly eroded. (In Butler 1985: 187)

The implication of the concept of internal difference is not necessarily to fragment the periphery so that it ceases to have any significant role in the production of meaning but to redefine it in ways that are closer to the lived experience of those within it. This distinction has been articulated succinctly by Mike Jenkins in an introduction to a selection of his own work:

> In the past, I've been called a local (Merthyr) poet, an urban poet and a political poet and I hope this selection will both prove and confound those terms. Living on the edge of a moor still owned by the Coal Board, teaching at a school overlooking the Brecon Beacons yet drawing pupils from council estates and older communities and, above all, seeing politics in terms of people's lives: all these contribute to a tension which questions categories. (Stephens 1991: 155)

But Jenkins also suggests here, in his allusion to the demise of the coal industry, that the material operations and cultural consequences of globalisation mean that we cannot think of the margins in purely cultural terms. We have to engage with economic and sociological factors. As I have argued elsewhere (1997), both Jenkins and Minhinnick can be seen as responding to the transition in the 1970s and 1980s from modernity to postmodernity. By postmodernity, I mean the quite evident shift at this

time from an industrial to a post-industrial society with its own organi-
sing principles, in which new forms of technology and information are
central. The poems dealing with a post-industrial society in Jenkins's
Invisible Times (1983) and *A Dissident Voice* (1990), and in Minhinnick's
volumes published about the same time, *The Dinosaur Park* (1985) and
The Looters (1989), offer a variant on the way in which the regions were
associated in the 1970s with an escape from centralisation and universalism. By the mid 1980s, the forces of centralisation were global rather
than metropolitan, international rather than national.

While Minhinnick and Jenkins are very different poets, the understanding of 'postmodernity' which emerges in their respective poetry is
not fundamentally different: the rise of an image/media-saturated society,
the increasing importance of consumption and of a social geography
based on consumer markets, and the erosion of traditional, collective and
personal identities. But what Jenkins and Minhinnick discover happening in post-industrial Wales is a phenomena experienced throughout the
Atlantic archipelago. There are fundamental parallels between, for
example, the image-saturated, multi-media packages based on what
were once real working mines by the Welsh heritage industry in Mike
Jenkins's poem, 'Industrial Museum' and the simulacra that develop
around Einstein in Robert Crawford's 'Alba Einstein' to which I referred
on p. 106. But while there are similarities in the post-industrial world
emerging in Minhinnick's Wales or Crawford's Scotland, it is experienced differently in different regions. Jenkins' and Minhinnick's critique
of 'postmodernity', and their means of arguing for resistance, is based on
the importance of interaction with the natural environment, an especially strong motif in Minhinnick's work, and on an identifiable fusion of
people and place at the level of microgeography, characteristic preoccupations of Welsh, English-language poetry.

If it is appropriate to think of the poets of working-class origin and
sympathy who came to prominence in the 1980s as 'postmargin', the
concept might be equally applicable to women poets who achieved prominence at that time, many of whom – such as Liz Lochhead, Gillian
Clarke, Grace Nichols and Jackie Kay – are not only from cultures which
had been marginalised by the centre but cultures in which women had
been marginalised. Both the Scottish poet Lochhead and the Welsh,
English-langauge poet Clarke have emerged from social and economic
circumstances which, as Cairns Craig says of Lochhead, had entrapped
their foremothers (1996a: 355). In Clarke's case this is evident in her early
poem, 'Marged':

> I think of her sometimes when I lie in bed,
> falling asleep in the room I have made in the roof-space
> over the old dark parlwr where she died
> alone in winter, ill and penniless.
> Lighting the lamps, November afternoons,
> a reading book, whisky gold in my glass.
>
> (1985: 105)

But while insisting on difference, the poem seems to want to seek out an 'essence' to turn into essentialising notions. It concludes: 'What else do we share, but being women?' This is a recurring danger in Clarke's poetry, even in her major long poem of the 1990s, *The King of Britain's Daughter* (1993), but one that for the most part she avoids. However, it is also a danger of which we must be aware as critics. Lochhead's experiences are different from Clarke's, rooted in different personal, geographical and sociocultural circumstances, as are Robert Crawford's or Robert Minhinnick's experiences of postmodernity. There is nothing in Gillian Clarke's poetry comparable to Lochhead's view of the mother, in Cairn Craig's words, 'hemmed in by fearful daughter fantasies' (1996a: 352):

> Everybody's mother
> was the original Frigid-
> aire Icequeen clunking out
> the hardstuff in nuggets, mirror-
> silvers and ice-splinters that'd stick
> in your heart.
>
> (Lochhead 1984: 94)

The importance of resisting received notions of nationality, as well as unified concepts of gender, have become increasingly recognised in poetry criticism. But one of the problems is that the geographical groupings that have been used to indicate the heterogeneity of race and region in women's writing have tended to enforce a homogeneity of particular races and regions. In the recent study of poetry in the Atlantic archipelago from non-metropolitan perspectives which I cited at the beginning of this essay, Christopher Harvie warns that 'one cannot see the periphery whole, or even the individual nationalities whole: one can try to see a constant dialogue of communities with their individual members and with one another' (1995: 6). The need to recognise complex lived experience is important in the case of black writers who, as C. L. Innes says, tend to be associated with group identities and enterprises (1996: 315). But this does not mean taking writers out of place, and out of group identities and enterprises. It means being true to how poetry recomposes itself in dialogue with place or group identity, with the way in which places map ourselves, and with the occluded histories of power relationships.

Most of the poems in the black British section of *The New British Poetry* (Allnutt *et al.* 1988), like much of the work selected for the anthology, provide examples of how concepts and experiences may be redefined when taken outside the centre-periphery paradigm, as is evident in Fred D'Aguiar's 'Half-caste' which he included from his own work:

> explain yuself
> wha yu mean
> when yu say half-caste
> yu mean when light an shadow
> mix in de sky
> is a half-caste weather /
> well in dat case
> england weather
> nearly always half-caste
> in fact some o dem cloud
> half-caste
>
> (Allnutt *et al.* 1988: 6)

Here the mocking and ironic voice of the poet/narrator is located not simply in difference but a mental space that has its own configurations. The posing of the question, 'wha yu mean', arrests the fictitious formulation on which absolute notions of identity, race and the centre are based. But like Dabydeen's employment of Creole, D'Aguiar's use of dialect emphasises how identity is always both personal and social, linked in the dominant symbolic order. Different concepts of identity are brought together and clash with each other, a recurring feature also of *British Subjects* (1993), which should compete with Dabydeen's *Turner* (1994) as the most significant work by a black poet in the 1990s, where he mockingly observes on re-entering the country,

> my passport photo's too open-faced,
> haircut wrong (an afro) for the decade;
> the stamp, British Citizen not bold enough
> for my liking and too much for theirs.
>
> ('Home', 1993: 14)

It is difficult to compare, say, the experience of Wales by Welsh poets writing in English with those of black British poets, although sometimes postcolonial criticism invites us to do so. However, what is clear is that many poets of Welsh or black British origin writing in the 1980s and

1990s locate themselves in a place that they do not see only in terms of a centre-margin paradigm. They tend to see themselves increasingly in a place that is different. This is especially true of those black British poets to whom I referred at the beginning of this chapter, who, from the point of view of the centre, have not received the recognition of David Dabydeen, Fred D'Aguiar or John Agard. These writers, such as Kwesi Owusu, Amon Saba Saakana or Lemn Sissay, locate themselves in a space which owes more to the African diaspora, to black history, African roots and orature, embracing poetry as performance, and to music more than a British-African paradigm.

Performance poetry, poetry readings, a plethora of small press publications and little magazines still constitute from even the 'new' centre's point of view a marginal cultural activity. Many of these literary magazines, as David Kennedy says of *Bête Noire*, demonstrate 'how the blandishments of the centre should be resisted' (1991/92: 29). *Bête Noire* and *Verse* are placed at the front line of resistance because Hull and Scotland are good 'locations from which to focus on multi-cultural and international concerns', but *The North*, published by The Poetry Business in Huddersfield, has proved itself similarly well situated, as has *The Wide Skirt*, edited by Geoff Hattersley, one of the most significant North of England poets of the 1990s, in South Yorkshire. At a grass roots level, the same might be said of much performance poetry. But, as Simon Armitage's review of a poetry performance by Adrian Mitchell in the same issue as Kennedy's 'magazine roundup' exemplifies, discussion of it usually gets bogged down in definitions and a 'readerly' and 'performance' binarism. However, so-called performance poets, such as Attila the Stockbroker, challenge not only what we might think of as poetry but also conventional definitions of the margins. *Scornflakes* (1992) includes satiric responses to subjects of popular concern, such as the High Court Judge who told a hitchhiker who was raped late at night that she was guilty of contributory negligence. Like the black British poets Lemn Sissay, Benjamin Zephaniah and Linton Kwesi Johnson, whose collections *Rebel Without Applause*, *Propa Propaganda* and *Tings on Times* were also published by Bloodaxe, he employs simplistic rhymes and discomforting social aggression. But, like theirs, his work is also direct, spontaneous, witty and humorous. It employs arresting imagery, original social juxtapositions, and a defamiliarising use of language. It challenges what is meant by 'poetry', especially when we remember that many so-called 'readerly' poets include in their volumes a range of work from across the readerly–performance continuum. In fact, Liz Lochhead, as Robert Crawford has pointed out (Crawford and Varty 1993), relies heavily on puns that work better in speech than writing, and draws upon radio and music hall, especially its tradition of comic monologue. The distinction between readerly and performance work is further complicated by the pressure exerted on poets by their agents and publishers to give more readings and public appearances and by the presence of writers such as Jo Shapcott (1992, 1999) who have created poems for the stage that work as well on the page.

In fact, the startling unpredictability that characterises the work of many contemporary poets can be linked to a fusion of the readerly and the oral. In becoming the new centre, the margins have brought with them a renewed interest in 'other tongues', which extends to the mother tongue, to formerly silenced gender and sexual discourses, to the communication of a wide range of non-metropolitan experiences, but also to oral cultures and traditions marginalised by the emphasis upon the printed word. Whether it be the Scottish ballad, the Irish story-telling tradition, the comic monologue of the music hall, the oral culture of the school playground or of the new housing estate, the oral often contains the seeds of subversion. Material presented orally is always more susceptible of interruption and disruption than material presented in writing. One wonders whether Liz Lochhead is so much more a radical poet than Gillian Clarke partly because she draws so much on oral modes while Clarke's work is rooted in written forms often associated with women, such as the diary and the letter.

In aesthetic terms, the centre-margin debate is based upon the centrality of familiar assumptions about poetry which professional critics often reiterate unquestioningly. Despite Gary Day's generally incisive appraisal of what he perceives as the dominant political idiom in poetry criticism in the mid 1990s, he lapses into unchallenged assumptions such as 'poetry is private, almost intimate', or 'poetry aims to soften the language to receive the impress of the personal' (1997: 7, 8). Despite his rejection of the political idiom, Day argues for poetry in terms of resistance, to 'endlessly proliferating jingles, slogans and sound bites of consumer culture', to 'the rigidities of headline culture' and to 'public rhetoric' (8). Unfortunately, Day's singular model of what constitutes poetry does not recognise that in the work of many leading poets, whether of readerly or performance persuasion, Robert Crawford, Mike Jenkins, Liz Lochhead, Attila the Stockbroker and Fred D'Aguiar, there is a dialectic with the characteristic forms of communication in consumer society.

The use of modes of speech and writing in the 1980s and 1990s not normally associated with mainstream poetry two or three decades ago, however, is a linguistic as well as a political phenomenon, although ultimately the two cannot be easily separated. Drawing on the Russian critic Mikhail Bakhtin's notion of 'heteroglossia', Robert Crawford points out that 'if language is normally made up of languages, if discourse is always a blend of discourses', then the linguistic hybridity we associate with Anglo-Welsh, Scottish and black British poets 'becomes typical rather than eccentric' (1993: 7). This is to say that the multilayered linguistic and ideological nature of formerly marginalised groups is itself being recognised as typical.

One of the salient features of poetry in the 1990s is the cross-currents of influence, evident in poetry from the North of England in Geoff Hattersley's *Don't Worry* (1994), drawing on a diverse range of American poetic influences and, to a lesser extent, in Graham Mort's *Snow from the North* (1992), both of which interweave northern environments with international perspectives and viewpoints. In this respect, it is perhaps the second generation of post 1970 Northern Ireland poets, more than any other, that has established an important presence in the poetry of the Atlantic archipelago; their work often amounts to a complex amalgam of differences and border crossings. As Neil Corcoran has observed of Paul Muldoon, 'collations, collisions and collusions' in their work create an 'extraordinarily open and free poetic space' (1993: 211). The truth of this is evident in Paul Muldoon's long poem *Madoc* (1990), which along with Medbh McGuckian's *Marconi's Cottage* (1991), marked the transition in particular Northern Ireland poetry circles to the kind of work Corcoran has in mind. But what Corcoran does not go on to consider is that the confluence of intellectual currents produces a conjunction between dominant and marginal modes of discourse. Clair Wills, however, argues that the fragmented and self-reflexive nature of Tom Paulin's, Paul Muldoon's and Medbh McGuckian's work can serve to marginalise poetry since its meanings are so often inaccessible, except to readers educated in different poetic traditions, able to respond to the juxtaposition of different styles and not put off by enigmatic statements and semantic indeterminacy (1993: 13ff). There are a number of possible explanations for the prevalence of this type of writing among late twentieth-century poets, many of the features of which can be clearly associated with postmodernism. One is that the way in which the marginal has become central is itself a reflection of a much wider cultural sea change in which monologism, centricity and the notion of the speaking subject have been rendered untenable. Laudable as this development may be, postmodernism can now be seen as the new universalism, capable of incorporating postmodernist writing from different parts of the globe in an all encompassing internationalism. While the work of poets from different cultures and traditions may appear to share postmodernist characteristics, it is important to distinguish between them, to recognise that different writers may employ similar strategies for different purposes and derive their knowledge of them from different sources, and to develop ways of discussing 'postmodernist' writing that recognise cultural nuances. The focus for poetry's continuing interest in the political, in identity and resistance in the new millennium, is the future of poetry in a globalised, electronic culture, which will itself create, of course, new centres and margins.

7

Sounding out the margins: ethnicity and popular music in British cultural studies

SEAN CAMPBELL

Introduction

In their discussion of the development of British cultural studies,[1] Jon Stratton and Ien Ang point out that the 'energizing impulse' of the field has 'historically ... lain in [a] critical concern with, and validation of, the subordinate, the marginalized [and] the subaltern within Britain' (1996: 376). Accordingly, many of the field's principal practitioners have paid a considerable amount of attention to questions of 'race'[2] and ethnicity in post-war Britain (CCCS 1982; Gilroy 1987; Hall *et al* 1978). Much of this work has, in turn, centred on popular culture in general, and popular music in particular (Gilroy 1987: 117–35, 153–222; Hall 1992a; Hebdige 1979, 1987a; Jones 1988).

This chapter concerns itself with the ways in which Britain's multi-ethnic margins have been handled in British cultural studies, and particularly that strand associated with the Birmingham Centre for Contemporary Cultural Studies. Taking popular music as a case study, it explores the field's reception of immigrant-descended cultural practitioners, focusing specifically on its treatment of second-generation Irish rock musicians.[3]

To this end, the chapter re-examines Dick Hebdige's *Subculture* (1979), a formative endeavour in the field's engagement with questions of race, ethnicity and popular music, before going on to consider the more recent response of cultural studies' practitioners to 'Britpop'. This discussion draws attention to the narrow parameters of the 'ethnicity' framework underpinning this body of work. For if the field's reception of second- and third-generation African-Caribbean and South Asian cultural practitioners has tended to foreground questions of race and ethnicity, it has been almost axiomatic in cultural studies simply to overlook the particular immigrant background of the second-generation Irish, who have instead been subsumed in an all-encompassing, and largely undefined, 'white ethnicity'. Moreover, in a great deal of work on questions of race, ethnicity and popular music, second-generation Irish musicians have been recruited for a putative Anglo-Saxon 'centre' against which the descendants of African-Caribbean and South Asian immigrants can be differentiated.

This analysis of cultural studies' engagement with questions of race, ethnicity and popular music is explored in the second part of the chapter. I wish to begin, however, by re-considering the intellectual and institutional context from which this body of work has emerged. Here, I will retrace the development of questions of race and ethnicity in the field of British cultural studies,[4] before re-visiting what is widely considered to be a formative text in this project: the Birmingham Centre's *Policing the Crisis* (Hall *et al.* 1978) (hereafter *Policing*). My analysis demonstrates that while the Irish ethnic group in England has been almost comprehensively overlooked in cultural studies' engagement with questions of race and ethnicity, its presence has often been intrinsically relevant to this body of work. The chapter suggests that an acknowledgement of Irish ethnicity might have been beneficial for the field in its endeavour to engage with Britain's multi-ethnic margins.

The margins and the centre: 'race', ethnicity and British cultural studies

Stuart Hall has explained that the 'decisive turn' of the Birmingham Centre (and by implication the field of British cultural studies) towards questions of race and ethnicity was 'a profound theoretical struggle, a struggle of which *Policing the Crisis* was, curiously, the first and very late example'. This 'turn', for Hall, 'was only accomplished as the result of a long, and sometimes bitter – certainly bitterly contested – internal struggle against a resounding but unconscious silence' (1992b: 283).

Stratton and Ang have suggested that the 'unconscious silence' identified here by Hall 'revolved around the implicit racial assumptions of Britishness and British identity'. They go on to explain that many of the progenitors of cultural studies in Britain (referring specifically to Raymond Williams, and, in parenthesis, to 'many others', by which they presumably mean Richard Hoggart and E. P. Thompson) 'did not query the naturalized equation of Britishness with whiteness' (1996: 382). The initial concerns of the field had been largely determined by the class-based focus of Hoggart's *The Uses of Literacy* (1957), in conjunction with the field's other 'founding' texts: Williams' *Culture and Society* (1958), and Thompson's *The Making of the English Working Class* (1963) (Hall 1980b: 16). The apparent conflation of race and nation in these formative texts has been subjected to a substantial critique from black British cultural studies' practitioners, most notably Paul Gilroy (1987: 49–56). Roxy Harris has suggested that Gilroy 'signalled [a] moment of rupture' in the field 'when he attacked both Williams and Thompson for their silences or negative collusions on questions of "race"' (1996: 337).

By drawing attention to the 'naturalized equation' of race and nation in earlier work in the field, and providing some long overdue considera-tion of the historical experience of post-war African-Caribbean and South Asian immigrants and their descendants, this 'turn' towards ques-tions of race and ethnicity clearly served to contest the status of 'black' people 'as Other to a taken-for-granted "white" British imagined community' (Ang and Stratton 1995: 18). This is not to suggest, though, that the field's handling of visible immigrants was necessarily even-handed. In the preface to *The Empire Strikes Back* (1982, hereafter *Empire*), for example, Gilroy acknowledged the relative lack of attention that the authors had paid to the South Asian ethnic group in Britain, explaining: '[we] have struck an inadequate balance between the two black commun-ities. Only one of us has roots in the Indian subcontinent whereas four are of Afro-Caribbean origin. This accounts for the unevenness of our text' (CCCS 1982: 7).

Notwithstanding this particular asymmetry, though, the point that I want to make here is that while the field's 'turn' was effective in its endeavour to deconstruct the implicit conflation of whiteness and Britishness in previous work (and thereby pointed to a more ethnically diverse sense of Britishness), it simultaneously re-inscribed, albeit tacitly, the homogeneity of whiteness in England by taking it at face value. In other words, in its crucial move towards 'historicising and denaturalising "blackness"' (Ang and Stratton 1995: 19), the field appeared to take for granted the ostensible homogeneity of whiteness in England, and thereby served to re-produce a kind of ahistorical and re-naturalised 'whiteness'.

The 'turn' towards questions of race and ethnicity, then, was informed by a particular definition of race politics that pertained specifically to visible (and largely African-Caribbean) immigrants and their descendants. This particular emphasis was, of course, hardly peculiar to the field of cultural studies. On the contrary, it was symptomatic of the dominant 'race relations' paradigm that had been practised by sociologists in post-war Britain.[5] As Mary Hickman and Bronwen Walter have pointed out, this emphasis on visible difference was 'understandable at one level because of the systematic racism and discrimination which has characterized the experience of different collectivities of mainly British citizens who have migrated from the New Commonwealth and Pakistan, and their British born children' (1995: 7).

If the administering of cultural studies' 'turn' towards questions of race and ethnicity was forged in the context of these particular sociological practices and historical circumstances, then it was perhaps inevitable that, in the process of this manoeuvre, the field tended to overlook the ethnic heterogeneity of whiteness in England. However, by adhering to the dominant 'race relations' paradigm in this way, British cultural studies' engagement with questions of race and ethnicity has, like the sociology of 'race relations', 'dovetailed well with the concern of the British state to construct the problem of "immigrants" and of racism as narrowly constituted' (Hickman 1995: 4). In other words, this engagement with questions of race and ethnicity has, in one sense, taken at face value particular ahistorical notions about black immigrancy and white indigineity in which the Irish have been 'undifferentiated as an ethnic minority, part of an undeconstructed whiteness' (Sharkey 1997: 128–9).

Consequently, in the process of cultural studies' imperative endeavour to construct 'a more pluralistic, postcolonial sense of British culture and national identity' (Gilroy 1992: 190), the presence of a predominantly white ethnic group, such as the Irish, could only be rendered invisible. Accordingly, if the emphasis on class in the 'founding' texts and initial theoretical positions of British cultural studies had marginalised questions of race and ethnicity in general, then in the subsequent effort to foreground these issues, this Irish dimension was, once again, overlooked, and thereby doubly elided.

This abiding absence of an Irish dimension seems particularly anomalous in light of the fact that the formative years of British cultural studies coincided historically with an increasing Irish presence in England (Paul 1997: 90–110). And even if the presence of these immigrants, and their English-born children, was less visible than that of other post-war immigrant groups, a series of acts of political violence carried out by militant Irish republicans in the 1970s and 1980s served to heighten awareness, as well as generate anxiety, about the presence of the Irish ethnic group in England. Indeed, the city of Birmingham, the location in which cultural studies had been institutionalised (Hall 1980a: 58; Nelson, Treichler and Grossberg 1992: 9), and which had been an important receptor for post-war Irish Catholic labour migrants (Ziesler 1989: 171–

347), was, in November 1974, subjected to a bomb attack that demolished a section of the city, killing twenty-one (and injuring 162) of its inhabitants. In the traumatic aftermath of this bomb, Irish people in Birmingham were evidently subjected to particular forms of differentiation, and many Irish-related institutions were attacked (Ziesler 1989: 340–1).

Significantly, the manifestations of anti-Irish prejudice that unfolded in the aftermath of such acts of political violence made little attempt to distinguish between Irish-born immigrants and their English-born children. According to John Gabriel, second-generation Irish people became 'the object of attacks' in English schools, 'during and after IRA bombing campaigns' (1994: 85). Johnny Marr of The Smiths, one of the groups that practitioners of British cultural studies have conventionally theorised in terms of a homogeneous 'white ethnicity' (Stringer 1992: 21), has explained that, at school in the 1970s, he was called an 'Irish pig' by Mancunian classmates 'who equated being Irish with explosions' (Simpson 1996: 30). At the particular moment of British cultural studies' initial engagement with questions of race and ethnicity, then, the Irish ethnic group in England was, in some ways, becoming increasingly visible, not least because of the malign consequences of Irish-related political violence. Moreover, at approximately the same time, particular academic and political discourses about ethnicity in contemporary Britain were endeavouring to provide recognition of Irish ethnicity (Greater London Council 1984; Ullah 1981, 1983). What the elision of Irish ethnicity in British cultural studies appears to point to, then, is the rigidity and vigour of the black/white binary division underpinning the field's 'turn' towards questions of race and ethnicity.

Despite the fact that one of the co-authors of *Empire* concluded an endnote by asking 'on what grounds … have the "ethnicity studies" researchers singled out only the darker-skinned "ethnic minorities" as fitting objects of study?' (CCCS 1982: 136), the adherence of cultural studies' practitioners to the dominant 'race relations' paradigm has received little consideration in the field. It has on occasion, though, been informally broached. For instance, at the 'Cultural Studies Now and in the Future' conference held at the University of Illinois in April 1990, Paul Gilroy was asked by one of the conference discussants 'why discussions of race and class in Britain never discuss the Chinese in Britain'. This question, which could arguably have been equally concerned with the exclusion of white ethnic groups, such as the Irish, from the agenda of British cultural studies, elicited an interesting response from Gilroy, who suggested that: 'it's probably got to do with who owns and manages and controls the spaces in which such discussions appear and the *particular definition of race politics* that they want to trade in'. He also ventured that the reason some 'experiences aren't addressed or recorded as having any significance is because they're *perceived to be peripheral* to where the real action is supposedly identified' (quoted in West 1992: 701, my emphases).

Gilroy's remarks provide a useful perspective from which to consider the absence of an Irish dimension in *Policing*, the field's first major engagement with questions of race and ethnicity (Hall 1992b: 283; Turner 1996: 227). My decision to concentrate on *Policing* is based not only on its status as a formative text in the development of cultural studies, but also on the fact that its adherence to the dominant 'race relations' paradigm has been characteristic of much of the field's subsequent work on race and ethnicity.

Policing the Crisis: 'race', ethnicity and the Irish in England

As I have pointed out, the specificities of the dominant 'race relations' paradigm may explain, at least in part, the absence of an Irish dimension in British cultural studies' work on race and ethnicity. However, a further problem is presented by the fact that, in some of the field's major interventions in this area, the Irish presence in England has been intrinsically relevant, not to say centrally important. In other words, while the absence of an Irish dimension may be understandable when the express purpose of a particular project is to engage with, say, African-Caribbean or South Asian experience in England, this becomes problematic when, as has often been the case, the Irish ethnic group in England is implicitly relevant to the discussion at hand. In these particular instances, however, the Irish ethnic group is only tacitly included, and Irish ethnicity is simply rendered invisible. Gilroy's remark about perceived peripherality might be worth considering here: 'other experiences aren't addressed', he suggests, 'because they're *perceived to be peripheral* to where *the real action* is supposedly identified' (quoted in West 1992: 701, my emphases). By 'real action', Gilroy is presumably referring to instances such as the mugging in the Handsworth district of Birmingham in 1973 that instigated the project of *Policing*. We can perhaps infer, then, that the experience of the Irish in post-war England was 'perceived to be peripheral' to this putative focal point. This particular example of 'real action', however, had special resonances for the Irish ethnic group in England.

The absence of an Irish dimension in *Policing* is, of course, understandable, as its authors were primarily concerned with the 'moral panic' about the culturally constructed notion of the 'black mugger' in Britain in the 1970s (Hall *et al.* 1978: 3–28). However, the particular historical event that initiated the project of *Policing* had a peculiarly Irish dimension. In their introduction to the text, the authors explain:

> Until we started the study, crime was not a special field of interest to us. We became involved in a practical way when, in 1973, sentences of ten and twenty years were handed down in court to three boys of *mixed ethnic background* after a serious incident in Handsworth, Birmingham, in which a man on the way home from a pub was 'mugged' on a piece of waste ground, robbed and badly injured. (viii, my emphasis)

This man, we later learn (by virtue of a quote from the *Daily Mail*), was Robert Keenan, 'an Irish labourer' (91). Meanwhile, one of the boys who had attacked him, James Duignan, had migrated with his parents from Ireland to England as an infant. This detail is entirely absent in the text, despite the fact that the authors had implicitly described him as 'ethnic' in their description of the 'muggers', and subsequently quoted from a newspaper report that had made multiple references to Duignan's Irishness (Colling 1973; *Daily Mail* 1973). (His accomplices were Paul Storey, who had a West Indian father and white English mother, and Mustafa Faut, who was Turkish-Cypriot.) Here, the authors emphasise that this news report 'picked up the familiar themes of race and crime', quoting the paper's assertion that '[all] the sentenced youths are *either coloured or immigrants*' (Hall *et al.* 1978: 102, my emphasis). But they overlook the report's emphasis on Duignan's Irishness, and its distinction between 'coloured' and 'immigrants' (which clearly served as a tacit acknowledgement of Duignan's ethnicity and, by implication, that of the Irish in England).

Moreover, in the authors' lengthy analysis of letters that had been printed in local and national newspapers in response to the sentences of these boys (120–38), they quote from a particular letter that included a forthright expression of anti-Irish prejudice in tandem with other racist sentiments. The writer of this letter clearly drew attention to Duignan's Irishness, suggesting that 'by her name the woman who has 12 kids [Duignan's mother] is an alien too, an R.C. [Roman Catholic], she should be in Southern Ireland [sic] and you and the nigs and pakis back in the Jungle', before concluding: 'The 3 of them [the 'muggers'] have no rights in this country, just living off the Welfare State. Oh for Enoch Powell to clear the lot of you, back to your own land' (132). Although the authors of *Policing* record this reader's expression of anti-Irish prejudice, there is little consideration of this dimension, and the authors fail to point out that it was directed specifically at Duignan and his mother. This is regrettable, not least because an overlooked implication of the letter-writer's racist logic is that Keenan, the victim of the 'mugging', would also have been considered an 'alien' by this reader, and would therefore have been subjected to their racialist fantasy of Powellite repatriation.

The particular historical incident that instigated British cultural studies' first major endeavour to address questions of race and ethnicity was, then, immanently relevant to the experience of the Irish ethnic group in England. However, this dimension of the Handsworth 'mugging' evidently failed to coincide with the specific concerns of the authors of *Policing*, perhaps because the text, as Ang and Stratton have pointed out, 'relies on the continued reproduction of a rock-solid white/black dichotomy' (1995: 21). And while this binary division was, of course, symptomatic of the dominant 'race relations' paradigm, it is worth pointing out that a major sociological study of race and crime in Birmingham, published earlier in the 1970s for the Institute of Race Relations (John Lambert's *Crime, Police, and Race Relations*), had textually foregrounded the Irish presence in the city, and was permeated with references to both the first- and second-generation Irish (1970: vi, vii, xx, pp. 15–18, 45, 48, 53–4, 56, 60–5, 67, 73, 79–80, 88–90, 102–6, 123–7, 187–9, 212–26, 246, 266–9, 286–7). Admittedly, Lambert's work may have been somewhat of an exception in this regard, but it was nevertheless a project with which the authors of *Policing* were evidently familiar (Hall *et al.* 1978: 42, 44–5, 49–50, 280). In light of this, it would appear that the Irish dimensions of the Handsworth 'mugging' were considered to be especially inconsequential.

What this effectively constitutes, then, is a kind of disciplinary policing of Irish ethnicity in the field of British cultural studies, parti-cularly in its engagement with questions of race and ethnicity. This has rendered invisible the presence, not to say the historical experience, of the Irish ethnic group in post-war England. However, given the political imperatives underpinning British cultural studies' endeavour to address the experience of visible immigrant groups, it would be churlish simply to castigate the field's principal practitioners for their failure to acknow-ledge the presence of the Irish ethnic group in England. Indeed, if Irish ethnicity has been one of British cultural studies' absences and silences, this omission has perhaps been less by denial or design (a sinister erasure of Irishness), than indifference or default (an insentient elision of an anomalous ethnic group). Accordingly, I am not suggesting that texts such as *Policing* should *necessarily* have engaged with the experience of the Irish ethnic group (although, in light of the fact that the Irish were frequently relevant to the discussion at hand, it might have been useful to at least acknowledge their *absence*). Instead, my discussion of British cultural studies has primarily been an attempt to identify the particular critical and intellectual context from which scholarly discussions of immigrant-descended musicians have emerged. In the second half of this chapter, then, I will examine the ways in which these musicians have previously been contextualised, and the manner in which their ethnicities have conventionally been handled.

Ethnicity and popular music in British cultural studies

As Simon Frith has pointed out, 'the dominant forms [of popular music] in all contemporary societies have originated at the social margins – among the poor, the migrant, the rootless, the "queer"' (1996: 122). The field of British cultural studies has accordingly paid a considerable amount of attention to this realm of cultural production (Bradley 1980; Hebdige 1971; Willis 1972, 1974). In turn, much of this work has been specifically concerned with questions pertaining to race, ethnicity and popular music (Chambers 1976, 1985: 139–74; Gilroy 1987, 117–35; 153–222; Hebdige 1974, 1979, 1987a; Jones 1988). However, this body of work has tended to adhere to the practices of the dominant 'race relations' paradigm, re-producing the black/white binary division that has rendered Irish ethnicity invisible. This is not to say, though, that musicians of Irish descent have simply been overlooked. In fact, as I will demonstrate, musicians such as John Lydon have inhabited a crucial position in cultural studies' engagements with questions of race, ethnicity and popular music. However, with few exceptions, these discussions have appeared to be wholly oblivious to the fact that musicians such as Lydon, as well as The Smiths and Oasis, are the immediate descendants of post-war Irish Catholic labour migrants.

   The critical reception of other immigrant-descended musicians has, of course, been markedly different, and scholarly discussions of second- and third-generation African-Caribbean and South Asian cultural practitioners have tended to privilege questions of race and ethnicity, often at the expense of other considerations. For instance, in a discussion of 'black' independent film-making in Britain during the 1980s (particularly the work of the Black Audio Film Collective and Sankofa), Judith Williamson points out that 'the formal properties' of particular 'films have somehow, in most of the critical discourse surrounding them, been subsumed into their "blackness'" (1988: 110). In stark contrast, the field's reception of second-generation Irish musicians has rarely even acknowledged their particular immigrant background. The absence of an Irish dimension in discussions of these musicians is not, of course, inherently problematic. Clearly an 'ethnic' dimension is not necessarily relevant to *every* discussion of *any* cultural practitioner. Moreover, the second-generation Irish musicians with whom I am concerned have rarely engaged with recognisably 'Irish' issues, and have tended to eschew identifiably 'Irish' musical styles. Consequently, their work appears to bear little trace of an explicitly 'Irish' dimension, and this has undoubtedly been a fundamental reason for the field's apparent obliviousness to their particular immigrant background.

In the absence of this context, most cultural studies texts that have engaged with, or made reference to, the musicians with whom I am concerned, have customarily assumed that these musicians are straightforwardly and unambiguously English. Moreover, in some of the 'canonical' texts of British cultural studies, particularly those principally concerned with race, ethnicity and popular music, second-generation Irish musicians have functioned as representatives of a homogeneous white Englishness. Indeed, where questions of ethnicity have been invoked, it has been in terms of a largely undefined 'white ethnicity' that many of these texts have used to denote this ostensibly homogeneous white Englishness.

The musicians I discuss here are all English-born and have white skin colour, so to contextualise them in terms of a 'white Englishness' is, of course, hardly erroneous. I am not suggesting that these musicians should be excluded from discussions of 'white Englishness'. (In fact, they have often been theorised productively in this context (see, for example, Stringer 1992).) Instead, what I want to draw attention to is the fact that this Irish dimension has rarely even been acknowledged in scholarly discussions of these musicians and that, in its absence, this work has assuredly posited second-generation Irish musicians as a kind of 'white English' centre with which to differentiate more ostensibly marginal immigrant-descended cultural practitioners. In doing so, this work has not only assumed that the children of Irish Catholic labour migrants are straightforwardly and unambiguously English (when in fact, as has been demonstrated elsewhere, their relationship with the host culture has been complex and ambivalent (Campbell 1999; Ullah 1985)), but it has also overlooked the precarious position that the Irish have historically occupied *vis-à-vis* whiteness. For instance, Lynda Boose has explained that:

[if] 'race' originates as a category that hierarchically privileges a ruling status and makes the Other(s) inferior, then for the English the group that was first to be shunted into this discursive derogation and thereafter invoked as almost a paradigm of inferiority was not the black 'race' – but the *Irish* 'race'. (1994: 36)

Clearly such notions of Irish racial inferiority have been historically specific, and it is imperative that we do not overlook the fact that whiteness is a modality of power in which predominantly white ethnic groups, such as the Irish, are, as it were, always already located. Nevertheless, as Richard Dyer has pointed out, the Irish have been 'rather less securely white than Anglos, Teutons and Nordics'. Moreover, if, as Dyer has put it, 'some white people are whiter than others', then the Irish have historically provided one of the 'striking instances' of 'maybe, sometimes whites, peoples who may be let in to whiteness under particular historical circumstances' (1997: 12, 51, 19). And while the particular context of post-war England might have constituted one such historical circumstance (Paul 1997: 90–110), this point has received little consideration from practitioners of British cultural studies, many of whom have, of course, been primarily concerned with questions of race and ethnicity.

The uneven handling of Britain's multi-ethnic margins in British cultural studies is evident in Dick Hebdige's *Subculture* (1979) – arguably the field's first major engagement with questions of race, ethnicity and popular music (Clarke 1982: 13) – and which, like *Policing*, has 'become something of a milestone in cultural studies' (Davies 1995: 23–4). In light of its formative status in the field's development (it was published only one year after *Policing*), it is perhaps unsurprising that *Subculture* largely adheres to the dominant 'race relations' paradigm, and thereby reproduces a black/white binary division that foregrounds visible immigrant groups while simultaneously rendering invisible the presence of white ethnic groups, such as the Irish. Nevertheless, Hebdige introduces a particular notion of 'white ethnicity', and frequently makes references to a second-generation Irish musician, the former Sex Pistols' vocalist and lyricist John Lydon. It is this particular aspect of *Subculture*, then, that provides the kernel of my discussion here.

'Punky reggae party': *Subculture,* John Lydon and 'white ethnicity'

In *Subculture*, Hebdige endeavoured to theorise a variety of youth subcultural styles as a set of 'differential responses to the black immigrant presence in [post-war] Britain' (1979: 29), but I am primarily concerned here with his discussion of punk. In a particular sub-section entitled 'Bleached roots: punks and white ethnicity', issues of race and ethnicity are clearly foregrounded. Hebdige suggests, for example, that 'the punk aesthetic can be read … as a white "translation" of black "ethnicity"' (64), proffering the notion that punk itself constituted a 'white ethnicity' (62–5). In the context of this discussion of punk, Hebdige makes numerous references to John Lydon, who was widely considered to be the principal icon of that particular phenomenon (Burchill and Parsons 1978: 78; Murray 1977a: 28–9). Lydon is not, of course, the principal object of analysis in *Subculture*'s discussion of punk, which is more specifically concerned with punk style and its relationship with reggae. Nevertheless, Lydon (who is referred to in the text as Johnny Rotten, Lydon's adopted name as vocalist/lyricist for the Sex Pistols) pervades the text in a number of important ways, functioning as a representative icon of the broader cultural phenomenon of punk. For instance, a sketch of Lydon (based on a photograph in which a policeman stops Lydon in the street and takes his name; *Melody Maker* 1977) provides the illustration for the book's title page, and Lydon is subsequently mentioned and alluded to in various ways in the (140 pages of) main text (28–9, 61, 64, 90, 92–3, 98, 106, 109, 112) as well as in the endnotes (142, 151, 156-7, 161).

Moreover, Lydon is frequently positioned at a kind of interface in the punk–reggae nexus with which Hebdige is concerned. For instance, introducing Lydon's role in what he later refers to as punk's 'association' (66) with reggae, Hebdige quotes from a music paper in which an acquaintance of Lydon explained that reggae was 'the only music' that Lydon would 'dance to' (28–9). Hebdige also points out, here, that Lydon 'displayed a detailed knowledge of the more esoteric reggae numbers in a series of interviews throughout 1977' (28–9). Such points clearly serve to demonstrate the important position that Lydon inhabited in the affiliation between punk and reggae, and it is perhaps worth briefly re-tracing the development of this engagement here.

Before doing this, though, I should point out that despite Hebdige's emphasis on 'white ethnicity' in his discussion of punk, and the over-arching 'turn' throughout the text 'from an exclusive emphasis on class to assert the centrality of race in subcultural formations' (Clarke 1982: 13), *Subculture* offers no recognition of the ethnic diversity of whiteness in England. Accordingly, Lydon's particular immigrant background is simply rendered invisible, and remains a kind of 'present absence', to borrow a term from the text. However, by briefly revisiting Lydon's role in the punk–reggae interface, I will demonstrate that Irish ethnicity was a salient dimension of his public persona, one that was frequently alluded to in the context of his engagement with reggae.

Lydon had initially demonstrated his interest in reggae in a much celebrated radio interview (in which he also displayed a familiarity with Irish traditional music) in the summer of 1977 (Captain Nemo 1977). In addition, he frequently appeared during this period in promotional photos wearing badges that publicised reggae groups (see for example Vermorel and Vermorel 1978: 99), and often discussed his interest in reggae in press interviews (including those in which his Irishness was also mentioned: see, for example, Murray 1977b: 23, 26). In fact, the extent of Lydon's association with reggae was such that, in the immediate aftermath of his departure from the Sex Pistols, reports in the music press suggested that he would form a reggae band. Significantly, when a music journalist asked Lydon to confirm these rumours, he responded by playfully positioning his Irishness in a multi-ethnic musical context: 'I'm forming an Irish Cajun Disco Afro Rock band' (Goldman 1978c: 22).

Lydon's public association with reggae, though, was perhaps most clearly demonstrated when, in February 1978 (only a few weeks after his departure from the Sex Pistols), he visited Jamaica with Don Letts, a second-generation Jamaican film-maker and disc jockey, described by Hebdige in *Subculture* as a 'black Rastafarian d-j' (1979: 29). The ostensible purpose of this highly publicised three-week visit (it was subsequently recorded as a serialised interview in the music paper *Sounds* (Goldman 1978b, 1978c), as well as in other reports and interviews (Goldman 1978a; Salewicz 1978), was to 'scout' for unsigned Jamaican reggae musicians. In these interviews, both Lydon and the *Sounds* journalist, Vivien Goldman, frequently allude to the singer's Irishness. At one point, Goldman announces: 'John's roots are Irish, and on average twice a day something happens that reminds him of the old sod' (1978b: 18). This emphasis on Irishness is underscored by Lydon's own comments. For example, in a discussion of his alleged mistreatment by the Sex Pistols' management, he indicates that Vivienne Westwood (the then partner of the group's manager Malcolm McLaren) had made an apparently derisive public gesture about his Irishness: 'Just go to her shop now if you don't believe me', he tells Goldman, 'read what she's wrote [sic] on the window about my connections with being Irish' (Goldman 1978c: 21).[6]

Significantly, Don Letts' recollections of the trip to Jamaica also make reference to Lydon's Irishness (Lydon 1994: 287). Moreover, he has framed his relationship with Lydon in terms of Jamaican and Irish ethnicity, maintaining that 'Irish and Jamaican people are definitely alike in spirit' (a point with which Lydon concurs: 'Irish and Jamaicans definitely have a common bond') (1994: 287), and drawing attention to the ways in which Lydon was received in London reggae clubs: 'He could walk into places white people could never go with total immunity'. Letts goes on to explain that 'We all felt like society's outlaws', suggesting 'I think that's why John and I get on so well. In the development of England's history, there was a time when John's mob – the Irish – and blacks and dogs were thrown together' (Lydon 1994: 280, 287). (This is, of course, an allusion to the discriminatory notices in post-war London hotels from which Lydon's autobiography, *Rotten: No Irish, No Blacks, No Dogs* takes its title.)

Given that, in *Subculture*, both Letts and Lydon emerge as components in the punk–reggae interface, it is perhaps significant that Letts should frame his relationship with Lydon in terms of Jamaican and Irish ethnicity, a dimension that has clearly been overlooked by practitioners of British cultural studies.[7] This is not to suggest, however, that Lydon's engagement with reggae pertained specifically to his Irishness, nor to imply that there is an inevitable or innate affinity between the second-generation Irish and other second-generation ethnic groups. Instead, what this demonstrates is the fact that this Irish dimension was considered to be significant (both at the time and in retrospect) by Lydon himself, by ethnic minority colleagues in the music industry (such as the Jamaican Letts and the Jewish Goldman), and by his white English band members: the other Sex Pistols apparently called him 'Paddy' (Murray 1977b: 23). In turn, this would appear to suggest that Lydon's position in the white English working class was not as straightforward as Hebdige seems to imply.

In *Subculture*, then, Irish ethnicity is entirely absent and, as a consequence, Lydon is implicitly situated on one side of a binary division between (black) immigrancy and (white) indigeneity, functioning as a straightforward representative of what Hebdige calls the 'indigenous working-class culture' (1979: 68). Indeed, there appears to be a quiescent convergence in *Subculture* of the terms 'immigrant' with 'black', and 'host' with 'white English', which implicitly racialises both immigration and indigeneity. Accordingly, the term 'second-generation' is tacitly racialised as non-white: Hebdige explains that '*second-generation immigrant* youth culture was closely monitored by those neighbouring *white* youths interested in forming their own subcultural options' (43, my emphases).

This is not to suggest that *Subculture* demonstrates an even-handedness towards visible immigrant groups. For instance, Gary Clarke has pointed out that, in *Subculture*, 'Asians are particularly noted by their absence'

(1982: 17). Accordingly, if, as Clarke has maintained, Hebdige 'tends to equate black culture with Jamaican culture' (1982: 17), then there is perhaps a corresponding equation of whiteness with Englishness. Lydon's Irishness is therefore absorbed into an ethnically undifferentiated working-class whiteness, and in the process of *Subculture*'s formative engagement with questions of race and ethnicity, the second-generation Irish appear to have been remaindered, as it were, in the modality of class (although they were, of course, equally absent, or at least invisible, in many of the class-based accounts of earlier practitioners of cultural studies).

Hebdige's discussion of punk as a 'white ethnicity', and the text's implicit positioning of Lydon in this context, has frequently been restated in subsequent cultural studies' engagements with questions of race, ethnicity and popular music (Chambers 1985, 178; Gilroy 1987, 123–5; Jones 1988, 95–6). Consequently, despite the fact that Hebdige would eventually offer recognition of Lydon's Irishness (albeit in passing) in a later essay (1987b: 63), other accounts have served to (re)position Lydon in this 'white ethnicity'. Moreover, the particular critical paradigm that emerged in these texts has continued to be practised in more recent work, although with some important deviations.

Deconstructing Britpop: whiteness, 'race', and the politics of inclusion

In his discussion of Englishness and popular music in the 1990s, Martin Cloonan points out that while 'black English-born (or resident) artists [referring specifically to bands such as Cornershop and Fun-Da-Mental] have ... commented about the *condition* of England, they have seldom been held to *represent* it'. In an endeavour to demonstrate this point, Cloonan draws attention to a second-generation Irish musician, the former Smiths' vocalist and lyricist Morrissey, pointing out that 'while it is quite possible for the *Guardian* to talk of Morrisey [sic] as "a signifier of our (i.e. England's) broader disorder" ... such signification is rarely accredited to the 6% of the population who form the ethnic minorities' (1998: 69).

Cloonan is quite correct in making this point. Second-generation Irish musicians have, as I have demonstrated elsewhere (1998), functioned in journalistic discourses as representative icons of Englishness, a position that the descendants of other post-war immigrants have seldom held in critical discourses. Moreover, Cloonan's tacit assumption that Morrissey and, by implication, the second-generation Irish, should not be considered 'ethnic' is also understandable, particularly in light of the apparent vigour and longevity of the dominant 'race relations' paradigm. Rather than simply disputing Cloonan's argument, then, the point to note is that in a scholarly discussion of ethnicity and popular music, a second-generation Irish musician is taken to be a representative of a white English 'centre' against which more ostensibly marginal musicians can be differentiated.

However, in a modified version of this article, Cloonan included an important endnote that offered recognition of the Irishness of second-generation musicians. In this version, Cloonan explained that '[there] is nothing inevitable about [the fact that 'black' musicians have rarely been held to represent England], as Wade has shown how in another context the music of an ethnic minority, namely blacks in Colombia, came to be associated with concepts of the nation. But mainstream pop Englishness has generally been defined by whites who have been born in the country' (1997: 59). At this point in the revision, Cloonan suggests that:

> it is worth noting that the most strident nationalists – such as many campaigners for national language – are often not born in the country they espouse. This is replicated in pop, where some of the most allegedly 'English' of voices have had their roots elsewhere. In punk Johnny Rotten was of Irish descent, and Oasis – often portrayed as both 'English' and part of 'Britpop' – are led by the Gallagher brothers, who are also of Irish descent. (1997: 67)

If, in this adapted version of Cloonan's article, Irish ethnicity makes a kind of transition from absence to endnote, then in more recent work Irishness has made a further transition, from endnote to main text (albeit parenthetically). For instance, in a discussion of 'independent' music in 1990s Britain, David Hesmondhalgh makes a brief but insightful comment about Britpop, stating that 'the narrow nationalism of the term ... hardly needs comment (though the Irish roots of the two brothers, Noel and Liam Gallagher, at the centre of Oasis, make the[ir] relationship ... to the phenomenon quite complex)' (1999: 52). Clearly this acknowledgement registers an important shift in terms of the recognition of Irish ethnicity in British cultural studies. I want to develop Hesmondhalgh's point here, as it raises an important question about 'Britpop' and white homogeneity.

'Britpop' – which is perhaps best understood as a critical discourse (rather than an aesthetic style) – initially emerged in the London-based music press in the mid–1990s (see, for instance, Bennun *et al.* 1995; Richardson 1995). Although I do not have sufficient space to fully consider the politics of Britpop, which in any case have been discussed by Bennett

(1998) and Cloonan (1997), it is perhaps worth pointing out that the 'Britishness' of this 'defiantly nationalistic' (quoted in Shuker 1998: 36) discourse tended to manifest itself as a white Englishness. It is perhaps unsurprising, then, that many second-generation African-Caribbean and South Asian musicians have expressed particular concerns about the racial connotations of Britpop. For instance, Aniruddha Das of Asian Dub Foundation has argued that 'Britpop is an attempt to reassert a sort of mythical whiteness. In that respect, I'd say it's implicitly racist' (Stubbs 1998: 46). Musicians of Irish descent have also made similar criticisms of Britpop. For instance, in 1996, former Smiths' guitarist Johnny Marr expressed his 'despair' about the 'nationalism' of Britpop in an interview in which he recalled his personal experience of anti-Irish prejudice (Simpson 1996). Marr underlined this point by expressing a particular antipathy towards the Union Flag, the principal signifier of Britpop (Boyd 1999).

However, despite the fact that musicians of Irish descent, such as Marr, have articulated an aversion to Britpop, they have nevertheless been critically appropriated as key Britpop figures, and have therefore been a crucial component in its construction of a 'mythical whiteness'. For instance, during the summer of 1995, at the height of Britpop, Marr's former group The Smiths (who had disbanded in 1987) were conscripted for what *Melody Maker* called 'the Home Guard of Britpop', while Marr, specifically, was honoured as a 'Britpop icon' (Bennun *et al.* 1995: 32–3). Accordingly, if Britpop was, indeed, implicitly racist, then this was arguably due not only to its exclusion of musicians of African-Caribbean and South Asian descent, but also its symmetrical *inclusion* of second-generation Irish musicians. In other words, Britpop's incorporation of the descendants of post-war Irish Catholic labour migrants suggests that its principles of exclusion were determined less by the historical fact of having an immigrant background, than by a discursive conflation of race and nation.

This convergence of race and nation has not, of course, been restricted to discourses about popular music. In fact, for Walter, such '[exclusionary] ideas about "race" lie at the heart of British national identity':

> The term 'immigrants' has a racialized meaning which makes it synony-mous with black skin colour … Shared whiteness is thus a central reason for Irish inclusion. The power of racialized exclusion on grounds of skin colour would be seriously weakened if similar divisions within the white population were exposed. (1999: 93)

Clearly Walter's point, here, recalls the practices of the dominant 'race relations' paradigm (and thereby the origins of Irish exclusion from British cultural studies' engagement with questions of race and ethnicity). However, it also raises crucial questions about Britpop's assertion of a 'mythical whiteness'. For instance, in the face of Britpop's tacit construction of a monolithic 'white Englishness', perhaps an acknowledgement of Irish ethnicity in England could, by drawing attention to the immigrant-descended heterogeneity of this ostensibly homogeneous category, make visible the racialising logic that underpinned Britpop's mechanisms of inclusion.

However, discussions of Britpop in British cultural studies, and particularly those that have been concerned with questions of race and ethnicity, have been primarily concerned with its exclusionary practices. For instance, Andy Bennett has drawn attention to Britpop's apparent disregard for musicians of African-Caribbean and South Asian descent (1997: 29), a point that has been broached in other scholarly accounts (Cloonan 1998: 69). Britpop's principles of inclusion, however, have been taken at face value, and the particular implications raised by its incorporation of the second-generation Irish have tended to be overlooked.

Conclusion

The discernible shift towards a recognition of Irishness in recent scholarly work about music and ethnicity has coincided with an analogous departure in popular discourses. The British music press has conventionally overlooked the particular immigrant background of second-generation Irish musicians (Campbell 1998), whilst simultaneously privileging questions of ethnicity in discussions of musicians of African-Caribbean and South Asian descent. This practice has, however, undergone significant modifications in recent journalistic discourses. In the summer of 2000, for instance, the British music magazine *Q* ran a special theme issue, replete with glossy Union Flag cover, entitled 'The 100 greatest British albums'. In an apparent endeavour to quell simplistic celebrations of a racially exclusive Britishness, the issue included an ethnically sensitive editorial overview essay, entitled 'One nation under a groove'. Indeed, a pull-out quote from this article, used to illustrate the text, emphasised that 'Britain's multi-ethnic mix and links with the Commonwealth have contributed to a potent shebeen of home-grown music' (Maconie 2000: 83). In the actual text itself, though, this assertion was punctuated with a parenthetical recognition of Irish ethnicity, that read: 'Britain's multi-ethnic mix (wherein the immigrant Irish have proved most crucial, from The Beatles to Oasis) …' (84). Clearly this acknowledgement marks a striking deviation from previous journalistic discourses about ethnicity and popular music, for rather than being omitted, the Irish are in this instance privileged as the 'most crucial' ethnic group. And while the significance of this assertion may be somewhat diminished by its parenthetical status (not to mention its omission from the pull-out quote), it nevertheless serves as a gesture towards prising open the narrow parameters of the dominant paradigm.

This inclusion of an Irish dimension in recent journalistic discourses about popular music is perhaps indicative of a potential shift in contemporary thinking about ethnicity in Britain. In the recent report on *The Future of Multi-Ethnic Britain* (Parekh *et al.* 2000), the commissioners (including, significantly, Stuart Hall) endeavoured to incorporate an Irish dimension, demonstrating an awareness of the presence of the Irish ethnic group, as well as an understanding of their particular historical experience (*Guardian* 2000). And while this report has been widely received as a critical repudiation of the racial connotations of conventional notions of Britishness (Travis 2000), it might also be understood as a corrective to similarly conventionalised assumptions, held within British cultural studies, about white homogeneity. The conceivable paradigm shift that this might engender could perhaps facilitate a fuller understanding of the complex and diverse contours that constitute Britain's multi-ethnic margins.

Notes

1 As Kobena Mercer has pointed out, 'when people talk about "British Cultural Studies" they often seem to be involved in the construction of a new mythology which implies a unitary and homogenous field of endeavor' (1992: 447). Cultural studies, in Britain as elsewhere, has, of course, been a complex and contested field encompassing a diverse range of often disparate intellectual projects. A number of published accounts have endeavoured to chart the development of the field. See, for example, Clarke 1991a; Davies 1995; Hall 1980a; Turner 1996: 38–77.

2 Although Tariq Modood has suggested that it is 'a waste of ink to put race in scare-quotes' (quoted in Fenton 1996: 145), I have done so in this instance to indicate the term's problematic status. However, subsequent references to the term will, in light of its frequent usage in the text, not be placed in quotation marks.

3 I will focus specifically on John Lydon, perhaps better known as Johnny Rotten, former vocalist and lyricist for the Sex Pistols (1975–78). However, I will also make reference to The Smiths and Oasis. The Smiths (1982–87) despite their

adoption of an archetypal English surname, consisted of four second-generation Irish musicians (Rogan 1994: 10–15). All five original members of Oasis (1992–) were also second-generation Irish (Hewitt 1997).

4 Mark Gibson has explained that 'There is a noticeable weariness in some quarters with attempts to trace the history of cultural studies, particularly where that history is British. The theoretical development of the field has now been recounted so many times as to have become almost a catechism' (1999: 139). However, there has been little consideration, in this narrativisation of the trajectory of British cultural studies, of the handling of Irish ethnicity in the field. In my endeavour to address this point, then, it has been necessary to trace, from this particular perspective, the field's engagement with questions of race and ethnicity, and in turn, to consider, albeit briefly, the development of British cultural studies as a field of scholarly activity.

5 According to Mary Hickman, this paradigm was 'primarily designed to explain patterns of racism and discrimination experienced by migrants from Britain's ex-colonies in Africa, the Caribbean and the Indian sub-continent. Its main premise … is that racism is about "colour": that is, about visible difference', hence the 'automatic exclusion' of white immigrant groups, such as the Irish (1995: 4).

6 Lydon fails to specify the particular nature of this evidently anti-Irish gesture.

7 A notable exception in this regard is Simon Jones's *Black Culture, White Youth: The Reggae Tradition from JA to UK* (1988). This was an ethnographic research project – based at the Birmingham Centre – on ethnicity and popular music in the city of Birmingham. In the study, Jones draws attention to the family background of Jo-Jo, a second-generation Irish youth who emerges as one of the dominant voices in the text. Jones explains: 'Like many of the Irish families in the area, they had developed close ties with black neighbours by sharing the same survival strategies, living spaces and supportive child-care networks. (The parallel experiences of Irish and black migrant workers generally was an important foundation of much of the interaction between the two communities)' (129–30). Later on, Jones points out that some working-class white youths in the city had 'attempted to forge an identity with black people by drawing attention to parallel forms of ethnicity, such as Irishness' (192).

8

Cool enough for Lou Reed?: The plays of Ed Thomas and the cultural politics of South Wales[1]

SHAUN RICHARDS

In the conclusion to his 1985 book *When Was Wales?* the historian Gwyn A. Williams declared that the Welsh were now 'nothing but a naked people under an acid rain' (305). Written in the aftermath of the anti-devolution vote of 1979 and the fatal blow delivered to the economy and confidence by the defeat of the 1984 miners' strike, Williams's work, for all its tentative faith that some form of Wales will survive, is a litany of loss. Above all it mourns the loss of a Welshness of class and community which provided illuminating moments of inspiration, and in particular the loss of a righteous communal resistance to injustice captured in the triumphant mass resistance to the government's 1934–5 Unemployment Assistance Board Act. This victory of grass-roots radicalism, argued Williams, buoyed up the flagging confidence of a people ravaged by unemployment and 'carried [them] into their liberating World War on a surge of socialist and Labour hope' (264).

While the cultural and linguistic reality of Wales encompasses far more than the heavy industry and socialism of the predominantly English-speaking southern valleys it is that Wales which is home to the highest percentage of the population. It is also the Wales which has come closest to extinction. For despite the ravages experienced by the hill farmers of rural Wales it is the south which has seen the erasure of the very sources of income upon which the community was founded and through which its identity was forged. In the aftermath of what Williams termed 'the terrible year 1979, *blwyddyn y pla*, the year of the plague … The elections of that year seemed to call into question the whole basis on which Welsh history had hitherto been written' (1990/91: 57).

Such an analysis might appear idiosyncratic in the light of the rock band Catatonia's celebratory 'Every day when I wake up/I thank the

Lord I'm Welsh' (1998). Coming at the end of the 1990s, a decade which saw the triumph of the Manic Street Preachers, this unironic paean to a nationality whose future Gwyn Williams had doubted only a decade earlier suggests either an inadequacy in his analysis or a staggering reversal of economic and cultural fortunes. As the decade closed with the establishment of a Welsh Assembly it might appear that Williams was simply wrong in pronouncing that with the 1979 anti-devolution vote, and the swing to Conservatives throughout almost all of Wales in the General Election of that year, the Welsh had identified themselves with southern England and 'finally disappeared into Britain' (1985: 305). The socialism forged in the inter-war years can still be found in the self-confessed 'classic labour' (Maconie 1998: 96) lyrics of the Manic Street Preachers whose 'A design for life' (1996) announced 'Libraries gave us power/Then work came and made us free'. Yet even this anthemic assertion of the cultural and material foundations of traditional valleys socialism acknowledges the extent to which it is an historical memory in the bleak contemporaneity of the next line: 'What price now for a shallow piece of dignity?' However, out of this complex of economic despoliation, a burgeoning cultural confidence and residual socialism has emerged a fledgling theatre movement which captures the trauma consequent on the fact that, in the words of Ed Thomas, foremost among these playwrights, 'old Wales is dead' (1997).

But Thomas is not here reflecting on the loss of Williams's cauldron of radicalism. His reference point is a Cymru of clichés whose longevity was demonstrated by Shirley Bassey's Welsh-dragon dress at the 1999 Welsh Assembly celebrations. The reference to Max Boyce in the title of Thomas's 1997 article, 'A land fit for heroes (Max Boyce excluded)' neatly captures the image which he wishes to dispel: the caricature of Welshness whose soft sentimentality eases away the necessity of self-analysis. The thrust of Thomas's argument is that a people can only live in, and live up to, the images of themselves which circulate in the culture. As one of the characters in his first play, *House of America* (1994b [1988]), expressed it: 'look at Wales, where's its kings, where's our heroes? ... one answer, mate, we haven't got any. I mean let's face it Boyo, Harry Secombe isn't a bloke I'd stand in the rain for, is he?' (46–7). And as suggested by Thomas's extended list of images capable of producing a cultural cringe, '[the] Wales of stereotypes, leeks, daffodils, look-you-now-boyo rugby supporters singing Max Boyce songs in three-part harmony while phoning Mam to tell her they'll be home for tea and Welsh cakes' (1997) is one whose demise he would welcome.

Negative or disempowering stereotypes are an integral part of political and cultural colonialism. While efforts to locate Wales within any post-colonial paradigm inevitably looks strained owing to the fact that the undeniable colonisation 'happened seven centuries ago, rather than in the last century' (Aaron 1995: 15), the implications of the nursery rhyme 'Taffy was a Welshman/Taffy was a thief' are clear. Evelyn Waugh's description of the Welsh in *Decline and Fall* as 'low of brow, crafty of eye, and crooked of limb ... [slavering] at their mouths, which hung loosely over their receding chins' (1937 [1928]: 65–6) finds its 1990s equivalent in A. A. Gill's *Sunday Times* claims that the Welsh are an assortment of ugly trolls. Although Rhys Ifans's portrayal of a Welshman stole the screen in *Notting Hill* through the force of its comic brio, that image only served to reinforce images of the Welsh as voluble sexual obsessives. Thomas, however, insists that '[we] can't just blame the ignorance and stereotypes on people from outside' (quoted in McLean 1995: 6). Self-generated images have themselves ensured that the Welsh are incarcerated in a cultural landscape formed of an amalgam of John Ford's *How Green Was My Valley* and Dylan Thomas's *Under Milk Wood*.

Loren Kruger has written persuasively on the role of the theatre in establishing a national hegemony by 'summoning a representative audience that in turn recognizes itself on stage' (1987: 35). The vibrant contribution of theatre to establishing a rejuvenated sense of nation in countries and moments as diverse as nineteenth-century Norway and twentieth-century Ireland suggests the possibility of a Welsh equivalent. The reality, however, is captured in Carl Tighe's 1986 observation that despite the 'enormous social and political and industrial changes that have swept over Wales in the last ten or fifteen years' (251), its stages have seen merely 'a parade of West End copies, examination texts and amnesiac froth' (258). 'There is', he argued, 'a general refusal to engage with the idea of Wales' (255), or rather to explore realities as opposed to an idea of Wales where 'sentimental twaddle' (257) dominates and the country is seen as populated by 'barmy eccentrics, loonies and no good boyos' (256). Tighe's dispiriting summary provides the context within which Thomas's observation that 'we haven't created enough fictions ourselves' takes its force (quoted in McLean 1995: 6). His objective is to create what he terms 'a vibrant and invented contemporary mythology ... a landscape of fiction that reflects the way we live, love and die; a fiction that shows us our experiences are particular and at the same time universal' (Thomas 1997: 18). With the establishment of Y Cwmni (now Fiction Factory) in 1988, Thomas engaged in the process of first analysing then generating adequate fictions to live by; a process which continued across the 1990s. In addition to Thomas's plays this decade saw the proliferation of alternative Welsh images across a variety of genres, most particularly music and film. In a 1997 interview with Thomas, Heike Roms speculated that contemporary Welsh youth would 'find their role-models in films like *Twin Town* rather than in the writings of Jack Kerouac' (1998b: 190), which drove the protagonist of Thomas's *House of America*. While *Twin Town* (1997) blasts open images of Wales as an extended Llareggub, a closer analysis suggests a less progressive set of values than implied by Roms and forms a useful point of comparison to Thomas's attempts to stimulate 'a multicultural Wales with a myriad of sustainable myths' (Davies 1998a: 117).

After the sweep of the camera across the expanse of Swansea Bay and fleeting glimpses of the city's loveable, if slightly eccentric, normality, the film roars into action as two teenagers, the Lewis twins, joy-ride, *Bullit*-like, down the steep streets of the city before stopping outside a doctor's surgery and picking up a pensioner couple. 'Now don't forget, there's a welcome for you both in the choir practice. Your father was a fine tenor, be a shame to break the mould, innit?' are the words of the husband to the blank-faced boys. The penetration of such residual values into a culture of joy-riding and joints is complicated by the fact that the pensioners are fuelling the boys' drug habit by selling them their Diazepam prescription: 'The boys have this with their cider ... To have a good time see' is the streetwise comment of the wife. Clashes of con-temporary culture with remnants of a glory that is gone continue throughout the film in which language and attitudes have the gloss of contemporaneity: 'karaoke is what's killing the fucking male voice choir music', the police are corrupt, the sex is brutish and the patron of the rugby club, Bryn Cartwright, is funding Swansea's cocaine traffic. When the boys' family are burnt to death as a result of an escalating feud over compensation demanded in recompense for the father's accident while working for Cartwright, they initiate a scheme of revenge which results in the death of both Cartwright and Terry, the corrupt policeman who was the direct cause of the family's murder. As the production team of *Trainspotting* were involved in *Twin Town*, comparisons between the films are readily made. The way in which *Twin Town* ends, however, lends itself to a reading more confirmatory of 'residual' cultural values than is suggested by this particular Welsh connection.

At the film's close the boys enact a ceremony of simultaneous homage and revenge, providing the father with the burial at sea he craved and executing Terry by strapping him to the coffin. As the coffin sinks beneath the waves the boys cast a Welsh flag on the sea, the whole final sequence being accompanied by the strains of 'Myfanwy' from a male-voice choir standing at the end of Mumbles pier. This excess of national signifiers might be taken as ironic were it not for the fact that the executed Terry has not only committed murder but aggressively mocked the Welsh throughout the film, finally deriding the national rugby team as a 'crap-shite rugby team that can't even beat Canada'. Terry is Scots, and it is worth noting that the moment of past rugby glory which is reflected on at some length, with individual moves being recited in sequence by three Welsh characters, refers to a 1977 Welsh victory at Murrayfield. Terry is also responsible for extending the volume of cocaine traffic in Swansea, the drug being brought in by a Londoner whose anti-Welsh prejudice matches his own. Although Cartwright is Welsh, his *parvenu* lifestyle suggests that he has cut himself off from any authentic communal values. The fact that the choir turns up on the pier at the request of the boys demonstrates that while the Lewises are delinquent they are not to be read as excluded. What they inflict is a communal punishment rather than an act of personal revenge and triumphantly demonstrate whose is the victory by placing the Welsh flag on the water, smothering the last sight of Terry even as it memorialises their father. While this moment is far from the radical communality recalled by Gwyn Williams, it is still closer to that sense of innate opposition to injustice than it is to the alienation of the world of Irvine Welsh. Its political impotence lies in the fact that while the Lewis twins triumph, the film ends as they head out to sea in a stolen motor launch, their only concern whether they have enough fuel to reach Morocco. The final shot of the choir on the illuminated pier is set against the dark night of the Welsh mainland and as the film credits roll the strains of the choir are replaced by the sound of the Super Furry Animals' 'Bad Behaviour'. The victory of the old Wales is fleeting, all that is left is a sense of what once was, for the values finally upheld by the brothers are 'residual', and too readily mourned and memorialised rather than mobilised.

The use of rugby failure as shorthand for a more extended cultural malaise is a feature of the film and, as argued by Glyn Davies, 'Welsh rugby, once a source of national pride, [has] now become part of that rapid erosion of national identity which has thrown a big question mark over what it means to be Welsh today' (1991/92: 4). Davies neatly summarises those elements of the culture which once represented Welsh-

ness: 'close communities sustained by heavy industry, the Welsh language, male-voice choirs, chapels, hill-farms, rugby', and the fact that now
'they are things in decline' (4). Having suffered defeats by Canada and
Western Samoa, the rugby players of the early 1990s, and the nation
whose pride they once embodied, saw themselves as 'figures of fun, out
of date and out of fashion, searching for their "*hwyl*" [emotional ecstasy]
amongst the wreckage of old securities' (1991/92: 6). The issue which is
addressed directly by the theatre of Ed Thomas is how to rescue
something from the ruins.

Thomas's decade-long dramatisation of the trauma of his native
culture is born of his own sense that 'the only thing I see in Wales is
defeat' and, he continued, 'I personally find defeat difficult to live with'
(Davies 1994/95: 58). In the bleak *Song From a Forgotten City* (1995)
Thomas takes this pervasive sense of terminal decline to an ultimate low
as Wales, defeated in Cardiff by the English national rugby team,
spawns desolate characters who, faced with the fact that 'THE
WHOLE FUCKING WORLD IS BEATING US AT OUR OWN
GAME', now cry 'I'm Welsh and I'm fucked in the head' (4). The grim
sense of cultural meltdown is absolute. Despite the echo of Thomas's
own sentiments in the assertion of Carlyle, the protagonist, that 'we
must play our part on the world stage. We've got to show that the way
we live, love and die means something, that we are part of the world, not
unique but similar, universal, like small countries all over the world!' (17),
it is the quality of lament which distinguishes the play, coupled with
traces of a cultural anguish which drives Carlyle into excesses of self and
national disgust which confirms defeat far more than it liberates desire.
Thomas, as observed by Katie Gramich, may 'believe in the tragic
potential of the cliché' (1998: 168), but Carlyle's masturbatory release over
a Cindy doll in the aftermath of a rugby defeat runs perilously close to
confirming rather than interrogating the most negative images of
Welshness. Gwyn Williams noted that images of a cosy Welsh world
were a badge of subordination, 'the diminishing and sometimes debilitating shorthand of a subordinate people cultivating a re-assuring self-
indulgence in the interstices of subordination' (1990/91: 59). With *Song
From a Forgotten City* Thomas is so concerned with demolishing cosy
images that he fails to see that self-indulgence and subordination can
take several forms. Far more significant both in cultural and dramatic
terms are *House of America* (1994b [1988]), *East From the Gantry* (1994d
[1992]) (which form the first and last plays of the *New Wales Trilogy*) and
Gas Station Angel (1998), all of which interrogate the pressing need for

sustaining national images, passing through the inadequacy of those imported from another culture to tentatively alight on the possibility that Wales itself contains the necessities of renewal. But as is clear from *The Myth of Michael Roderick* (1990, unpublished) where the arms of stretcher bearers are wrenched out by the strain of carrying the dead who are 'heavy with nostalgia for a golden age there never was and they never saw' (Savill 1991: 86), this renewal is not to be grounded in images which sustained the Wales of the past.

Thomas's most successful play, *House of America*, takes a traumatised Welsh family living on the edge of an opencast mine as a metaphor for Wales itself. As noted above, a central question of the play is 'where's our heroes?' and, faced with the vacuity of those on offer, Sid Lewis and his sister Gwenny indulge in a progressively incestuous and ultimately murderous identification with Jack Kerouac and his lover Joyce Johnson. A more pertinent question, however, is as to what has created the pressing need for heroes; an issue which is acknowledged in Thomas's work, but only tangentially, and in increasingly elliptical ways, as his plays go through their various drafts in the process of production and publication.

In the second play of the *New Wales Trilogy*, *Flowers From the Dead Red Sea* (1994c [1991]), which is stripped down to a Beckettian bleakness in its published form, one character proclaims that 'the good bit' 'is already crushed, like my mother's and my father's, my grandparents and theirs. I am the progeny of crushed good brain, the history of crushed good brains, I am the future of a million crushed good brains' (124). And as becomes clear in this exchange from the final play in the trilogy, *East From the Gantry* (1994d [1992]), this sense of extinction is grounded in specific historical and material realities:

> Bella: It's a shame it died out … mining.
> Trampas: It is.
> Bella: It's a real shame.
> Trampas: Miners used to bring down governments.
> Bella: They did.
> Trampas: There were thousands of them.
> Bella: Yes.
> Trampas: Pits all over the place.
> Bella: And now there's none.

(197)

As recorded in a review of one production of the play, this moment was accompanied by 'big black-and-white photos emerging from dust-sheets which conjure up images of old Wales – rugby teams, stone farmhouses, pitheads' (McMillan 1998: 225). Thomas has expressed his doubts about the 'old Wales' of clichés and stereotypes but this other 'old Wales' – while less apparent in his work, and while this moment is excised from the published version of the play – still underpins the essential tragedy which unfolds in *House of America*. For this is a Wales of unemployment where Sid's failure to obtain work at the open caste mine, and the fact that at thirty 'the only job I've ever had is fucking gravedigging', drives him inexorably into the 'game' of Jack Kerouac and Joyce Johnson which he 'plays' with Gwenny because 'I was Jack for a bit, felt good' (97). Escaping from this downward spiral of despair leads to Gwenny's pregnancy, and final drug-induced death, and his being beaten to death by his brother, Boyo, who is outraged at their incestuous liaison. Dreams, specifically American dreams, have a death-dealing power when cherished in lieu of reality. The fact that the mother's murder and burial of the father, which has always been referred to by her as his escape to America, is soon to be revealed by the encroaching opencast mine makes explicit Thomas's association of America with deaths which are both physical and cultural. He is scathing in his attitude to American commercialism and culture. In an interview in 1997 he commented that 'America is eminently successful at exporting crap all over the world – Mickey Mouse, Macdonald and KFC … it supports a kind of monoglot culture, a dangerous simplicity' (Davies 1998a: 116, 118). But what it possesses, Thomas continues, is a sustaining power such as Wales lacks. There is then 'nothing wrong with Sid, he just selects the wrong dream. But the quality of his imagination is terrific' (126). However, while the play is explicit in its presentation of the consequences of the wrong dream, it is muffled on the causes of such a choice and limits alternatives to hints and suggestions which flit across the dialogue but are not embodied in either theme or action.

'I tell you one thing', says the Mother to Boyo, 'if you don't stand up to it, your roots are going to fly out of the ground to wherever the wind blows them' (1994b: 85). Apart from her fears that the mining operation will expose her own guilty secret, the explicit reference here is to the fact that it is their house, 'home', which will be destroyed by this new enter-prise. The company operating the mine is given no national affiliation but what is made clear is that this is work lacking in all dignity and direction. In the desolate self-analysis of the labourer employed at the mine, 'the dreams have just fallen out of the ears' consequent on engaging in a work in which 'I've got to go now, see the machine's started walking, got to follow the machine' (66). This is the low-skill employment produced in the postmodern economy which Fredric Jameson described as the global expression of American capitalism (1984: 57), and its all-pervasive quality is captured in Sid's observation that pretty soon the company will want their house 'and you'll say "You can't have it, it's part of our street," and they'll turn round and say, "We know, but we own the street"' (73). The paradox of Sid, and Gwenny, is that they are destroyed by the culture which they embrace as an escape from the ravages effected by its economy.

What is interesting is the position of Boyo: 'I drink coke, eat pop-corn, wear baseball hats, watch the films' (76) is his comment on the perceived excessive identification of his brother with America as, by implication, he suggests that he draws the line at a purely physical consumption of that culture, denying the dominance of what he derides as 'yankage' (97). And when Sid and Gwenny offer him a baseball cap in the intensity of their Kerouac fantasy he 'scrunches it and throws it to the floor and spits' (89). While there is a difference between the conscious-ness expounded by Kerouac and the corporate capitalism from which the beat generation was in flight, the implication of *House of America* is that the commerce and the culture come as one imported and indivisible package, inhabiting dreams as readily as they control daily schedules. Both are equally invidious. 'Some of us don't forget' (81) is the Mother's comment as she commemorates St David's Day, and while this is articulated from within a hospital to which she has been consigned for mental illness the issue of holding to origin as an antidote to oblivion is echoed by Boyo's resolute 'this is where I belong, and I'm staying, no fucking tinpot dreaming for me' (73). While strong in this assertion, however, *House of America* is clearer in its analysis of cultural inadequa-cies than it is in explicating their causes and, while allowing Boyo's identification with 'home' full articulation, the play closes as he holds the dead Gwenny in his arms; the curtain falling on the failure of the false dream rather than on the reconstitution of an alternative.

The success of *House of America* led to its being made into a film in a Wales nominally quite other than that of its first production. The soundtrack for the stage production in 1988 was dominated by tracks from The Velvet Underground and The Doors. Such was the extent of the felt inadequacy of contemporary Welsh culture in this period that the significance of John Cale's birth in 'Ponty or somewhere' (Thomas 1994b: 32) is denied: 'I don't care if Cale came from fucking Ystrad, he's living in New York now' (32). And as for Cale's partner in boho cool,

Lou Reed, Wales is 'not cool enough for him, no way' (32). By the time of the film production in 1997, however, not only had Welsh culture taken on a different tone from that defined by Harry Secombe but Thomas's attitude to his native culture had consequently modified. Celebrating the explosion of Welsh bands he said '[we're] all outed now. Wales is full of different voices and the more the merrier. Take the bands, for example, Catatonia, Super Furry Animals, the Manic Street Preachers, they all have a different sound but they're all Welsh' (Hitt 1998: 5). Indeed, far from his 1994 sense of a prevalent defeat in the culture, by 1998 he was speaking of the fact that '[kids] growing up today now think it's OK to be Welsh, it's groovy, hip, cool, whatever you want to call it' (Hitt 1998: 5). However, the choice of a soundtrack which included successful Welsh bands not only for the film, but also for the 1997 tour of a drama nominally concerned with the inadequacy of the indigenous culture to sustain a demoralised people poses certain problems. Thomas acknowledged that 'the question will come up why these people don't get their act together', responding to this self-interrogation by asserting that rather than criticising Sid for dreaming, 'what I would give him a row for is buying an American dream off the shelf' (Roms 1998b: 190). The film, he went on to say, would not be played 'with the same moral correctness as the original stage version' (190) and the script has clearly been modified in the light of a perceived transformation in the cultural domain and Thomas's own analysis as it developed through subsequent plays.

The film of *House of America* provided a more complex psychology for Sid; his American dream is driven by his knowledge of his father's death, exacerbated rather than caused by unemployment. Rather than being killed by Boyo he commits suicide. The causal factors for the family tragedy are far more personal than social; indeed Sid's possession of a Harley Davidson casts him as romantic rebel rather than economic victim with his death imaged as a release and redemption when he rides through an *Easy Rider* landscape to be reunited with his father in the last of the black-and-white 'American' dream moments which have been interspersed through the film. With this resolution of Sid's trauma, it is suggested, the family regains some form of normality: the film closes as Mother and Gwenny discuss a name for the latter's baby while Boyo is heard from as working as a mechanic in Poole. Unemployment and its attendant despair are still present in a Wales imaged as bleached of colour but they are factors essentially external to the Lewis's intense domestic agony.

Despite the optimism which Thomas spoke of as entering Wales in the decade between the production of the play and that of the film, and its expression in the perpetuation of the family and the self-realisation of Boyo in work, its substantial elements are less evident. The film makes clearer the reality of America's economic colonisation of the valleys as the mining company's title, Michigan, towers in HOLLYWOOD-high red letters above the Lewis home. Despite the opening up of the drama into the streets, pubs and countryside of south Wales, however, there is a contraction of the scope of its analysis. Causes of social optimism are limited to the inclusion of the Manic Street Preachers and Catatonia on the soundtrack, in addition to three songs from Tom Jones. While Jones is approvingly acknowledged in the original play for being 'back now in the Vale' (1994b: 46) his presence in the film is an expression of his transcendence of ironic appreciation to iconic status. This, coupled with the fact that John Cale supplies the film's original music, suggests a more confident culture than that of the 1988 theatrical production. The problem posed by the film, however, is in many ways paradigmatic of the culture itself in that the optimism is generated at a superstructural level.

Thomas has frequently asserted that the real problem confronting Wales is its cultural invisibility: 'the way we live our culture doesn't mean anything to anyone else, and moreover, we've never seen that culture reflected back at us.' The result, he argued, being that 'the Welsh are paralysed by a lack of self-esteem and lack of confidence' (Davies 1994/95: 56). It is this lack of self-esteem, and what Thomas terms 'global myths ... exportable myths' (Davies 1998a: 116), which drives Sid Lewis into his destructive American dream. But if Sid's conviction that 'I've been born in the wrong country' (1994b: 45) is to be rectified for the culture of which he is, in part, the expression, then a sense of Wales as a country possessing indigenous sustaining myths has to be developed; a process which Thomas initiates with *East From the Gantry* (1994d [1992]).

In many ways Thomas's most technically interesting work, and one which demonstrates his acknowledged debt to Sam Shepard's American Expressionism, the play is set 'in Southern Powys ... In Wales' (182). But this grounded specificity of place is countered by the characters' fluid sense of time and memory as a feuding couple, Ronnie and Bella, and her potential lover, Trampas, reflect on the loss of love, life and dreams, the whole summarised in Trampas's recollection of a friend's despairing comment "'You haven't got a home man," he said, "it don't exist, it disappeared, it shrunk, it fucked off, it took a walk, it died, it no longer continued to be"' (182). The desolation evokes that of *House of America*, and Trampas, like Sid Lewis, has sought consolation in an American identity which is both culturally and temporally regressive: that of 'Trampas' the cowboy drifter in the 1960s TV series *The Virginian*. However, *East From the Gantry* marks an advance on the earlier play where lines of resistance were limited to Boyo's rejection of 'yankage' and the Mother's feeble insistence on holding to roots. As the three characters converse in the fire-gutted house which was once a home, *East From the Gantry* moves to a sense of undefined, but optimistic progression. Recognising that '[the] home I knew has gone forever' Trampas accepts Ronnie's suggestion that it is '[time] to make a new start then', marking this with a return to his own name, 'Billy' (212). As the play closes, the three characters move to the table where Bella pours wine and lights some candles: 'The table looks beautifully laid, ready for something good to happen' (213).

The moment is one of anticipation rather than achievement, but in returning to his proper name Billy is laying claim to a future which is located in 'southern Powys'. His 'Trampas' declaration, 'I'm either going to fly or fall from the sky with a crash' (192), evokes the death of Martin Bratton who was killed in an attempt to fly east from the gantry. Attempts at flight, whether literal or metaphoric, effect their own kinds of death. And as Katie Gramich argues, 'what Edward Thomas seems to be suggesting is that the only place of salvation and fulfillment is not west, not east, but here' (1998: 160). While the resolution is suggestive rather than prescriptive, the play's opening, and Thomas's dense intertextuality, provides a clearer sense of the direction of his regenerative cultural analysis.

East From the Gantry opens with Trampas's story of how his uncle Ieu, when a child, had accidentally killed his mother with a shotgun, a traumatic event which affected both Ieu and his younger brother Jim: 'they were never the same again' (169). The bare bones of this story forms the narrative of Thomas's TV play, *Fallen Sons* (1994e). Here the boys, Iorry and Danny, are twins, and it is the father rather than the mother who is killed. The death splits the family as the 'guilty' Iorry is sent to live with relatives and a deep animosity created between him and his brother which lasts through into their old age. The moment of the play is that of their collective birthday, the day on which their father was killed, when Danny escapes the celebrations guiltily engineered by his *parvenu* son, and seeks out Iorry who has lived in an isolation compounded by his trauma-induced stammer. The play closes as Iorry stammers out '*damwain*' (accident); the final image is of the brothers' laughing reconciliation drifting in a boat on a lake high in the hills. *Fallen Sons* suggests an ability to accommodate even the past's most devastating moments and lay the foundations for a sustaining future; the work is given an extra cultural resonance by the use of Welsh for the moment of reconciliation. It is the clearest expression of Thomas's acknowledgement of his preference for 'epiphany to comprehension' (Davies 1994/95: 61); the piece evoking a mood rather than concluding a thesis. For while as engaged as G. B. Shaw in the failings of his contemporary moment, Thomas is no exponent of the Shavian 'Problem Play', rejecting '"well-made" plays that have an argument and a counter-argument and a message' (Davies 1998: 121) in favour of a theatre that 'should release the imagination for people who want to be taken on a journey' (129).

Although this move away from the desolation of the original stage version of *House of America* was followed in 1995 by the bleak *Song from a Forgotten City*, that play, while open to criticism as 'a resumé of his message about inferiority' (Adams 1998: 148), is the final expression of anguish at no longer belonging to 'a nation that was fucking good at something' (Thomas 1995: 8). *Gas Station Angel* (1998), Thomas's last play to date, was described by him as 'a new kind of play for me. It's very optimistic', and for reasons which set it directly against the stage desolation of *House of America*: '*Gas Station Angel* is about how these two people – white trash I call them – make themselves up and realise they've got their own mythology. The future is theirs, if they come to terms with the past. Instead of the past destroying them like in *House of America*, they survive the past, so it's quite hopeful' (Hitt 1998: 6–7). Surviving the past then becomes a crucial facet of Thomas's sense of a regenerated Wales, one complemented by 'imagination', since '[to] be Welsh at the end of the Twentieth Century you need to have imagination' (Davies 1998a: 118).

The play's central characters, Ace and Bron, are the products of dysfunctional families who are unknowingly united by the finally revealed secret that Bron's missing brother was assaulted in error by Ace before being killed by his mother. As in *East From the Gantry* and *Fallen Sons*, the thrust of the play is towards the realisation of Bron's perception that 'maybe if we faced up to the past then maybe we wouldn't find the world so confusing' (1998: 20). As Ace and Bron become lovers capable of accommodating the knowledge of his and his mother's culpability for her brother's death there is a clear expansion of horizons. While *House of America*'s Sid Lewis can only see the limitations of his homeland, rejecting the idea that he could ride to Pembroke – 'don't give me Pembroke, what happens when you reach the sea, the end of the line?' (1994b: 44) – Ace is capable of imagining beyond Wales while remaining firmly within it. 'I could see for miles', he says, 'all of Europe spread out in front of me' (1998: 75). Thomas's own desire for Wales's future to be as 'an eclectic, modern European society' (Davies 1998a: 117) is captured in Ace's declaration 'I felt in my bones that the times are a-changing. Maybe I can soon call myself a European. A Welsh European, with my own language and the rudiments of another on the tip of my tongue' (1998: 75). This inclusive sense of Welshness echoes Raymond Williams's hopes for a modern, 'European' Wales; what he termed 'the moment when we move from a *merely retrospective* nationalist politics to a *truly prospective* politics' (1989: 118, original emphases). However, while Ace can recognise what Williams called 'the living complexity' (118) of a changing Wales and echo verbatim Thomas's dictum that to be Welsh in the twentieth century requires imagination, there is no decisive advance into action. Despite the acknowledgement that youth in this society has 'no roots … no morality … no religion … no family … no values … no hopes … no desires … no dreams' (1998: 32), there is no suggestion as to the alleviation of that condition beyond the power of imagination. The limitations of this are captured, albeit unintentionally, in Ace's stated preference for stories: '[life] in storyland I could control, the on-going war against the sea and real life I couldn't' (11).

Thomas has expressed his distrust of art 'that tells you what to think', acknowledging that he doesn't 'claim to be prescriptive' (Davies 1998a: 122). His rejection of the role of the dramatist as being equivalent to that of 'journalists discussing the issue of unemployment in the south Wales valleys' is legitimised by the claim that his fictions 'contain possibilities of telling certain truths or reflections about the world' (Davies 1998a: 124). As noted above, the redemption of individual and social malaise is realised through imagination and the ability to first face and then transcend the past. The difficulty with this analysis is that Thomas sees the past only as the source of debilitating memories rather than a resource on which the present can draw.

At the time of *Song From a Forgotten City* in 1995 the reviewer of the *Socialist Campaign Group News* commented '[whether] they [Y Cmwni] will want to address current economic and social issues any more concretely seems doubtful' (Trott 1998: 236). In large part this is because Thomas's dramas are essentially domestic rather than social, his characters frequently traumatised by the deaths of parents or siblings with the social and economic dimensions to those tragedies, while alluded to, never becoming central to the work. This is in striking contrast to the works of 1930s South Wales writers such as Lewis Jones, who has the protagonist of his novel *We Live* make the fervently socialist declaration 'Keep close to the people. When we are weak they'll give us strength. When we fail, they'll pick us up and put us back on the road again' (1979 [1939]: 144). Thomas's dramas are set in the moment of that community's descent into extinction in which Jones's belief that the Red Flag 'shows the way to revolution and freedom' (1979 [1939]: 139) has become an embarrassing anachronism. There is then a painful realism to Thomas's projection of Wales into a future fuelled by imagination as for him the past is 'fucked-up' (1998: 20), and progress only a possibility when it is transcended.

Thomas is at one with Gwyn Williams in his advocacy of an imaginative shaping of a Welsh future, but he lacks his social(ist) engagement with the community's history as a repository of possibilities; a severing of the connective tissue binding the intellectual to the community which Williams locates as occurring at the onset of Wales's disappearance into Britain when 'Welsh politics had ceased to exist'. While 'most Welsh intellectuals since the eighteenth century had served as organic intellectuals ... [the] votes of 1979 dramatically registered the end of that epoch' (Williams 1985: 297). Stephen Knight has commented on the extent to which the socialist novel exemplified by *We Live* saw 'a tapering off in the post-war period, mostly into sentimentality or nihilism tinged with despair' (1993: 84), and Lewis's activism might appear redundant in the face of Wales's post–1979 exposure to 'the radical restructuring of an increasingly multinational capitalism in Britain' (Williams 1985: 297). The dismantling of Wales's industrial base and the social collapse consequent on this 'radical restructuring' has been addressed in recent drama, in Alan Osborne's *Redemption Song* (1999), or most notably in Patrick Jones's *Everything Must Go* (1999) in which the young protagonist attempts to inspire some resistance to the occupation of the valleys by the 'kabashio tv and video' company through his evocations of 'fucking chartists meeting in the rain soaked caves up in fucking cwm and brymawr ... aneurin bevan uppona hill speaking to fucking thousands of people bout life an stuff' (9). And it is Jones's comment on *House of America* which brings Thomas's intention to create a Welsh future into sharp focus: 'I don't think it was political enough really – I think it could have been a lot more angry, a little bit more politicised' (Parry 1999: 7).

Heike Roms has argued that Thomas is committed to a political cause, but that his work should not be confused with 'the often crude literalness that characterised the agitprop theatre of the 1960s and 1970s' (1998a: 131). The rejection of naturalism in his work, the fluid use of space and preference for non-linear narratives is all part of a search for a distinctly and innovatively Welsh theatre, one which, for Thomas, 'is part of the argument for a new and invented Wales' (1994c [1991]: 17). In rejecting imported images and dramatically invoking individuals' power to override inherited limitations and inhibitions Thomas intends to provide a theatrical parallel for a Wales which will be 'fast, maverick and imaginative, and innovative ... a grown-up Wales, which is self-defined and not stereotypical' (Davies 1998a: 117). Thomas has argued that he 'very much agree(s) with Gwyn Alf Williams's view of the history of South Wales' particularly of Welshness as 'an idea that is constantly being reinvented' (Davies 1994/95: 56). However, while both Thomas and Williams advance a view of what Williams termed 'Welsh making and unmaking of themselves' it is only Williams who argues that 'a sense of history has been central' (1985: 304). And in the moment of post-modernity that sense of history is crucial.

Thomas's open-ended compositional technique, in which 'plays mutate in text, in form, in medium', has been cited by David Adams as 'a clear example of what postmodernists mean when they assert that all writing is a rewriting' (1998: 156). Moreover, according to Katie Gramich, Thomas's plays embody the 'postmodernist ideology' explicated in Deleuze and Guattari's *Anti-Oedipus*: 'We no longer believe in a primor-dial totality that once existed, or in a final totality that awaits us at some future date' (1998: 170). While the end of the grand narratives may have proved a liberation for many, the implications of an end of any 'totality' for a historically validated sense of national identity and difference are obvious. History may have a part to play in the world of the postmodern but, according to Gwyn Williams, it is on the level of 'pits turned into tourist museums' and is 'rarely to be brought to bear on vulgarly contem-porary problems'. This, he concluded, 'is not to encapsulate a past, it is to sterilize it. It is not to cultivate an historical consciousness; it is to eliminate it' (1985: 300). And this prophetic sense of Welsh history and identity as commercial commodities is made chillingly apparent in the pronouncement by the International Officer with the Welsh Arts Council that

> the image of Wales abroad as represented by its artists is one of a distin-ctive, individual culture, of a dynamic, self-confident and risk-taking people, a place of innovation as well as tradition, richness and diversity.

These attributes are of interest to potential investors both in terms of representing the positive qualities of our people – self-motivation, commitment and flexibility – as well as providing an interesting environment in which to relocate. (Vaughan Jones 1997/98: 46)

As argued by Fredric Jameson, postmodernity's malign reality is that of 'the internal and superstructural expression of a whole new wave of American military and economic domination throughout the world' (1984: 57) in which 'historicity and historical depth, which used to be called historical consciousness or the sense of the past, are abolished' (Stephenson 1989: 4). The threat of such a 'thinning' of the historical consciousness is seen by Jameson as being as disastrous for the individual as for the nation; indeed the former is the paradigm of the latter:

> when the links of the signifying chain snap, then we have schizophrenia in the form of a rubble of distinct and unrelated signifiers [and as] personal identity is itself the effect of a certain temporal unification of past and future with the present before me; and second, that such active temporal unification is itself a function of language, or better still of the sentence, as it moves through its hermeneutic circle through time. If we are unable to unify the past, present and future of our sentence, then we are similarly unable to fulfil the past, present and future of our own biographical experience or psychic life. (Jameson 1984: 72)

In shedding the 'old Wales' of Max Boyce, male-voice choirs and daffodils Thomas aims to enable the unencumbered nation to make the leap into the future. However, there is a risk that along with the past of tired stereotypes goes that of the regenerative possibilities evoked by Gwyn Williams, as Wales has 'repeatedly employed history to make a usable past, to turn a past into an instrument with which a present can build a future' (1985: 304). Wales may now be cool enough for Lou Reed but what may be generated through cultural 'chilling' alone is open to question.

Notes

1 I am indebted to the generosity of Ed Thomas and Patrick Jones in providing me with copies of the unpublished *Song From a Forgotten City* and *Everything Must Go* respectively.

9

Waking up in a different place: contemporary Irish and Scottish fiction

GLENDA NORQUAY AND GERRY SMYTH

In his 1994 essay entitled 'The lie of the land: some thoughts on the map of Ireland', the Irish journalist and cultural commentator Fintan O'Toole made the point that although Dublin and Edinburgh are equidistant from the Rhine, the latter city, according to a certain German map of Europe's new economically defined regions, was

> part of the core whereas Dublin is part of the outer periphery, simply because Edinburgh is more accessible and richer. In this sense, the new map of post-1992 Europe is one in which Dublin, and Belfast, are in the West, along with Warsaw, Bucharest and Lisbon, while Edinburgh and London are in the East along with Stuttgart and Nice and Rome. Where space is measured, not in miles or kilometres, but in marks or francs, it is hard to get your bearings. (30)

A decade later, it is unlikely if that particular analysis still holds. Without any corresponding shift in the earth's tectonic plates, Ireland's tigerish economy has rocketed the Dublin-dominated island into the European heartland, while Edinburgh, with the advent of the Scottish Parliament and a host of new employment opportunities has continued to prosper, albeit through its acknowledged difference and distance from the metropolitan 'core'.[1] O'Toole's main point, however, continues to hold good, namely, that the meanings attributed to 'places' like Edinburgh and Dublin (and indeed Scotland and Ireland) rely in large measure on the criteria whereby they are spatially constructed.

As the updating of O'Toole's example demonstrates, however, we appear to have entered a period of history in which the spatial constructions of Scotland and Ireland are almost changing faster than cultural representations can cope with. Roddy Doyle's advice for the citizens of the Republic is apposite for those living throughout these islands: 'You should bring your passport to bed with you because you're going to wake up in a different place' (quoted in Smyth 1997: 102). It is also pertinent advice for writers of contemporary fiction in Ireland and Scotland. Nevertheless, the established cultural institutions continue to service the notion of place as a significant factor impacting on modern identity formation, while at the same time engaging with new possibilities for mapping location. Given this dynamic tension between cultural representation and spatial construction, it is a particularly interesting time at which to undertake a comparison of the fiction being produced in different parts of the Atlantic archipelago.

Traditionally such comparisons have been conducted through a limited core-periphery model. Even such a self-conscious comparativist as Susan Bassnett comments that '[the] relationship of the Celtic diaspora to the English mainstream still remains to be properly investigated' while the 'difficulty' of such an enterprise is explained as due to the complex history of political and linguistic development (1993: 62). Such (un)critical endorsement of ideological space (English centre, Celtic periphery) contributes to the process whereby that hegemonic space is reproduced and perpetuated. This chapter aspires to an alternative critical project: an analysis of contemporary Scottish and Irish fiction through a comparison of the ways in which relations between cultural representation and spatial construction are negotiated in each case to produce places called 'Scotland' and 'Ireland'. In the innovations of recent writing, challenging new maps of archipelagic spaces have emerged; yet in the reception of such writing in mainstream culture we can also discern the perpetuation of older patterns of assimilation.

I

In the preface to the 1829 edition of his novel *Waverley* (first published in 1814), Walter Scott cited amongst his influences the Anglo-Irish writer Maria Edgeworth, and particularly her first novel *Castle Rackrent* published in 1800. He noted:

> the extended and well-merited fame of Miss Edgeworth, whose Irish characters have gone so far to make the English familiar with the characters of their gay and kind-hearted neighbours of Ireland, that she may be truly said to have done more towards completing the Union than perhaps all the legislative enactments by which it has been followed up.
>
> Without being so presumptuous as to hope to emulate the rich humour, pathetic tenderness, and admirable tact, which pervade the

works of my accomplished friend, I felt that something might be attempted for my own country, of the same kind with that which Miss Edgeworth so fortunately achieved for Ireland – something which might introduce her natives to those of the sister kingdom, in a more favourable light than they had been placed hitherto, and tend to procure sympathy for their virtues and indulgence for their foibles. (reproduced in Williams 1968: 413)

This was praise indeed from such a well established man-of-letters, someone who was to go on to become one of the century's most influential writers. Scott's regard was responsible in no small part for the consolidation of Edgeworth's reputation at a time when her pseudo-Enlightened 'novels' must have been suspect to a culture in deep reaction against Enlightenment-inspired revolution (Butler 1981: 94–8). In articles, reviews and prefaces throughout the first quarter of the nineteenth century, Scott alluded to Edgeworth's exemplary fiction, and subsequent criticism has by and large endorsed his view.[2] *Castle Rackrent* continues to be invoked as a crucial moment in the archipelago's literary history, widely cited as an early (if not the first) example of a number of subsequently significant subgenres: the regional novel, the historical novel, the saga novel, the 'Big House' novel, the 'found-and-edited' novel. The engagement of Scott, a writer whose influence on cultural formations of national histories has been equally long-lasting, with Edgeworth, and his subsequent adaptation of her breakthrough discourse, provides an early example of what Luke Gibbons has called an 'unapproved road' in archipelagic cultural history, an exchange along the margins – from Ireland to Scotland and back again – which threatens to 'short-circuit the colonial divide' (1996: 180). This concept of unapproved roads is one to which we shall return as we examine the ways in which contemporary writers also cross and map a terrain that does not require polarisation with a 'core' to give it significance.

At the same time, however, Scott's understanding of the peculiar merits of Edgeworth's art is cast in terms which were to encumber much subsequent Irish and Scottish fiction. The merit of *Castle Rackrent*, it appears, is that it makes 'the English familiar with the characters of their gay and kind-hearted neighbours of Ireland', while representing the 'natives' in ways likely to procure the 'sympathy' and 'indulgence' of a supposed 'sister kingdom'. Edgeworth's novel, in other words, performs an important political function – amelioration and union – with England providing the explicit cultural norm against which Irish and Scottish 'virtues' and 'foibles' may be regarded. The attempt to induce (English)

understanding of the peripheries through more sympathetic representations was widespread in archipelagic cultural discourse at this time, but
for the novelist in particular this was an undertaking fraught with
dangers and difficulties. Pointing out that Thady M'Quirk (the narrator
of *Castle Rackrent*) 'is a character only a hairsbreadth away from caricature',
Seamus Deane continues:

> This transition from the analysis of a society to the stereotyping or
> exploitation of it was rapid in those 'national' novels which became so
> popular in the early nineteenth century in Ireland and in Scotland (with
> Scott and John Galt). For the novelist who subscribed to this idea in
> any of its forms, the problem of representation was severe, largely
> because the possibility of misrepresentation was so easy ... In the Irish
> colonial situation there was an irresistible temptation to impersonate
> the idea of oneself which was entertained by others. Landlord or
> peasant, English improver or Gaelic remnant, played out roles ascribed
> to them by a situation which had robbed them of the central sense of
> responsibility, by effectively denying them basic executive power. Thus
> it was very Irish to be irresponsible and very English to be responsible
> and very typical of the English-Irish confrontation to find that neither
> could learn from or teach the other. This was a paradigm for much of
> the century's voluminous writings on the issue. It was a stylized repre-
> sentation of a powerless condition. (1986: 94, 97)

Scott's own fiction has been seen by some to have had an equally
powerful effect – as Cairns Craig comments: 'No issue has been more
debated in Scotland over the past thirty years, in terms of its political and
cultural consequences, than the falsification of Scotland's history initiated
by Walter Scott' (1999: 116). Scott, it is argued, was not alone in deploy-
ing the Jacobite cause and Highland culture to offer a distorting and
empty symbolism of national identity, in a 'project of sealing off the
Scottish past as a source of contemporary political inspiration' (Beveridge
and Turnbull 1997: 95) and the continuing critical negotiations of his
influence reinforce his key role in cultural representation (Kidd 1993;
Nairn 1981; Pittock 1999). While Edgeworth and Scott therefore offer an
instance in which it is possible to travel by unapproved roads, reading
across the margins, taken in conjunction they also present an example of
collusion with that which the centre 'approves'.

Nearly two centuries later, many writers from across the islands are
still labouring in the wake of the 'stylized representations' of Scott and
Edgeworth, still searching for forms and voices through which to
articulate experiences which are definably 'Scottish' and 'Irish', whilst
simultaneously attempting to avoid the 'powerless condition' inscribed in

received definitions of those terms. Yet in some respects the Edgeworth/ Scott dynamic provides a more apposite paradigm for writing from Scotland and Ireland in the last decade than it might have done over the last century. For fiction produced over the past ten years, notions of a 'centre' no longer provide the point of definition or difference: a significant feature of recent Scottish and Irish writing has been a tendency towards self-referentiality, an impetus towards reconfiguring the spaces of its own national landscapes and reshaping and/or challenging a perceived body of writing from within its own boundaries – what Patrick Kavanagh might refer to, in his redefinition of the term, as a necessary parochialism (1988: 205–6). Some of the newest and most recognisable of these voices belong to Roddy Doyle and Irvine Welsh, two young writers whose rapturous receptions outside Ireland and Scotland further problematise questions of acceptable and popular representation, both within and outwith their respective national cultures. The similarities and differences between their debut novels reveal much about the fortunes of the Scottish and Irish novelistic traditions in the years since *Castle Rackrent* and *Waverley*, while also offering a point of contrast for work by less well-known but no less engaged contemporary Scottish and Irish novelists.

A comparison of two key texts by Doyle and Welsh – looking not only at distinguishing features, but also at why their work has received such acclaim elsewhere – offers a powerful illustration of the ways in which this dynamic between 'margins' and 'centre(s)' is still being played out but also reconfigured. The similarities are obvious. Both *The Commitments* (1992b [1987]) and *Trainspotting* (1993) drew on, and to an extent were aimed at, 'youth' culture. With the take-off into an information revolution, and with the imminent demise of extended prose fiction once again a topic for the London reviewers, Doyle and Welsh succeeded in making the novel an attractive proposition for the non-standard reader – a reader, in other words, who was not that metropolitan, adult subject encoded into mainstream novelistic discourse at every level from composition through marketing and on to the various modes of critical engagement. Young working-class Dubliners finding common (if strategic) cause with African-American soul music; an alienated working-class generation from Edinburgh finding temporary solace in heroin – it is always difficult to appreciate *after* the event, but these were unlikely topics for successful novels in the respective cultural climates of 1987 and 1993.

As aesthetic possibilities, after all, both 'Scotland' and 'Ireland' still trailed an array of well-established connotations from earlier points in their cultural history. Both figured predominantly within the popular imagination as signifiers of the pastoral and the past: even at the outset of a new century, the Celtic north and west continue to be depicted in terms – non-Newtonian, uneven, liminal – which stress their essential difference from a putatively 'normal' southern centre. Magnificent landscape, cultural simplicity, charming locals, places offering literal (touristic) as well as imaginative relief from the pressures of the present – these are the images which continue to signify 'Scotland' and 'Ireland' for many throughout the Atlantic archipelago, produced and reproduced in a variety of televisual and cinematic examples. With regard to fiction, both were subject to a peculiar 'chronotope', the theory developed by Bakhtin to describe the particular ways in which time and space are represented in differently empowered cultural contexts (1981: 84–258). In the case of Ireland the emphasis was predominantly on small rural communities characterised by 'eccentricity', warmth and emotional purity. Scotland's fictional traditions encompassed a rather different dynamic, with a well-established tradition of novels exploring urban life through the frame of class conflict, 'masculine' industries, but also individualistic desires to escape from the soul-denying city to fresher, greener spaces. Although more urban in setting the rural still functioned as a powerful imaginative trope. It was, however, against both sets of images which Doyle and Welsh so obviously and so strenuously set their work.

One of the ways in which they did so was by locating their fictions in places different from the established representations of their respective countries. Traditionally, if Scotland and Ireland *had* to have cities, they should be ones that complement their chronotopic identities. Thus, Dublin was and should remain the city of Joyce – which is to say, not a city at all but an urban village amenable to peripatetic traversal unlike real (that is, English, European or American) cities. By the same token, Glasgow – Scotland's 'real' city – should provide the backdrop for the emergence of the authentic Scottish (working-class) identity, an identity amenable to tragic or comic inflection depending on the artist's response to the Scottish subject's essentially displaced and alienated condition. Doyle's Dublin, however, was unrecognisable as that 'word city' around which Stephen Dedalus and Leopold Bloom strolled earlier in the century. Indeed, it was not really 'Dublin' at all but a community of former city- and country-dwellers displaced from their native locales to housing estates on the edge of what was rapidly becoming a vast city-region (Smyth 2000). All the Commitments live, work and socialise in Barrytown, not in Dublin. One of the first things we learn about the central character is that '[you'd] never see Jimmy coming home from town

without a new album or a 12-inch or at least a 7-inch single' (Doyle 1992b
[1987]: 7). The most frequently remarked characteristic of Barrytown's
youth is their familiarity with and desire for non-Irish, late twentieth-
century popular culture, represented throughout the text (and in the
above sentence) in the form of English and American music. Also note-
worthy, however, are both the movement and the function described
here: movement from the centre to a home on the periphery after an
economic exchange. Like every other Dublin estate-dweller, in other
words, Jimmy has become a tourist in his own city, a 'Dubliner' with only
limited access to a place defined increasingly in material terms.

   In *The Commitments* Doyle represents Ireland in ways which disrupt
the established chronotope, depicting an urban rather than a rural milieu,
making that place unrecognisable in terms of established traditions, and
peopling his text with aggressive, immature young adults rather than
deliberating mature subjects. We find many of these characteristics
repeated in *Trainspotting*. The mean streets of Leith (the working-class
port in which Welsh sets his autopsy of contemporary Scottish life) are a
long way from the romantic 'Highlands and Islands' of the chronotopic
imagination.[3] But they are also some way removed from traditional urban
representations of Scotland – invariably set in Glasgow, centred around
traditional heavy industries such as shipbuilding and mining, and engaged
with received, and supposedly 'universal', discourses of gender, class and
race. What also sets Welsh apart from previous writing is that the definitional relationship is no longer the city against the country, epitomised
in the titles of novels such as *A Green Tree in Gedde* or *The Dear Green
Place*, in which an opposition between the urban present and the lost
green past construct the co-ordinates of identity (Gifford 1985). Building
on transitions offered by Alasdair Gray's *Lanark* (in which hill-walking
offers rather ambivalent pleasures to the young Duncan Thaw), Welsh
refuses to engage with such romantic narratives of escape and polarisation. As Mark Renton (the principal character and focaliser) repeatedly
points out, however, those discourses that order meaning in the 'real'
world stand for nothing when confronted with the 'reality' of heroin.
Speaking as the inheritors of a disabled cultural tradition, the implicit
question asked by Renton and his fellow smackheads – following on
from Renton's rather more explicit comment: 'Ah've never felt a fuckin'
thing aboot countries other than total disgust' (1993: 228) – is: What have
gender, class and race ever done for us? *Trainspotting*, like *The Commitments*, thus serves as an intertextual rejoinder to an entire tradition
founded on a set of disabling chronotopic representations.

This challenge extends to novelistic conventions of language, narrative and character. Both novels deviate from standard English in narrative voice and dialogue. Both dispense with what Joyce called 'perverted' commas, those scriptive markers of different voice-zones by means of which the textual world is orchestrated in line with established discourses of power. *The Commitments* has a third-person narrator, but this figure does not adopt the traditional authorial role of realist fiction, by and large avoiding any intrusion into the world of the story aimed at offering 'real' interpretations of the characters' motives, words or actions. Doyle achieves an ensemble effect by refusing much of the time to specify which individual is speaking. In a soul group, after all, the individual is less significant than the ways in which individuals combine and inter-relate. Welsh also employs this technique, although his greatest formal challenge to conventional narrative discourse is to combine limited authorial narrative with a range of focalisers so as to produce a text decentred in terms of focus and identification. As with Doyle, this narrative technique is linked to the subject matter, as the loss of narrative control highlights the loss of individual self-control brought on (in many cases, actively sought) by the characters' substance abuse.

The most obvious formal signal of their difference from standard novelistic discourse, however, is the adoption of 'regional' voices, and the related attempt to produce an immediacy of effect that would fly in the face of any 'literary' pretension. *Trainspotting* is more obviously exotic than *The Commitments* in terms of reproducing a specific class-regional dialect, but the language used in each text constitutes an attempt to accurately capture a local urban patois in terms of rhythm, accent and slang. More significant, however, is the fact that both texts aim to expose the ideological distance between 'colourful' vernacular and a controlling metalanguage, an effect going back at least to Scott and Edgeworth, and one which has played a crucial role in enabling the spatial construction of each place.[4] Welsh had immediate precedents such as James Kelman and Jeff Torrington for his formal assaults upon such a disabling tradition, although their use of the demotic was again firmly embedded within the context of a west of Scotland culture. The work of Janice Galloway and Alasdair Gray had also offered patterns for Welsh in his challenge to the conventional typographies of fiction. Doyle, however, found himself in the early 1980s working in a cultural context in which working-class Dublin speech was available only in comic and/or heavily ironic mode. Apart from Flann O'Brien, one has to go all the way back to Joyce – to *Ulysses* and more obliquely *Finnegans Wake* – to find any sustained attempt to reproduce a meaningful written rendition of the Dublin accent. Of course, *The Commitments* appears to bear out this comic/ironic inheritance; one of the common criticisms levelled against the novel is that it represents a mere updating of 'Paddy's Progress', an anthropological rendering of working-class subjects in their natural environment, with a large number of swear-words added to provide extra *frisson* for the encoded middle-class reader. There is a lack of sentimentality in *The Commitments*, however, a certain edginess of tone that was to evolve in Doyle's subsequent fiction into a desire to explore the dark corners of Barrytown, and to expose the emotional depths of a supposedly 'comic' working-class language.

Like Doyle, Welsh writes with a hyper-awareness of the ideological implications of novelistic discourse, a condition that can lead the 'regional' writer either towards the Scylla of effusive self-consciousness or the Charybdis of debilitating silence. The achievement of these novelists is their reproduction of a local voice that manages to steer clear of both dangers: neither the 'colour' of self-conscious regionalism, nor the solipsism of cultural exceptionalism. One irony in this particular context, of course, is that the Scottish novelist is in fact more difficult for the 'ordinary' (that is, English) reader to understand than his Irish counterpart. A more significant irony, perhaps, lies in the fact that although both Doyle and Welsh clearly set their artistic stalls against an established novelistic discourse possessing little scope for the expression of their own experiences, they were at the same time partaking of a well-established archipelagic tradition whereby the cultural produce of the margins is co-opted by the centre to revitalise what are seen as decadent metropolitan practices. A further irony lies in the fact that what makes both Welsh and Doyle so acceptable to other literary establishments is the ways in which the very extremity of their endeavour to place different kinds of experiences, milieus, and voices at the centre of their texts, leads to easy metropolitan acceptance of their 'marginality'. Doyle's promise was realised with the Booker Prize-winning *Paddy Clarke Ha Ha Ha* (1993), and a decade or so after the publication of *The Commitments* it seemed as if all the budding novelist needed was an Irish accent and a few hundred words to secure the interest (and more) of the big London publishing houses. The 'Irvine Welsh Effect' likewise became an established phenomenon of the late 1990s, and as supposed principal spokesperson for 'the chemical generation' his influence was pervasive. In the case of Welsh, however, explicit references to 'schemie' culture, and implicit links with post-colonial experience, signalled fairly crudely in *Marabou Stork*

Nightmares (1996), appeared to produce for readers a frame of interpretation that makes sense of, but also renders less threatening, the 'alien' cultural representations offered. There is a sense then (as Ian Bell has pointed out), that '[no] matter how strongly novelists feel their sense of dissidence from the authorized version of our culture and no matter how deeply run their local affiliations, the novel – by its very form – often implicitly reproduces the hegemonic gaze' (1995: 2).

II

It would be an even greater irony if the many significant similarities between these two writers were allowed to congeal into some species of marginal essence permanently at odds with metropolitan practices – thus consolidating the divide between centre and periphery – or to mask what are in fact a number of crucial differences between them in terms of style, subject matter and intention. One means, therefore, of reading Welsh and Doyle together, but without reinforcing their function within a centralising metropolitan culture, is to place them within the context of other contemporary writers in Scotland and Ireland. Another is to foster awareness of the differences between cultural configurations between Scottish and Irish writing.

Although they remain high-profile writers within a wider archipelagic context, Welsh and Doyle are but part of highly active and diverse scenes in their respective literary formations. To that extent, while perhaps not unrepresentative, their novels should be read in relation to works by other writers in order to understand the wider dimensions of culture across the islands. In the case of Welsh, the effect of wide acclaim has been to separate him from a number of other writers whose work has also been strikingly experimental both in terms of narrative technique and linguistic innovation. Experiments with narrative form have been characteristic of Scottish writing from the early nineteenth century onwards – with James Hogg's *Confessions of a Justified Sinner* (1824) a much-cited example – through the fiction of Muriel Spark and, more recently, Alasdair Gray. Linguistic experimentation and disruption of literary hierarchies has also been characteristic of the work of James Kelman, Jeff Torrington and Janice Galloway. To see Welsh as an iconoclast is therefore to ignore the literary context in which he has developed as a writer and also to diminish the significant work of contemporaries. Within Scottish culture the writers with whom his name is often linked – Alan Warner and Duncan McLean through personal connections, Janice Galloway and A. L. Kennedy through more formal parallels – present equally radical challenges.

Alan Warner, for example, has made a conspicuous and conscious engagement with 'youth' culture. He goes much further than Welsh in reconfiguring the polarisation of the rural and the urban, by locating his fiction in small-town 'highland' settings which nevertheless contain many aspects of urban culture, while retaining differences in community structures that signal their separateness from the major conurbations. Warner also represents what might be seen as one of the key character- istics of contemporary Scottish and Irish writing – a literature that engages with its own parameters and does not define itself through its situation in relation to a supposed English 'centre'. Epitomised in the striking image from *Morvern Callar* (1995) of Morvern burying parts of her lover's body throughout the landscape, Warner is engaged in mapping out the speci- ficities of a particular cultural location and constituency. His concern with the co-ordinates of youth identity, however, is not dependent upon boundaries between Scotland and a core elsewhere. Rather, he is pre- occupied with the codes of naming and of community relations that exist within but also across the communities he depicts – be they in Oban, Ibiza or Edinburgh. It is the supposed centre itself – London – which has at its heart an absence of memory: it is here that Morvern is confronted by a war memorial on which the names (of battles) obscure the indivi- duals: such names signify nothing except the grand narratives of history.

While a writer such as Warner represents an explicit challenge to previous chronotopic modes, other, equally distinctive manifestations of this new cultural consciousness have also emerged within the past ten years. A second characteristic of contemporary fiction is writing which operates within recognisable cultural paradigms, but feels no pressure to make issues of national identity an explicit issue. While writers such as A. L. Kennedy or John Burnside may demonstrate concerns which could be identified as 'national pre-occupations' – such as Kennedy's inheritance of Muriel Spark's trio of concerns: lies, duality and punishment – their interests need not be translated into metaphors of national identity. Conversely, it could be argued that a third body of writing has emerged which flags its own nationality, making clear its location within a geographically specific and 'national' space, but which operates through forms of genre fiction in which the narrative conventions offer an equally significant, and for the reader perhaps more powerful, spatial demarcation. Thus Iain Banks has developed within the genre of fantasy fiction novels which are clearly set within Scotland, clearly 'Scottish' in many of their concerns but also preoccupied with other aspects of identity formation – such as gender, desire, violence (Schoene 1999). Andrew Greig has produced a number of novels which might be marketed as 'romance' but which again are identifiably Scottish in location. In *When They Lay Bare* (1999), for example, with its potent evocation of Border Ballads and feuding Border history as context for its exploration of desire and identity, Greig works within a frame of specifically Scottish (in both historical and geographic terms) spaces but issues of 'national identity' are not central as 'thematic' material. Ian Rankin, in his highly successful 'Inspector Rebus' detective stories, has carved out a landscape of crime particular to Edinburgh, and given rise to the development of a whole sub-genre of Edinburgh hard-boiled detectives. While asserting the particular inheritance and terrain of his chosen location, Rankin has shown an increasing engagement with that city as representative ground for the games of nationalist politics; if the novels contain hidden polemic, however, that lies as much in testing of genre boundaries as in the reconfiguring of city space.

In the Irish context, the great Joycean project to forge the uncreated conscience of the race is pursued in less lofty though no less compelling ways in the work of writers such as Anne Enright, Joseph O'Connor and Colm Tóibín. The novel would still appear to be one of the principal forms through which a particular (that is, national) reality may be observed and deconstructed. There is still, as the critic Timothy Brennan observed, a 'national longing for form' (1990), and the novel is still one of the most popular and malleable media for that longing to be realised. One marked difference, however, is the fact that the Irish reality addressed by the typical novel of the 1990s was not that of a 'paralysed' provincial culture, but a complex social milieu animated by an aggressive economy and the awareness of a greater Ireland beyond the geographical confines of the island. If, as Fintan O'Toole suggests, 'Ireland is something that often happens elsewhere' (1994: 27), then the Ireland that happens 'here', so to speak, is unrecognisable as the country that existed one hundred, forty, even ten years ago. The novels of Tina Reilly and Neville Thompson, as well of those of genre writers such as Marian Keyes and Colin Bateman, depict an Ireland – north and south – in which film and fashion, drugs and data, take their place alongside politics as the touchstone of contemporary Irish identity. We still await, however, the great modern satirist capable of doing justice to the seemingly endless tribunals that, throughout the latter half of the 1990s, revealed the corruption at the heart of public life in the Republic. Perhaps twenty-first-century Ireland is not so far removed from 'Ivy Day at the Committee Room' as many would like to believe.

At the same time, many writers attempt to mitigate the anxiety of Joyce's influence by locating the action of their 'Irish' stories offshore – in Africa (as in Ronan Bennett's *The Catastrophist*, 1997), in Central America (as in Joseph O'Connor's *Desperadoes*, 1994), or in New York (as in Colum McCann's *This Side of Brightness*, 1998). Others still trace a movement *between* Ireland and other places – places such as Spain (as in Tóibín's *The South*, 1990), London (as in Robert Cremins' *A Sort of Homecoming*, 2000), or continental Europe (as in Desmond Hogan's *A Farewell to Prague*, 1995) – as if to show the ways in which Irish identity is becoming necessarily nomad and dispersed rather than rooted and stable. As in certain Scottish contexts, the intention would appear to be to represent nationality as an incidental rather than a defining factor. And as in Scotland, this may have something to do with increased cultural confidence in the wake of greater political and economic success. In any event, whether within or outwith the geographically defined national territory, novelists seem more willing and more able to transcend the imaginative boundaries of the nation than ever before, even as the nation remains a factor at both the thematic and formal levels.

Another similarity between Irish and Scottish fiction lies in the fact that a desire to play with established parameters of novelistic discourse did not emerge from a literary–historical vacuum. There is in fact a long experimental tradition in Irish literature that continues to impact upon contemporary novelistic discourse. During the nineteenth century, the novel's troubled status was primarily to do with the anomalousness of the colonial society which Irish writers were attempting to represent. Long before international modernism rendered self-conscious the relationship between form (representation) and content (reality), the complex resonances accruing from that relationship were laid bare (often unconsciously or unwittingly) by novelists such as Maria Edgeworth, Sydney Owenson (Lady Morgan) and William Carleton. As Luke Gibbons has written with reference to such shattering developments as the loss of a national language and the Great Famine: 'In a country traumatized by a profound sense of catastrophe, is there really any need to await the importation of modernism to blast open the continuum of history?' (1991: 3). In such a context, simply putting pen to paper was an act fraught with all manner of potential affiliations and betrayals. In this respect, James Joyce (invariably invoked alongside Marcel Proust as the key modernist exponent of the novel) emerges as a much more complex figure when placed within the context of Irish colonial history. In this respect also, and *pace* Doyle's populist realism, the post-Joycean Irish novelist is heir to a tradition in which the very form with which she/he is working is itself suspect, and in which the *act* of representation – with all its connotations of power and identity – frequently becomes the *subject* of representation.

John Banville is perhaps the major contemporary heir to this Irish 'anti-tradition'. All his fiction contains a level of discourse – wielded with greater or lesser self-consciousness – in which art itself operates as a key metaphor for the 'real' world represented in the narrative. Like many of the novelists mentioned in the preceding paragraphs, Banville's nationality is incidental rather than central. To use familiar terms in a perhaps unfamiliar context, nationality is 'peripheral' rather than 'core' in his writing, the means to an artistic end (concerned with larger 'human' issues) rather than the end itself. In *Athena* (the final part of his loose 'art' trilogy), for example, the Dublin underworld (if it is such) functions only as background for Morrow's musings on the nature of the relationship between reality and representation. Paradoxically, the peripheralisation of nationality as a determining factor in Banville's work has the effect of revealing the manner in which supposedly universal 'human' issues are always anticipated at a less general or, to be frank, national level. Again, in an early text such as *Birchwood* (1973), the local context (nineteenth-century rural Ireland) functions as an under-developed backdrop for a Wittgensteinian reflection upon the relationship between consciousness and narrative. But the slightest engagement with that context reveals that such a theme goes to the heart of national experience during the nineteenth century – a time when cultural narratives (histories, novels, poetry, and so on) were systematically deployed in the development of a national consciousness.

In less intellectualist though no less interesting ways, other contemporary novelists have engaged with the Irish anti-tradition, whether filtered through the discourse of fantasy (as in Anne Enright's *The Wig My Father Wore*, 1995), popular culture (as in Patrick McCabe's *Breakfast on Pluto*, 1998) or myth (as in Dermot Healy's *A Goat's Song*, 1995). Despite new times, (Irish) novel and (Irish) nation still appear to be caught in a bind of mutual fascination. For all these writers, even when the action is set elsewhere, or when the subject matter appears overtly non-national, the national narrative is still there, hovering in the background, still exercising influence at a deep structural and/or conceptual level. With Joyce as interlocutor, the modern Irish novelists might be imagined as saying: It's Ireland, Jim, but not as you knew it!

III

Reading Doyle and Welsh in relation to other writers, a more complex
process of spatial reconfiguration and cultural representation emerges.
Within this different context, their work appears less directed as a
challenge towards a metropolitan centre and less amenable to representation as the embodiment of an 'other' culture. The complexity of the
picture outlined also suggests that while there are similarities in the ways
in which the novelists mentioned here might be located within, and be
seen as responding to, new archipelagic cultural formations, it would be
too easy to homogenise and elide all differences.

Perhaps the most striking difference between fictions produced in
Ireland and Scotland has continued to be in their confrontations with
history. This is not to suggest that such writing can only be understood
in historicist terms, but rather that the dynamic with history itself
produces rather different spatial configurations. While the novel in
Ireland has been described in terms of a 'fixation on the ways in which
the past persists into the present' (Smyth 1997: 53) – manifested for
example in the Gothic form – the Scottish novel has been seen as
engaged in 'a confrontation with the limits of the historical as a mode of
understanding human experience' (Craig 1996b: 81). The ways in which
a small selection of recent Scottish and Irish novels from the 1990s
attempt to construct and imagine collective and personal 'pasts' offers
then some sense of how these different versions of history interact. Irish
writing engages with the past as lived in the present, not only in the
form of memories of events from Ireland's turbulent political history but
also through stories of ghosts and the supernatural (Deane 1996; Enright
1995; Healy 1995; McCabe 1995). Such novels offer very different manifestations of the ways in which houses, streets, subjects are mapped out
through narratives of the past which shape boundaries and meaning.
The modern Scottish novel, by contrast, has been described as resting on
a paradox: 'the forms of history that it charts in its narratives are what it
seeks to negate through its creation of narrative forms which will defy
and deny the primacy of the historical as the mode in which we should
comprehend the nature of human experience' (Craig 1999: 166).

Benedict Anderson's assertion that personal and national histories
are constructed through different narrative teleologies offers a point of
entry into an assessment of the implications for an understanding of
social and psychic 'national' identities. In the secular story of the
'person', he notes, 'there is a beginning and an end ... Nations, however,

have no clearly identifiable births, and their deaths, if they happen, are never natural … the nation's biography is marked by deaths, which, in a curious inversion of conventional genealogy, starts from an originary present' (1991: 205). Such a distinction would seem to function well as an image of the dynamic within both Irish writing and Irish politics. But as Murray Pittock suggests, the idea of 'imagined communities' has in a sense more application in an Irish context where

> the sound of ancestral voices has been forcibly and continuously projected through imaginative writing, literature and culture representations that lie at the heart of its generative power, whether for good or ill. In Northern Ireland uniquely in the British Isles, this imaginative dynamo is not simply the property of protest against a central state: it is divided against itself, with mutual incomprehension between the communities, not only because they have different myths but because they squabble over the same ones. (1999: 130)

Contemporary Scottish fiction may have moved away from a concern with Scottish history as a vacuum (as identified by Cairns Craig in his essay 'The body in the kit-bag': 1996c), the configuration of pasts and presents they offer (and the emphasis placed on such issues) does still, however, differ strikingly from the Irish novels described (Craig 1996b). In Alan Warner's *Morvern Callar* (1995), Andrew Greig's *Electric Brae: A Modern Romance* (1992), and Janice Galloway's *Foreign Parts* (1994), writers can be seen as adopting experimental narrative structures which juxtapose different versions of the past, but also addressing with a growing confidence the significance of community, familial, and personal (rather than national pasts) in relation to the present. If we contrast the image of Morvern boldly carrying her own past (her lover's head banging around in her knapsack, or striding out to the island with a child in her belly) through the Scottish landscape with her bafflement at the London war memorial, or Cassie's incomprehension of history in the French war cemetery – 'It was dubious territory indeed, the fantasy you could understand a bloody thing by looking at the likes of this. Rows of dead people. Dead men. Dead boys' (1995: 50) – her embrace of laughter, the sea and a lack of direction at the close of *Foreign Parts*, challenges to the grand narratives of history might be detected (Norquay 2000). In that sense, whereas in Irish fiction the past functions as a metaphor for the difficulty of coming to terms with conflicting national narratives, contemporary Scottish fiction appears to be developing a concern with 'personal' histories, moving from the past towards birth or rebirth.

Yet within both Irish and Scottish fiction a central similarity remains in the explicit concern with delineating the narratives of culture, the parameters of space which shape us. Which brings us back to the notion of unapproved roads. In *Foreign Parts* Galloway's characters make a crucial mistake when trying to find their way through France: thinking it more pleasant to take backroads, they become completely lost in a sterile and confusing landscape. 'We thought backroads would be prettier. But coming from a wee country, we forgot' (1995: 64). In *Reading in the Dark* the moral of McIlhenney's story about the man on the bus is: 'people in small places make big mistakes. Not bigger than the mistakes of other people. But there is less room for big mistakes in small places' (Deane 1997: 211). In each instance the reader is reminded that small countries make different navigational demands but also have something different to offer: space appears both more tightly structured yet also more multiple in its signification. Having recognised this difference, writers may then produce works which depart from a disempowering dynamic with supposedly core cultures and enjoy the potential fluidity, that rapidity of change recognised by Doyle. As critics, we also need to produce more complicated and complicating navigational aids if we are to do justice to the reality of 'waking up in a different place'.

Notes

1 On Scotland's post-devolution take-off see *The Scotsman* 17 January 2000.
2 For Scott's citations from 1810, 1816, 1823 and 1827, see Williams 1968: 174, 190, 206, 231 and 428.
3 With regard to the Celtic chronotope, Joep Leerssen writes: 'Once identified, the chronotope appears to be operative in almost all descriptions of outlying Celtic-language districts during the nineteenth and twentieth centuries, even in twentieth-century cinema – witness the prototypical Brigadoon (about a Scottish valley, Shangri-La-style, where time has literally stood still), or Powell and Pressburger's *I know where I'm going* (set in the extratemporal dreamscape of a Hebridean island) or the more recent *Local hero*. As regards Ireland, the treatment such as we have encountered it … is practically standard over the last two centuries, from the novels of Lady Morgan until films like *Un taxi mauve*' (1996b: 190).
4 On the ideological underpinnings of cultural regionalism, Raymond Williams writes: 'And then what is striking, in matters of cultural description, is the steady discrimination of certain regions as in this limited sense "regional", which can only hold if certain other regions are not seen in this way … Yet this is no longer a distinction of areas and kinds of life; it is what is politely called a value-judgement but more accurately an expression of centralized cultural dominance … The life and people of certain favoured regions are seen as essentially general, even perhaps normal, while the life and people of certain other regions, however interestingly and affectionately presented, are, well, regional' (1991: 230).

10

Finding Scottish art

MURDO MACDONALD

Nationality and art

The relationship between nationality and art, or something like it, has
been central to the history of art – scholarly or popular – whether in the
minimal form of this national school or that national school, or in a more
focused way as in 'the Italian Renaissance' or 'French Impressionism'.
The art in question is seen as directly related to a national or quasi-
national set of circumstances, and indeed the art is seen as having some
significant link to the nationality of those who carried it out.

A question that tends to be begged in such approaches is: what is
nationality? It seems to be assumed that words like Scottish, French,
English, and so on, do not require any particular analysis before one
tacks them on to some body of work. This approach to nationality is
often convenient but a little more must be said about the idea of a nation,
for it is an easily misunderstood thing. The most common misunder-
standing is that a nation is simply a culturally homogeneous group of
people who share certain attitudes, traditions and habits due to long
historical association within a geographical area. This idea of the nation
as depending on some sort of cultural homogeneity is a strongly propagated one, not least by governments in time of war. Yet in fact, nations
are intrinsically heterogeneous, and such diversity, far from being a
threat to a national identity is a necessary characteristic of it. Cultural
diversity is one of the things that defines a nation. Nations are identifiable as meaningful cultural units as a result of their internal cultural
diversity, not as a result of an internal homogeneity. Perhaps my view
here is coloured by my own experience as a Scot, for in Scotland it is very
obviously impossible to make any meaningful claim of cultural homogeneity. For example, for many hundreds of years there have been three

languages spoken and two of these – what is now called Scots and what is now called Gaelic – have been spoken in some form in Scotland for at least a millennium, while the third – what is now called English – has been in wide use since the seventeenth century.

Thus, even when considered without reference to twentieth-century immigration from Europe and the British Empire, Scotland has historically and presently an overtly diverse cultural identity. Regardless of what language or languages are spoken at present, most Scots are aware of the linguistic diversity of their own backgrounds. A working-class woman from a post-industrial Ayrshire steel town whose first language is Scots may share with a middle-class man born in Edinburgh whose first language is English the fact that each has a great-grand-parent who was a native Gaelic speaker. This shows the degree of threat to that particular language, but it also shows how small the historical distance to Gaelic culture is among many people who might be thought to have no link to it whatever. This is the context for the present wide-spread support for Gaelic studies across Scotland, and the related interest in the products of that culture which range from the *Book of Kells* (c. 800) to the art of Will Maclean (b. 1941). This support is thus engaged rather than nostalgic.

An interesting example of the cultural diversity that characterises Scotland is the 'division' between Highland Gaelic culture and Lowland Scots culture. This is very often seen as a site of conflict rather than unity in Scotland, and certainly on occasion it has been. Yet it can be recalled that it was the unity of Highland and Lowland that assured a Bruce victory at Bannockburn in the fourteenth century and thus asserted Scottish independence after three hundred years of varied incursions from south of the Border. The point is that Bannockburn, far from asserting the nation as culturally homogeneous, asserted national independence as dependent on cultural diversity. Similarly, and moving on over four hundred years, although the Battle of Culloden is normally stereotyped as a Highland versus Lowland clash in fact – as Murray Pittock (1995) has pointed out – Jacobites were drawn from both Highlands and Lowlands in substantial numbers, as were Hanoverian supporters. Again, what characterised both sides in this struggle was diversity not homogeneity. Although very obvious, these points have to be made because the stereotype of nations as homogeneous unities is so prevalent and yet so wrong, and one cannot start any useful study of how a nation relates to art, literature or whatever, without understanding that it is an intrinsically diverse thing.

But surely a nation has some cultural uniqueness? If so, what can this be if a nation lacks what would at first sight seem to be the key, namely homogeneity? The answer to this is quite simple. A nation's uniqueness, its national quality if you like, derives from the fact that the combination of cultural aspects which make it up is indeed unique (if not in principle, at least in practice). One can note that these cultural aspects themselves might be unique but are much more likely to be shared with other nations. For example, Scotland shares many cultural aspects with Ireland, many others with England, others still with Norway, France and the Netherlands. But the way these aspects combine in Scotland is unique to Scotland, and is mediated and transformed by further aspects such as geography. A nation is thus somewhat like a person. Each person shares a great deal with others, but in practice personalities – like nations – are unique. But this uniqueness claim is an assertion of a unique diversity, not an insistence on a unique homogeneity.

Stereotypes and Scottish art

By applying this idea of diversity to a particular area of activity such as art, one can see that it is only by appreciating an interplay of different currents that one can appreciate the Scottishness of Scottish art. While one can give some of these traditions names like classicism and Celticism, the first thing to note about such an approach is that the Scottishness of Scottish art is a consequence of the combinations involved, not merely a matter of content. This is an obvious point but it illuminates the inadequacy of the view that a painting can be thought of as Scottish only if it has an overtly Scottish content, or that architecture can be thought of as distinctively Scottish only if it makes some kind of Scots-Baronial reference. Such impoverished ideas of 'national art' as by definition stereotyped and inward-looking are odd to say the least. They have, however, bedevilled the perception of Scottish art. Such stereotyping is a method of concealing cultural realities, but at the same time creating a powerful imagery that seems to reflect that culture. What is wrong with stereotypes is not that they exist (indeed they normally correspond to some aspect of reality), but that they are selective and inflexible, that is to say they fail to reflect the plural nature of any culture. A particularly interesting example of stereotyping with respect to Scottish art is the over-use of the painting by Sir Henry Raeburn of *Colonel Alastair Macdonell of Glengarry*. This is one of the images that has stood in for the wider body of Scottish art for many years. It is an interesting picture in its own right, but one rarely has the opportunity to consider it as such. Usually it is simply used as a stereotypical shorthand for the idea of Scottish art, for example as a cover illustration. It was used in this way for Sir James Caw's guide to the National Gallery of Scotland published in 1927. Again one finds it used for the cover of the book published by the National Galleries of Scotland in 1990 to accompany the *Scotland's Pictures* exhibition. Well-written and well-illustrated, this latter book contained over a hundred full-colour illustrations. Perhaps three or four of these showed a person dressed in tartan. And yet the work taken to be representative of Scottish painting for the cover was one of those tartan images. I have nothing against tartan, but such a choice of cover image opens the way for a stereotype to dominate a tradition of art. Journalists talk about 'putting a kilt on an issue' when giving it a Scottish perspective. Here we see this literally in the case of Scottish art. The cover invites us to find Scottish art, if we can, within the stereotype, when we should really be doing the reverse, exploring stereotypical imagery within the broader context of Scottish art.

That relationship between cover and book is a metaphor for the relationship between stereotype and reality in Scottish culture. *Scotland's Paintings* reflected with considerable insight the real history of Scottish painting, but the cover subsumed that reality within a stereotype. As one might expect such stereotyping is just as evident in guidebooks. A particularly good example is the Jarrold Regional Guide to *Art in Scotland* published in 1980. Despite being a seriously written guide, its front cover illustration is *The Monarch of the Glen* by Landseer. Here that other stereotype of Scotland, the red deer in a deserted landscape, is employed. The fact that the landscape may be deserted because it has been cleared of people in favour of sporting interests, is not part of the painting's message. Because Landseer is an English artist the use of *The Monarch of the Glen* might seem to give the additional message that Scottish art is so unthinkable as to be not even worth reproducing on the cover. But the key issue is stereotyping, not the nationality of the artist. A Scottish work by the German artist Joseph Beuys or by the English artist John Latham would have challenged the stereotype nicely, but despite the fact that one could argue that Joseph Beuys has just as much relevance to Scotland as does Edwin Landseer, such approaches are notable by their absence in literature relating to Scottish art. One suspects that work by the English painter J. M. W. Turner of Scottish subjects is largely neglected because it does not conform to the antlers and tartan stereotype.[1] To consider Turner's work as appropriate to the representation of

Scotland would be to threaten the stereotype. Displacing *The Monarch of the Glen* in favour of such thoughtful explorations of topography and culture would risk forcing consideration of images of Scotland into the range of the modern and the thinkable.

Scottish art and the English model

It is equally interesting to consider how a Scottish artist or architect is considered when no stereotypical interpretation can be put on his work. For example, Nicolaus Pevsner in his book *The Englishness of English Art* (1956) seems determined to appropriate them to 'Englishness'. He considered it necessary for his argument that Robert Adam be assimilated into his idea of Englishness. But he knew that Adam was a Scot, so he suggested that for the purposes of his book, in the case of Adam, 'no distinction can be made between Scottish and English qualities' (125). This is convenient but not entirely convincing. Perhaps the real point that underlies Pevsner's argument is not so much that there is no distinction between Adam's Scottish and English qualities (whatever they may be) but that in much of his work he is developing a classical tradition shared throughout Europe. So Pevsner's underlying argument seems to be that because of Adam's Europeanness one can ignore his Scottishness and appropriate him as part of the Englishness of English art. But, of course, if one looks more closely at what was interesting to Scots at the time of Adam – both within Scotland and abroad – it was indeed the classical tradition not just in architecture but in all fields, not least mathematics and philosophy. The fact that most of the philosophers who could be called British at that time were Scottish (or, in the case of Berkeley, Irish) simply underlines this fact. One could argue just as Pevsner does for Adam's architecture that 'no distinction can be made between Scottish and English qualities' in Hume's philosophy. But – even if one held that position – it would be prudent to take note of the fact that during the period of the Scottish Enlightenment there was a great deal of philosophy of consequence written in Scotland and at the same time a distinct lull in the contribution to philosophy from England. The point here is that both Adam and Hume were part of this Scottish intellectual culture. It is no coincidence that the pioneer of European neo-classical painting in the time of Adam was another Scot, Gavin Hamilton.

Must this mean that Adam, by virtue of being an part of a Scottish intelligentsia (which Pevsner does not so much deny as side-step), cannot be part of the English tradition? Well, no it does not mean that, but the point is that Adam is part of the English tradition in the same way as Hume is part of it, or Berkeley is part of it, or indeed Nikolaus Pevsner himself or, for that matter, Wittgenstein is part of it. He is not part of the English tradition in the same way as, for example, Wren or Hawksmoor or Locke or Newton are. Adam may be an influential part of that tradition, but he does not himself find his origins within it, and that is the distinction which must be made if one is to understand the manner in which the Scottish and English traditions co-exist. At least, in the case of Adam, Pevsner acknowledges his Scottishness, even if he claims that it does not matter for his argument. By comparison one finds Pevsner absorbing Colen Campbell fully into the English tradition without further comment, although the comment that is made makes clear that he pioneered Palladianism in England in the early eighteenth century (1956: 113). He is thus presented, by default, as an architect entirely in the English tradition, which conflicts with the fact that (in a British context) he helped to pioneer Palladianism not in England but in Scotland along with William Bruce and James Smith. He did, of course, then work in England and there is no doubt that he considered himself part of the English tradition, but the fact that he was a Scottish architect does at least seem worth acknowledging.[2]

To do that, however, would be to threaten Pevsner's intriguing justification of 'English' Palladianism. He begins by noting that a 'connexion between the middle class as a carrier of rationalism and the Palladian style in England seems less convincing at first' (113). He then goes on, however, to imply that rationalism and reasonableness are the same thing and that the English have always been characterised by reasonableness so therefore the rationalism of the Palladian approach makes sense with respect to the Englishness of English art. Any Scot, or indeed any Italian or Frenchman, could have told Pevsner (as he could, no doubt, on reflection have told himself) that the rationalism of Palladianism is concerned with returning to first principles of proportion, which is to say, it is a radical architectural doctrine which if one were to transpose it to society would be more likely to herald revolution than the middle-class reasonableness with which Pevsner attempts to associate it. The Scottish artist Ian Hamilton Finlay puts it this way: 'In the foreground of every revolution, invisible, it seems, to the academics, stands a perfect classical column' (quoted in Abrioux 1992: 224). One might argue against this that the return to first principles could as easily take one to a consideration of balance within society rather than revolution. Again, however, this cannot be associated with the reasonableness Pevsner invokes for this is clearly concerned with pragmatic compromise rather than a rational scheme of social organisation. One can note that this reflects the difference in principle between English and Scots law, the former based on custom and convention, the latter closer in its origins to the legal rationalisations of ancient Rome.

If one makes such acknowledgement what begins to emerge is that Scottish architects (and James Gibbs is yet another example) were disproportionately influential on the English tradition during the eighteenth century, just as were Scottish philosophers. From a Scottish or genuinely British perspective this is interesting, but such a perspective is at variance with Pevsner's absorption into the English tradition of these pioneers who came from a different cultural and intellectual background. With respect to art and architecture, Pevsner's view seems to parallel that held by T. S. Eliot with respect to literature. In Cairns Craig's words, Eliot identifies the fact that 'the real function of Scottish, Irish and Welsh writers is to contribute, not to their own culture, which will not have "a direct impact on the world", but towards the tradition of English literature' (1996b: 16). Craig has described this phenomenon as a state of being 'out of history'. Arguments against Scottish independence are often couched in similar language. If Scotland were separated from England, Scotland would no longer be able to have a direct impact on the world, due to the loss of the association with the greater power of the sister nation. Militarily this is no doubt true, but few Scots would mourn Trident. Culturally, the fact that the British literary establishment never thought of Sorley MacLean as a writer who merited backing for the Nobel prize for literature puts a different complexion on such arguments.

The Englishness of British art

The problem of mislaying cultural identity when Scottish material is diffused into an English model has been illustrated. The problem is no less when ostensibly 'British' models are used.

In 1996 the British Broadcasting Corporation showed a series of programmes entitled *A History of British Art*. This series (British both in terms of its title and its commissioning body) provides an interesting example of the problematic use of the word 'British' with respect to Scottish culture. Consider the following: in the introduction to the book which accompanied the series (reprinted in 1999 as a handsome large-format paperback), the author, Andrew Graham-Dixon, writes of his disappointment with the negative attitudes expressed in an earlier book called *Art in England*, published in 1938, and goes on to say that this approach 'seemed to sum up the spirit in which the British have historically treated British art' (1999: 9). Already, only a few paragraphs into the book, Britain and England risk being conflated. In the introduction he mentions three books – two in his view bad, one good. Along with the one already noted these books are *The Englishness of English Art*, and *England's Iconoclasts*. Thus, the key examples for defining attitudes to British art, positive or negative, are primarily concerned with English art. Linked to this he notes that the negative views expressed about English art in the works he refers to are mirrored elsewhere in Britain.

Writing, as I am, from a Scottish perspective, this is confusing. For example, in 1938 – the same year that the first book on English art referred to was published – John Tonge's book on Scottish art was published to accompany a major exhibition at the Royal Academy in London. That book can hardly be considered a negative view of Scottish art. Furthermore, three other histories of Scottish art (Cursiter 1949: Finlay 1947, 1948) were written between that date and 1956, when the other book on English art which is criticised, ironically enough in the light of my argument above, Pevsner's *The Englishness of English Art*, was published. Reading this introduction it is as though such publications about Scottish art had never happened, let alone the publication of full-length histories of Scottish painting in 1889, 1906 and 1908, not to mention the numerous works published since 1956.³ These works are all devoted to giving Scottish art its due, and – while each author has different enthusiasms and opinions – can hardly be thought of as reflecting 'an air of abjectness and a consciousness of failure' to quote again from Andrew Graham-Dixon. Indeed as early as 1889 Robert Brydall was referring to Scottish art's 'pre-eminence'.⁴ In the light of the international recognition of the Glasgow School of painters in the 1880s one can see what he meant; however, the point here is not to defend Brydall's statement but simply to note that it seems to belong to a different discourse from that of *A History of British Art*.⁵ That may be summed up by noting that out of well over 200 works discussed in these programmes, less than three percent were by Scottish artists. Yet despite this emphasis in his programmes Graham-Dixon in his introduction explicitly extends the notion of 'abjectness and consciousness of failure' to 'Britain as a whole' (1999: 9). Although he has a clear interest in work from outside England, it is clear very early on that the paradigm of Britishness that he adopts is Englishness.

Note that these criticisms of *A History of British Art* stem from one word in the title. The programmes were interesting in their own right, they just were not about British art, unless one is prepared to accept that 'British' means 'English with a few references to other countries within, or once within, the UK'. Why was the series not called *A History of English Art*? This is a puzzle. Such a title certainly would not have prevented reference to influences on, or illumination of, English art from elsewhere in Britain and the rest of Europe.

But at least Scottish artists were mentioned in this series. Common also is the practice of not mentioning Scottish art at all in 'British' accounts. The Tate Gallery in London, for example, in the late 1990s had a room full of interesting early twentieth-century works by Epstein, Bomberg and painters associated with the Bloomsbury group. It was entitled something like 'Early British Modernism'. Again, as with *A History of British Art*, it was not uninteresting, it was merely misnamed. It is something of an irony that both Charles Rennie Mackintosh and J. D. Fergusson were both working within walking distance of the Tate Gallery during the period to which this display referred. The point is not to insist on quotas, but to suggest that understanding what words mean is appropriate in this sort of context. Every misuse of the word 'British' strengthens a redefinition of the word that excludes Scotland, and as a consequence Scottish art and Scottish culture in general may find the need to find themselves elsewhere.

Approaching the unthinkable

In 1906 one explanation of the problem of finding Scottish art within British accounts was suggested by W. D. McKay in *The Scottish School of Painting*. McKay states the obvious but essential when he notes the following: 'when, as in this case, one population far outnumbers the other, the less numerous is apt to be forgotten, or regarded as merely a sub-division of the larger' (1906: 1) A gloss on this was made by Hugh MacDiarmid half a century later in his 1950 essay *Aesthetics in Scotland*. There he wrote of the exhibition already noted, *The Arts of Scotland*, held in London just before the Second World War: 'It will be remembered that Sir William Llewellyn, the then President of the Royal Academy, confessed that he had had no idea before he saw that exhibition that Scotland had such a rich and distinctive tradition of its own in the art of painting' (1984 [1950]: 21). As recently as 1990, surprised comment could be heard in reaction to the publication of Duncan Macmillan's landmark book *Scottish Art: 1460–1990*. Such surprise is an index of cultural misrepresentation. It is related to a wider ignorance of Scottish history both within Scotland and further afield. The growth in research and teaching of Scottish history, including that of the history of Scottish art, as a tradition in its own right rather than as a sub-discipline of British history has begun to alter this situation.

There is thus at present a conscious redefining and refining of the relationship between Scottishness and Britishness. In 1969 the philosopher George Davie noted that when a writer 'proclaimed that modern Scotland was unthinkable apart from the union, he betrayed a point of view that takes for granted that modern Scotland does not bear thinking of at all.' (1990b: 38)[6] This comment can illuminate the present position. The idea that Scotland has been through a period in which a significant number of opinion formers did not consider it worth thinking about, apart from the Union, is an interesting one. In such a view Britain as an entity in its own right can be thought about, but Scotland as an entity in its own right can not. What Davie suggests is that this makes the reality of modern Scotland in any sense 'unthinkable' to such a commentator. Such 'unthinkability' is an example of what in a psychoanalyst would call 'denial', that is to say the insistence on the untruth of a particular truth: protesting too much at an unconscious or almost unconscious level, so to speak. To claim that Scotland is unthinkable apart from the Union is to protest too much. One might presume that with the devolution of power to a Scottish parliament and the clear possibility of independence, such attitudes no longer exist. But attitudes can lag behind political reality and from an attitudinal point of view the unthinkability of Scottish culture within a British context is alive and well. One question that must be considered is, how does one think about the unthinkable? Out of this paradox are born the stereotypes already referred to.

The model of 'Scotland as unthinkable' is easy to find even in writing relating to contemporary art. An illuminating example from the late 1980s is the keynote essay in a book entitled *The New British Painting* (Lucie-Smith, 1988) published by a major British art publisher to accompany a major exhibition of contemporary British painting shown in America. Scottish artists were well represented in both the exhibition and the book illustrations. It is therefore all the more ironic that in the essay in question, entitled 'The Story of British Modernism' the history of Scottish art is completely ignored. The essay is written as though the historical background to contemporary British painting were that of English painting. Scottish artists are mentioned, but only as part of the present. On reading this essay one would assume that there was no Scottish art prior to the decade in which the essay was written. William

Blake is the first English artist to be mentioned, the first Scottish artist to be mentioned, unless one counts the London-Scot Duncan Grant, is Steven Campbell, born two centuries later. Such writing is a further example of how the history of Scottish art becomes mislaid within 'British' accounts. It is an irony that the essay both asserts the value of contemporary Scottish art, and at the same time writes Scottish art out of history. This has the effect of making the production of Scottish artists seem to be either a sub-category of English activity or the miraculous production of savage purity, untarnished by the confusion of a recorded past, tutored only by the ghost of the monarch of the glen.

Semantic slippage

Such routine abuse of the word 'British' leads to it having no consistency of use except in so far as any use of the word tends to strongly imply 'English'. This duality in which it shares a kind of penumbra of loss of meaning with a fundamental Englishness is fascinating. We have in this use of the word 'British' a core of reference (the English) surrounded by a mantle of unthinkability (everybody else). In the political sphere this semantic slippage was neatly illustrated by John Major in February 1997 when, in an address to the Welsh Conservative Party, he spoke of proposals for Scottish devolution being a threat to 'one thousand years of British history'. Obviously enough, devolution could not be a threat to a thousand years of British history, for the British history to which the then Prime Minister referred has been in existence for either about three hundred years or about four hundred years, depending on whether you date it from the union of crowns or the union of parliaments. For Major the truth about Scotland was clearly unthinkable. Perhaps he had been reading another interesting example of such a 'British' view, journalist Polly Toynbee's leader for 'British Theme' week in the *Radio Times* from July 1996. The words 'Britain' or 'British' occur frequently, as one would expect. The words 'us' and 'we' also occur frequently. And the 'we' being referred to is apparently 'the British'. So far so good. The words England and English also occur frequently. And why not? But only one literary figure – William Shakespeare – is invoked. One sporting event is referred to, the 1966 World Cup, won by England. Two victories are mentioned, Agincourt and the Armada. These latter references are particularly telling for they refer to events well prior to even the union of the crowns. Indeed the only link to a British country other than to England is the film *Braveheart* but it is intriguing to note that this is only mentioned in the context of American (not even Scottish) anti-Englishness. Thus, Britishness is defined by English literature, English sport, English military achievements, and American anti-Englishness. A typical aspect of this exercise in 'Britishness' is that its writer seems oblivious to her own bias.

Again, the senior management of the British Broadcasting Corporation demonstrated such an attitude in an exemplary fashion in April 1995 by scheduling a *Panorama* interview with John Major three days before the local elections in Scotland and in direct contravention of their own guidelines. The Scottish law courts forced a rethink and very few people took seriously the subsequent claim by those responsible that they would have done the same three days before the elections in England and Wales. It was generally understood that at the root of the affair was ignorance. It is important to understand that this was not just ignorance in the sense of not knowing something, but more an attitude of ignorance, a culture in which certain kinds of ignorance are promoted. *Panorama* has built up expertise in this area. In a programme which purported to be about the negative attitude of the British man or woman on the street to the introduction of the Euro, broadcast in February 1999, it did not seem to cross the programme-maker's mind to reflect that the one part of Europe that has long-term experience of currency union, is in fact the UK. This was because the programme was not about Britain any more than Tony Blair's assertion that the British were attached to the image of the Queen's head on bank notes was about Britain: the point being, of course, that the Queen's head does not appear on Scottish banknotes.

Taken separately these examples are trivial to the point of tedium; taken together they reflect an ignorance so pervasive that you need a theory to account for it. Michel Foucault has helped greatly in this with his concept of 'silences', which captures the notion of actively ignoring something. It is appropriate to recall that the original panoramas were supposedly comprehensive – but in fact highly selective – views painted on the inside of windowless wooden huts. *Panorama* can thus be thought of as living up to an aspect of its own history. This kind of windowless-hut perception can be taken as characterising the information considered significant by London governmental and media bodies with respect to Scottish culture. Certainly the decision of the BBC not to have a separate Scottish six o'clock news in the wake of devolution betrays an assumption that a major rebalancing of the political constitution of Britain did not require a cognate media response.

Eternally recurrent renaissance

This attitude is not to be seen in terms of antipathy, but in terms of a kind of actively maintained ignorance. It can be manifested in periods of neglect followed by periods of overenthusiasm, a pattern that I have called elsewhere 'eternally recurrent renaissance' (1990a: 86). Since the London media is highly influential in Scotland this misperception from south of the Border puts Scots in the curious position of encountering their own culture both through local knowledge and through London interpretation. Thus a James Kelman novel may leave Glasgow as part of a developed literary tradition but it returns from London redefined as the spontaneous product of a Glasgow hard-man. As Kelman himself has noted, the St Andrews philosopher James Frederick Ferrier coined the word 'epistemology' for the theory of knowledge (in Davie 1990a: v). But Ferrier coined another word, which has not gained the same currency – 'agnoiology' does not even appear in most dictionaries. This refers to the theory of ignorance, which Ferrier saw as being the necessary complement of a theory of knowledge. One might object that a theory of knowledge must take ignorance into account and that therefore a separate theory of ignorance is not needed. This has been a popular view. But theories, if they are anything, are ways of giving emphasis, and to emphasise as one's starting point what is and can be known, draws one to see a different landscape of thought from that which one may encounter from a starting point of that which is not known and perhaps cannot be. To pursue the metaphor, an epistemological approach lets one look up and give names to the high features of the land, whereas an agnoiological approach allows an insight into the hidden geological movements which threw up the mountain ranges in the first place. This begins to sound like a description of a Freudian view of the conscious and the unconscious and that is no mistake, for it is just such interactions of the known or knowable with the unknown or unknowable that psycho-dynamic theories explore. There is a growing tendency to apply such theoretical models to the study of cultures, and Freud showed the way in this regard not least with his description of the 'uneasiness inherent in culture'.[7] Perhaps such an approach can be used to explore the ways in which Scottish cultural matters are presented or mislaid within British accounts.

Conclusion

While not all 'British' accounts ignore Scottish art, there is frequently a
problem of finding Scottish art within them. Scrutiny of such 'British'
accounts is, however, interesting, not least because the search for
Scottish art within them reveals their inadequacy. Consideration of such
inadequacy can lead one to consider the tendency to condone selective
cultural ignorance within the British establishment. More positively
such consideration can lead one to reflect on the growing interest in
reappropriating British history among thinkers who take the plurality of
Britishness as their starting point, rather than as something best avoided.
Linda Colley has made a significant contribution here in her book
Britons published in 1992. More recently Alexander Murdoch's *British
History* (1998) has been a notable addition. The prospect opens that by
finding Scottish art and properly acknowledging it, a set of critical
models of what might constitute a British art might follow.

Notes

1   This is not to discount the remarkable work of Gerald Finley.
2   It would be wrong to imply that Campbell's Scottishness is never acknow-
    ledged; see, for example, Tavernor 1991, 151ff.
3   See Brydall 1889; Caw 1908; McKay 1906. For a comprehensive account of
    histories of Scottish art see Macmillan 1990: 11.
4   Brydall concludes his preface thus: 'In placing the history of Scottish Art before
    the public, my object has been to fill a blank in our national literature, and to
    place on record the successive steps by which Art in Scotland has attained its
    present high pre-eminence' (1889: vi).
5   A further symptom of this is the way in which political history is referred to in
    this 'history' of British art: again it is that of England, not of Britain. To take an
    example from the first programme, Henry VIII of England is described as the
    reformation monarch who dissolved the monasteries. From an English
    perspective this is true. But for a Scot, Henry VIII was an invader, like Edward
    I before him and Oliver Cromwell later. So while the English experience of
    Henry VIII is of a reformation monarch operating within his own country, the
    Scottish experience is of a foreign king invading in order to make political and
    territorial gains. These are very different experiences, however similar the effects
    on religious establishments.
6   Compare the attitude here with that of Frank Johnson in the *Sunday Telegraph*
    (9 April 1995): 'The Conservatives behaved as if for them nowadays, Scotland
    does not matter. In this the Conservatives were correct … I hope the Scots do
    not mind my pointing this out. It is not my fault they are harmless' (quoted by
    Ian Macwhirter in *The Scotsman*, 12 April 1995).
7   This phrase is, courtesy of Bruno Bettelheim, a more accurate translation of the
    book title more often rendered into English as *Civilization and its Discontents*.
    For a recent use of psychodynamic theory with respect to cultural analysis see
    Kirkwood 1996.

Bibliography

Note: titles published in London unless otherwise stated. Where there is repetition in the case of university presses, the place of publication is omitted.

Aaron, J. (1995), 'Responses to the questionnaire', in Murray and Riach, 10–17.

Abrioux, Y. (1992), *Ian Hamilton Finlay: A Visual Primer*, 2nd edn, Reaktion Books.

Acheson, J. (ed.) (1991), *The British and Irish Novel Since 1960*, Basingstoke, Macmillan.

Acheson, J. and R. Huk (eds) (1996), *Contemporary British Poetry: Essays in Theory and Criticism*, New York State University Press.

Adams, D. (1998), 'Edward Thomas: negotiating a way through culture', in Davies (1998a), 145–58.

Ahmad, A. (1987), 'Jameson's rhetoric of otherness and the "national allegory"', *Social Text*, 17 (Autumn), 3–25.

—— (1992), *In Theory: Classes, Nations, Literatures*, Verso.

Allen, K. (1997), *Twin Town*.

Allnutt, G. *et al.* (eds) (1988), *The New British Poetry*, Paladin.

Amur, G. S. *et al.* (eds) (1985), *Indian Readings in Commonwealth Literature*, New Delhi, Sterling.

Anant, V. (1960), 'The three faces of an Indian', in O'Keefe, 79–92.

Anderson, B. (1991), *Imagined Communities: Reflections on the Origin and Spread of Nationalism*, Verso.

Anderson, C. (1992), 'Debateable land: the prose work of Violet Jacob', in Gonda, 31–44.

Anderson, C. and A. Christianson (eds) (2000), *Scottish Women's Fiction, 1920s to 1960s: Journeys into Being*, East Linton, Tuckwell Press.

Anderson, C. and G. Norquay (1984), 'Superiorism', *Cencrastus*, 15, 8–10.

Ang, I. and J. Stratton (1995), 'Speaking (as) black British: race, nation, and cultural studies in Britain', in van Toorn and English, 14–30.

Armitage, S. (1991/92), 'Hearsay', *Poetry Review*, 81:4, 73–4.

Asad, T. (1990), 'Multiculturalism and British identity in the wake of the Rushdie affair', *Politics and Society*, 18:4, 455–80.

Astley, N. (ed.) (1999), *New Blood*, Newcastle-upon-Tyne, Bloodaxe Books.

Attila the Stockbroker (1992), *Scornflakes*, Newcastle-upon-Tyne, Bloodaxe Books.

Attridge, D. (ed.) (1990), *The Cambridge Companion to James Joyce*, Cambridge University Press.

Attridge, D. and M. Howes (eds) (2000), *Semi-Colonial Joyce*, Cambridge University Press.

Bakhtin, M. (1981), *The Dialogic Imagination: Four Essays*, ed. M. Holquist, trans. C. Emerson and M. Holquist, Austin, University of Texas Press.

Banks, I. (1984), *The Wasp Factory*, Abacus, 1990.

—— (1986), *The Bridge*, Macmillan.

Bannerjee, A. (1989), 'The ideology and politics of India's national identity', in Hasan, Jha and Khan, 283–96.

Banville, J. (1992 [1973]), *Birchwood*, Minerva.

—— (1996 [1995]), *Athena*, Minerva.

Barker, E. (1992 [1991]), *O Caledonia*, Harmondsworth, Penguin.

Barker, M. (1992), 'Stuart Hall, *Policing the Crisis*', in Barker and Beezer, 81–100.

Barker M. and A. Beezer (eds) (1992), *Reading Into Cultural Studies*, Routledge.

Barthes, R. (1987 [1954]), *Michelet*, trans. R. Howard, Oxford, Basil Blackwell.

Bassnett, S. (1993), *Comparative Literature: A Critical Introduction*, Oxford, Blackwell.

—— (ed.) (1997), *Studying British Cultures: An Introduction*, Routledge.

Beer, G. (1990), 'The island and the aeroplane: the case of Virginia Woolf', in Bhabha (1990a), 265–90.

Bell, I. A. (1991), 'Diminished cities: contemporary poetry in Wales and Scotland', *Poetry Wales: Special Issue – The Poetry of Scotland*, 27:2, 28–31.

—— (ed.) (1995), *Peripheral Visions: Images of Nationhood in Contemporary British Fiction*, Cardiff, University of Wales Press.

Bennett A. (1997), '"Village greens and terraced streets": Britpop and representations of "Britishness"', *Young: Nordic Journal of Youth Research*, 5:4, 20–33.

Bennett, R. (1998 [1997]), *The Catastrophist*, Review.

Bennun, D. *et al.* (1995), 'Britpop', *Melody Maker* (22 July), 29–33.

Bersani, L. (1987), 'Is the rectum a grave?', *October*, 43 (Winter), 97–222.

Bery, A. and P. Murray (eds) (2000), *Comparing Postcolonial Literatures: Dislocations*, Basingstoke, Macmillan.

Beveridge, C. and R. Turnbull (1997), *Scotland After Enlightenment*, Edinburgh, Polygon.

Bhabha, H. K. (ed.) (1990a), *Nation and Narration*, Routledge.

—— (1990b), 'DissemiNation: time, narrative, and the margins of the modern nation', in Bhabha (1990a), 291–322.

—— (1991), 'The postcolonial critic: Homi Bhabha interviewed by David Bennett and Terry Collits', *Arena*, 2:2, 47–63.

—— (1994), *The Location of Culture*, Routledge.

Bhatnagar, O. P. (1985), 'Commonwealth literature: genesis and bearings', in Amur *et al.*, 23–38.

Boland, E. (1996), *Object Lessons: The Life of the Woman and the Poet in Our Time*, Vintage.

Boose, L. E. (1994), '"The getting of a lawful race": racial discourse in early modern England and the unrepresentable black woman', in Hendricks and Parker, 35–54.

Boswell, J. (1906 [1791]), *The Life of Samuel Johnson*, vol. I, Everyman.

Boyd, B. (1999), 'Johnny, we hardly knew you', *Irish Times*, *Arts Section* (8 May), 6.

Bradley, D. (1980), 'The cultural study of music: a theoretical and methodological introduction', Stencilled Occasional Paper, no. 61, University of Birmingham.

Bradshaw, B. and J. Morrill (eds) (1996), *The British Problem, c.1534–1707: State Formation in the Atlantic Archipelago*, Basingstoke, Macmillan.

Breitenbach, E. and F. Mackay (eds) (2001), *Women and Contemporary Scottish Politics: An Anthology*, Edinburgh, Polygon.

Brennan, T. (1990), 'The national longing for form', in Bhabha (1990a), 44–70.

Brown, A. (2001), 'Women and politics in Scotland', in Breitenbach and Mackay, 197–212.

Brydall, R. (1889), *Art in Scotland: Its Origin and Progress*, Edinburgh, Blackwood.

Brysson Morrison, N. (1933), *The Gowk Storm*, Edinburgh, Canongate Classics, 1988.

Burchill, J. and T. Parsons (1978), *'The Boy Looked at Johnny': The Obituary of Rock and Roll*, Pluto.

Burgess, A. (1982), *Here Comes Everybody*, Arena.

Butler, M. (1981), *Romantics, Rebels and Reactionaries: English Literature and its Background, 1760–1830*, Oxford University Press.

Butler, S. (ed.) (1985), *The Common Ground*, Bridgend, Poetry Wales Press.

Byers, T. B. (1995), 'Terminating the postmodern: masculinity and pomophobia', *Modern Fiction Studies*, 41:1, 5–33.

Cairns, D. and S. Richards (1988), *Writing Ireland: Colonialism, Nationalism and Culture*, Manchester University Press.

Calhoun, C. (1997), *Nationalism*, Buckingham, Open University Press.

Campbell, S. (1998), '"Race of angels": the critical reception of second-generation Irish musicians', *Irish Studies Review*, 6:2 (August), 165–74.

—— (1999), 'Beyond "Plastic Paddy": a re-examination of the second-generation Irish in England', *Immigrants and Minorities* 18:2 and 3 (July/November), 266–88.

Cannadine, D. (1995), 'British history as a "new subject": politics, perspectives and prospects', in Grant and Stringer, 12–28.

Captain Nemo (1977), 'The Johnny Rotten show', *New Musical Express* (23 July), 12.

Carlyle, T. J. (1868), *The Debateable Land*, Dumfries, W.R. M'Diarmid and Co.

Carson, C. (1988 [1987]), *The Irish for No*, Newcastle-upon-Tyne, Bloodaxe Books.

Carter, E., J. Donald and J. Squires (eds) (1993), *Space and Place: Theories of Identity and Location*, Lawrence and Wishart.

Carter, G. (1995), 'Women, postcolonialism, and nationalism: a Scottish example', *SPAN*, 41, 65–74.

—— (2000), 'Boundaries and transgression in Nan Shepherd's *The Quarry Wood*', in Anderson and Christianson, 47–57.

Catatonia (1998), *International Velvet*, Warner Music CD, 3984208342.

Caw, J. L. (1908), *Scottish Painting: Past and Present, 1620–1908*, T. C. and E. C. Jack.

—— (1927), *Hours in the Scottish National Gallery*, Duckworth.

CCCS (Centre for Contemporary Cultural Studies) (1982), *The Empire Strikes Back: Race and Racism in 70s Britain*, Hutchinson.

de Certeau, M. (1988 [1974]), *The Practice of Everyday Life*, trans. S. Randall, Berkeley, University of California Press.

Chambers, I. (1976), 'A strategy for living: black music and white subcultures', in Hall and Jefferson, 157–66.

—— (1985), *Urban Rhythms: Pop Music and Popular Culture*, Basingstoke, Macmillan.

—— (1993), 'Narratives of nationalism: being "British"', in Carter, Donald and Squires, 145–64.

Chambers, I. and L. Curti (eds) (1996), *The Post-Colonial Question: Common Skies, Divided Horizons*, Routledge.

Chaudhuri, N. C. (1959), *A Passage to England*, Hogarth, 1989.

Cheng, V. (1995), *Joyce, Race and Empire*, Cambridge University Press.

Chester, G. and S. Nielsen (eds) (1987), *In Other Words: Writing as a Feminist*, Hutchinson.

Christianson, A. (1993), 'Flyting with "A Drunk Man"', *Scottish Affairs*, 5 (Autumn), 126–35.

—— (1996), 'Imagined corners to debatable land: passable boundaries', *Scottish Affairs*, 17 (Autumn), 120–34.

—— (2000), 'Elspeth Barker, Candia McWilliam and Muriel Spark, writers in exile', in Hagemann, 339–47.

Christianson, A. and L. Greenan (2001), 'Rape crisis movement in Scotland, 1977–2000', in Breitenbach and Mackay, 69–76.

Christianson, A. and A. Lumsden (eds) (2000), *Contemporary Scottish Women's Writing*, Edinburgh University Press.

Clarke, Gary (1982), 'Defending ski jumpers: a critique of theories of youth sub-cultures', Stencilled Occasional Paper, no. 71, University of Birmingham.

Clarke, Gillian (1985), *Selected Poems*, Manchester, Carcanet.
—— (1993), *The King of Britain's Daughter*, Manchester, Carcanet.
—— (1997), *Collected Poems*, Manchester, Carcanet.
—— (1998), *Five Fields*, Manchester, Carcanet.
Clarke, J. (1991a), *New Times and Old Enemies: Essays on Cultural Studies and America*, HarperCollins.
—— (1991b), 'Cultural studies: a British inheritance', in Clarke (1991a), 1–19.
Clarke, P. (ed.) (1997), *Act One Wales*, Bridgend, Seven Books.
Cloonan, M. (1997), 'State of the nation: "Englishness", pop and politics in the mid-1990s', *Popular Music and Society*, 21:2 (Summer), 47–70.
—— (1998), '"What do they know of England?": "Englishness" and popular music in the mid-1990s', in Hautamaki and Jarviluoma, 66–72.
Colley, L. (1992), *Britons: Forging the Nation, 1707–1837*, Yale University Press.
Colling, K. (1973), 'Boys went mugging for "a bit of fun"' and 30p', *Daily Mail* (20 March), 13.
Connell, R. W. (1995), *Masculinities*, Cambridge, Polity Press.
Connolly, C. (2000), '*Reflections* on the Act of Union', in Whale, 168–92.
Connolly, S. J. (ed.) (1999), *Kingdoms United? Great Britain and Ireland since 1500: Integration and Diversity*, Dublin, Four Courts Press.
Corcoran, N. (ed.) (1992), *The Common Ground: Essays on the Contemporary Poetry of Northern Ireland*, Bridgend, Seren Books.
—— (1993), *English Poetry Since 1940*, Longman.
Corkery, D. (1924), *The Hidden Ireland: A Study of Gaelic Munster in the Eighteenth Century*, Dublin, Gill and Macmillan, 1989.
Coswajee, S. (1982), 'The partition in Indo-English fiction', in Dhawan, 51–69.
Craig, C. (ed.) (1987), *The History of Scottish Literature: vol. iv – Twentieth Century*, Aberdeen University Press.
—— (1996a), 'From the lost ground: Liz Lochhead, Douglas Dunn, and contemporary Scottish poetry', in Acheson and Huk, 343–72.
—— (1996b), *Out of History*, Edinburgh, Polygon.
—— (1996c), 'The body in the kit bag', in Craig (1996b), 31–63.
—— (1998), 'Scotland and the regional novel', in Snell, 221–56.
—— (1999), *The Modern Scottish Novel: Narrative and the National Imagination*, Edinburgh University Press.
Craik, D. M. (1850), *Olive*, Oxford University Press.
Crawford, R. (1990), *The Scottish Assembly*, Chatto and Windus.
—— (1992), *Devolving Scottish Literature*, Oxford University Press.
—— (1993), *Identifying Poets: Self and Territory in Twentieth-Century Poetry*, Edinburgh University Press.
—— (1995), 'Devolving Irish literature', *Bullán: An Irish Studies Journal*, 2:1 (Summer), 134–37.
—— (2000), *Devolving Scottish Literature*, 2nd ed., Edinburgh University Press.
Crawford, R. and A. Varty (eds) (1993), *Liz Lochhead's Voices*, Edinburgh University Press.

Cremins, R. (2000), *A Sort of Homecoming: A Novel*, New York, Norton.
Crick, B. (ed.) (1991), *National Identities: The Constitution of the British Isles*, Oxford, Blackwell.
Cursiter, S. (1949), *Scottish Art*, Harrap.
Curtis, T. (ed.) (1986), *Wales: The Imagined Nation*, Bridgend, Poetry Wales Press.
Dabydeen, D. (1984), *Slave Song*, Mundelsrup, Denmark, Dangaroo Press.
—— (1988), *Coolie Odyssey*, Coventry, Dangaroo Press.
—— (1994), *Turner: New and Selected Poems*, Cape.
D'Aguiar, F. (1993a), *British Subjects*, Newcastle-upon-Tyne, Bloodaxe Books.
—— (1993b), 'Have you been here long? Black poetry in Britain', in Hampson and Barry, 51–71.
Daily Mail (1973), 'Storm as boy gets 20 years' (20 March), 1.
Davie, G. (1990a), *The Scottish Enlightenment and Other Essays*, Edinburgh, Polygon.
—— (1990b), 'Nationalism and the philosophy of the unthinkable', *Edinburgh Review*, 83, 38–9.
Davies, G. (1991/92), 'The face in the mirror', *Planet* 90, 3–6.
Davies, H. W. (1994/95), 'Wanted: a new Welsh mythology' (an interview with Edward Thomas), *New Welsh Review*, 27, 54–61.
—— (ed.) (1998a), *State of Play: Four Playwrights of Wales*, Landysul, Gomer Press.
—— (1998b), 'Not much of a dream then is it?', in Davies (1998a), 115–30.
Davies, I. (1995), *Cultural Studies and Beyond: Fragments of Empire*, Routledge.
Davies, J. A. (ed.) (1994), *Writing Region and Nation*, Swansea, University of Wales, Swansea, English Department.
Davies, N. (1999), *The Isles: A History*, Basingstoke, Macmillan.
Day, G. (1997), 'Introduction: Poetry, politics and tradition', in Day and Docherty, 1–22.
Day, G. and B. Docherty (eds) (1997), *British Poetry from the 1950s to the 1990s: Politics and Art*, Basingstoke, Macmillan.
Deane, S. (1986), *A Short History of Irish Literature*, Hutchinson.
—— (1987), *Celtic Revivals: Essays in Modern Irish Literature, 1880–1980*, Faber.
—— (1990), 'Joyce the Irishman', in Attridge, 31–53.
—— (ed.) (1991), *The Field Day Anthology of Irish Writing*, 3 vols, Derry and London, Field Day and Faber.
—— (1997 [1996]), *Reading in the Dark*, Vintage.
—— (1997), *Strange Country: Modernity and Nationhood in Irish Writing since 1790*, Oxford, Clarendon Press.
Denning, R. H. (ed.) (1970), *James Joyce: The Critical Heritage, vol. II, 1928–1941*, Routledge and Kegan Paul.
Dent, G. (ed.) (1992), *Black Popular Culture*, Seattle, Bay Press.
Derrida, J. (1976 [1967]), *Of Grammatology*, trans. G. C. Spivak, Johns Hopkins University Press.

Devlin, K. J. and M. Reizbaum (eds) (1999), '*Ulysses*' – *Engendered Perspectives: Eighteen New Essays on the Episodes*, Columbia, University of South Carolina Press.

Dhawan, R. K. (ed.) (1982), *Modern Indo-English Fiction*, New Delhi, Bahri.

Docherty, T. (1992), 'Initiations, tempers, seductions: postmodern Mc-Guckian', in Corcoran, 191–210.

Doyle, R. (1992a), *The Barrytown Trilogy*, Minerva, 1992.

—— (1992b), *The Commitments*, in Doyle (1992a), 1–140.

—— (1992c), *The Snapper*, in Doyle (1992a), 145–340.

—— (1992d), *The Van*, in Doyle (1992a), 347–633.

—— (1993), *Paddy Clarke Ha Ha Ha*, Secker & Warburg.

—— (1996), 'Interview', *The Big Issue* 40 (21 March–3 April), 23.

Dreyfus, H. L. and P. Rabinow (1982), *Michel Foucault: Beyond Structuralism and Hermeneutics*, University of Chicago Press.

Duffy, C. A. (1985), *Standing Female Nude*, Anvil Press.

—— (1993), *Mean Time*, Anvil Press.

—— (1999), *The World's Wife*, Piicador.

Dunkerley, C. (1996), 'Bard for life', *The Scotsman Week End* (20 January), 8.

Dunn, D. (ed.) (1992), *The Faber Book of Twentieth-Century Scottish Poetry*, Faber and Faber.

Dyer, R. (1997), *White*, Routledge.

Eagleton, T. (1989/90), 'Comment', *Poetry Review*, 79:4 (Winter), 46.

Easthope, A. (1986), *What a Man's Gotta Do: The Masculine Myth in Popular Culture*, Boston, Unwin Hyman.

Edgeworth, M. (1995 [1800]), *Castle Rackrent*, Oxford University Press.

Elcock, H. and M. Keating (eds) (1998), *Remaking the Union: Devolution and British Politics in the 1990s*, Frank Cass.

Enright, A. (1996 [1995]), *The Wig My Father Wore*, Minerva.

Fallon, M. and D. Mahon (eds) (1990), *The Penguin Book of Contemporary Irish Poetry*, Harmondsworth, Penguin.

Fenton, S. (1996), 'Counting ethnicity: social groups and official categories', in Levitas and Guy, 143–65.

Finlay, I. (1947), *Art in Scotland*, Oxford University Press.

—— (1948), *Scottish Crafts*, Harrap.

Fitter, C. (1995), *Poetry, Space, Landscape: Towards a New Theory*, Cambridge University Press.

FitzSimon, C. (1998), 'Interview with Patrick McCabe: St Macartan, Minnie the Minx and Mondo Movies: elliptical peregrinations through the subconscious of a Monaghan writer traumatised by cows and the brilliance of James Joyce', *Irish University Review: A Journal of Irish Studies*, 28:1 (Spring/Summer), 175–89.

Foster, R. (1993), *Paddy and Mr Punch: Connections in Irish and English History*, Allen Lane.

Foucault, M. (1982), 'Afterword: the subject and power', in Dreyfus and Rabinow, 208–26.

Friel, B. (1989), *Making History*, Faber.

Frith, S. (1996), 'Music and identity', in Hall and du Gay, 108–27.

Gabriel, J. (1994), *Racism, Culture, Markets*, Routledge.

Galford, E. (1990), *Queendom Come*, Virago.

Galloway, J. (1991 [1989]), *The Trick is to Keep Breathing*, Minerva.

—— (1995 [1994]), *Foreign Parts*, Vintage.

Gibbons, L. (1991), 'Montage, modernism and the city', *The Irish Review*, 10 (Spring), 1–6.

—— (1996), *Transformations in Irish Culture*, Cork University Press.

—— (1997), 'Narrative, allegory and *Michael Collins*', *Éire-Ireland: An Inter-disciplinary Journal of Irish Studies*, 31:3 and 4 (Autumn/Winter), 261–8.

Gibson, M. (1999), 'Review of Tom Steele, *The Emergence of Cultural Studies 1945–65*', *International Journal of Cultural Studies*, 2:1 (April), 138–42.

Gifford, Don. and R. J. Seidman (1989), *'Ulysses' Annotated: Notes for James Joyce's 'Ulysses'*, University of California Press.

Gifford, Douglas (1985), *Dear Green Place: The Novel in the West of Scotland*, Glasgow, Third Eye Centre.

—— (1992), 'Honour where it's due', *Books in Scotland*, 41, 7–16.

Gifford, Douglas and D. McMillan (eds) (1997), *A History of Scottish Women's Writing*, Edinburgh University Press.

Gilroy, P. (1987), *There Ain't No Black in the Union Jack: The Cultural Politics of Race and Nation*, Hutchinson.

—— (1992), 'Cultural studies and ethnic absolutism', in Grossberg, Nelson and Treichler, 187–98.

—— (1993), *The Black Atlantic: Modernity and Double Consciousness*, Verso.

Goldman, V. (1978a), 'Johnny's Jamaican jaunt', *Sounds* (11 February), 12.

—— (1978b), 'Johnny Cool at the control: John Lydon in Jamaica', *Sounds* (4 March), 16–18.

—— (1978c), 'Man a warrior: John in Jamaica', *Sounds* (11 March), 19–22.

Gonda, C. (ed.) (1992), *Tea and Leg-Irons: New Feminist Readings from Scotland*, Open Letters.

Graham, C. (2001), *Deconstructing Ireland: Identity, Theory, Culture*, Edinburgh University Press.

Graham, C. and R. Kirkland (eds) (1999), *Ireland and Cultural Theory: The Mechanics of Authenticity*, Basingstoke, Macmillan.

Graham-Dixon, A. (1999 [1996]), *A History of British Art*, BBC Books.

Gramich, K. (1998), 'Edward Thomas: geography, intertextuality, and the lost mother', in Davies, 159–73.

Grant, A. and K. J. Stringer (eds) (1995), *Uniting the Kingdom? The Making of British History*, Routledge.

Gray, A. (1981), *Lanark: A Life in Four Books*, Edinburgh, Canongate.

—— (1984), *1982 Janine*, Jonathan Cape.

Greater London Council (1984), *Policy Report on the Irish Community*, GLC.

Greenblatt, S. (1985), 'Shakespeare and the exorcists', in Parker and Hartman, 163–87

Gregory, D. (1994), *Geographical Imaginations*, Oxford, Blackwell.

Greig, A. (1992), *Electric Brae: A Modern Romance*, Edinburgh, Canongate.

—— (1999), *When They Lay Bare*, Faber and Faber.

Grossberg, L., C. Nelson and P. A. Treichler (eds) (1992), *Cultural Studies*, Routledge.

Guardian (2000), 'Embracing the need to build an inclusive society' (extracts from the Runnymede Report), (11 October), 6.

Hagemann, S. (1997), 'Women and nation', in Gifford and McMillan, 316–28.

—— (2000), *Terranglian Territories*, Frankfurt, Peter Lang.

Hall, C. (1996), 'Histories, empires and the post-colonial moment', in Chambers and Curti, 65–77.

Hall, S. (1980a), 'Cultural studies: two paradigms', *Media, Culture and Society*, 2:1 (January), 57–72.

—— (1980b), 'Cultural studies and the centre: some problematics and problems', in Hall *et al.*, 15–47.

—— (1992a), 'What is this "black" in black popular culture?', in Dent, 21–33.

—— (1992b), 'Cultural studies and its theoretical legacies', in Grossberg, Nelson and Treichler, 277–94.

—— (1993 [1990]), 'Cultural identity and diaspora', in Williams and Chrisman, 392–403.

Hall, S. and P. du Gay (eds.) (1996), *Questions of Cultural Identity*, Sage.

Hall, S. and T. Jefferson (eds) (1976), *Resistance Through Rituals: Youth Subcultures in Post-War Britain*, Hutchinson.

Hall, S. *et al.* (1978), *Policing the Crisis: Mugging, The State, and Law and Order*, Hutchinson.

—— (eds) (1980), *Culture, Media, Language*, Hutchinson/CCCS.

Hampson, R. and P. Barry (eds) (1993), *New British Poetries: The Scope of the Possible*, Manchester University Press.

Hand, S. (ed.) (1996), *The Levinas Reader*, Oxford, Blackwell.

Harris, R. (1996), 'Openings, absences and omissions: aspects of the treatment of "race", culture and ethnicity in British cultural studies', *Cultural Studies*, 10:2 (May), 334–44.

Harte, L. and M. Parker (eds) (2000), *Contemporary Irish Fiction: Themes, Tropes, Theories*, Basingstoke, Macmillan.

Harvie, C. (1995), '"My country will not yield you any sanctuary": a polemic by way of preface', in Ludwig and Fietz, 1–12.

Hasan, Z., S. N. Jha and R. Khan (eds) (1989), *The State, Political Processes, and Identity: Reflections on Modern India*, Sage.

Hassan, G. and C. Warhurst (eds) (1999), *A Different Future: A Moderniser's Guide to Scotland*, Edinburgh, Centre for Scottish Public Policy/The Big Issue in Scotland.

Hattersley, G. (1994), *Don't Worry*, Newcastle-upon-Tyne, Bloodaxe Books.

Hautamaki, T. and H. Jarviluoma (eds) (1998), *Music on Show: Issues of Performance*, University of Tampere, Department of Folk Tradition, Publication 25.

Healy, D. (1995 [1994]), *A Goat's Song*, Flamingo.

Heaney, S. (1991), *Seeing Things*, Faber and Faber.

Hebdige, D. (1971), 'The style of the Mods', Stencilled Occasional Paper, no. 20, University of Birmingham.

—— (1974), 'Reggae, Rastas and Rudies: style and the subversion of form' Stencilled Occasional Paper, no. 24, University of Birmingham.

—— (1979), *Subculture: The Meaning of Style*, Methuen.

—— (1987a), *Cut 'n' Mix: Culture, Identity and Caribbean Music*, Comedia/Routledge.

—— (1987b), 'Digging for Britain: an excavation in seven parts', in Institute of Contemporary Arts, 35–69.

Hechter, M. (1975), *Internal Colonialism: The Celtic Fringe in British National Development, 1536–1966*, Berkeley and Los Angeles, University of California Press.

Henderson, S. and A. Mackay (eds) (1990), *Grit and Diamonds: Women in Scotland Making History 1980–1990*, Edinburgh, Stramullion.

Hendricks, M. and P. Parker (eds) (1994), *Women, 'Race', and Writing in the Early Modern Period*, Routledge.

Hendry, J. (1987a), 'The double knot in the peeny', in Chester and Nielsen, 37–45.

—— (1987b), 'Twentieth-century women's writing: the nest of singing birds', in Craig, 291–309.

Henke, S. A. (1990), *James Joyce and the Politics of Desire*, Routledge.

Herbert, W. N. (1994), *Forked Tongue*, Newcastle-upon-Tyne, Bloodaxe Books.

Hesmondhalgh, D. (1999), 'Indie: the institutional politics and aesthetics of a popular music genre', *Cultural Studies*, 13:1, 34–61.

Hewitt, P. (1997), *Getting High: The Adventures of Oasis*, Boxtree.

Hickman, M. J. (1995), *Religion, Class and Identity: The State, the Catholic Church, and the Education of the Irish in Britain*, Aldershot, Avebury Press.

Hickman, M. J. and B. Walter (1995), 'Deconstructing whiteness: Irish women in Britain', *Feminist Review*, 50 (Summer), 5–19.

Hind, A. (1984 [1966]), *The Dear Green Place*, Edinburgh, Polygon.

Hird, L. (1997), *Nail and Other Stories*, Edinburgh, Rebel Inc.

Hitt, C. (1998), 'Ed's outed with attitude' (interview with Ed Thomas), *The Western Mail Magazine* (16 May), 4–8.

Hofheinz, T. (1995), *Joyce and the Invention of History: 'Finnegans Wake' in Context*, Cambridge University Press.

Hogan, D. (1995), *A Farewell to Prague*, Faber.

Hogg, J. (1824), *The Private Memoir and Confessions of a Justified Sinner*, Longman.

Hoggart, R. (1957), *The Uses of Literacy*, Chatto and Windus.

Hooker, J. (1982), *Poetry of Place: Essays and Reviews 1970–1981*, Manchester, Carcanet Press.

Horton, P. (1997), '"Bagpipe music": some intersections in Scottish and Irish Writing', *Scotlands*, 4:2, 66–80.

Howard, M. and R. Jackson (1970), 'Empire to commonwealth and beyond', editorial of *The Round Table*, 240 (November), 375–80.

Hulse, M., D. Kennedy and D. Morley (eds) (1993), *The New Poetry*, Newcastle-upon-Tyne, Bloodaxe Books.

Humm, M. (1991), *Border Traffic: Strategies of Contemporary Women Writers*, Manchester University Press.

Innes, C. L. (1996), 'Accent and identity: women poets of many parts', in Acheson and Huk, 315–41.

Institute of Contemporary Arts, (1987), *The British Edge*, Boston, Institute of Contemporary Arts.

Irigaray, L. (1985 [1977]), 'The sex which is not one', in Porter, 23–33.

Islam, S. M. (1999), 'Writing the postcolonial event: Salman Rushdie's August 15th, 1947', *Textual Practice*, 13:1, 119–35.

Jameson, F. (1982a), '*Ulysses* in history', in McCormack and Stead, 126–41.

—— (1982b), *The Political Unconscious: Narrative as a Socially Symbolic Act*, Ithaca, Cornell University Press.

—— (1984), 'Postmodernism, or the cultural logic of late capitalism', *New Left Review*, 146, 53–92.

—— (1986), 'Third-world literature in the era of multinational capitalism', *Social Text*, 15 (Autumn), 65–88.

Jenkins, M. (1983), *Invisible Times*, Dufour Editions.

—— (1990), *A Dissident's Voice*, Bridgend, Seren Books.

—— (1994), *Graffiti Narratives*, Aberystwyth, Planet.

—— (2000), *Red Landscapes: New and Selected Poems*, Bridgend, Seren Books.

Jones, L. (1979 [1939]), *We Live*, Lawrence and Wishart.

Jones, P. (1999), *Everything Must Go*, performance script.

Jones, P. and M. Schmidt (eds) (1980), *British Poetry Since 1970: A Critical Survey*, Manchester, Carcanet Press.

Jones, S. (1988), *Black Culture, White Youth: The Reggae Tradition from JA to UK*, Macmillan.

Joyce, J. (1992 [1916]), *A Portrait of the Artist as a Young Man*, ed. S. Deane, Harmondsworth, Penguin.

—— (1989 [1922]), *Ulysses: The Corrected Text*, ed. H. W. Gabler, Bodley Head.

Kanga, F. (1991), *Heaven on Wheels*, Picador.

Kavanagh, P. (1988 [1952]), 'The parish and the universe', in Storey, 204–6.

Kay, J. (1991), *The Adoption Papers*, Newcastle-upon-Tyne, Bloodaxe Books.

—— (1992), *Other Lovers*, Newcastle-upon-Tyne, Bloodaxe Books.

—— (1998), *Trumpet*, Picador.

Kearney, H. (1989), *The British Isles: A History of Four Nations*, Cambridge University Press.

—— (1991), 'Four nations or one?', in Crick, 1–6

Kearney, R. (1988), *Transitions: Narratives in Modern Irish Culture*, Manchester University Press.

—— (2000), 'Towards a postnationalist archipelago', *Edinburgh Review*, 103, 21–34.

Keith, M. and S. Pike (eds) (1993), *Place and the Politics of Identity*, Routledge.

Kelman, J. (1995 [1994]), *How Late It Was How Late*, Minerva.

Kemp, A. (2000), 'In the beginning was the word: then they started arguing', *Observer, Review Section* (8 October), 12.

Kennedy, A. L. (1993), *Looking for the Possible Dance*, Secker and Warburg.

—— (1995), 'Not changing the world', in Bell, 100–2.

Kennedy, D. (1991/92), 'Magazines roundup', *Poetry Review*, 81:4, 28–30.

Kiberd, D. (1991), 'Contemporary Irish poetry', in Deane, vol. III, 1309–16.

—— (1995), *Inventing Ireland: The Literature of the Modern Nation*, Jonathan Cape.

Kidd, C. (1993), *Subverting Scotland's Past: Scottish Whig Historians and the Creation of an Anglo-British Identity*, Cambridge University Press.

Kirkland, R. (1999), 'Questioning the frame: hybridity, Ireland and the institution', in Graham and Kirkland, 210–28.

Kirkwood, C. (1996), *Scotland as a Learning Society: Identity, Difference and Relatedness*, Occasional Papers, no. 9, Centre for Continuing Education, University of Edinburgh.

Kirpal, V. (ed.) (1990), *The New Indian Writing in English: A Study of the 1980s*, New Delhi, Allied.

Knight, S. (1993), 'How red was my story?', *Planet*, 98, 83–94.

Kristeva, J. (1981), 'Oscillation between power and denial: [extract from] an interview with Xavier Gauthier', in Marks and de Courtivron, 165–7.

Kruger, L. (1987), '"Our national house": the ideology of the national theatre of Great Britain', *Theatre Journal*, 39, 35–50.

Kumar, K. (1995), 'Britishness and Englishness: what prospect for a European identity in Britain today?', in Wadham-Smith, 89–102.

Kureishi, H. (1981), *Borderline*, Methuen.

—— (1986), *My Beautiful Laundrette and The Rainbow Sign*, Faber.

—— (1989 [1986]), 'London and Karachi', in Samuel, vol. II, 270–87.

—— (1990), *The Buddha of Suburbia*, Faber.

Kwesi Johnson, L. (1991), *Tings on Times: Selected Poems*, Newcastle-upon-Tyne, Bloodaxe Books.

Lambert, J. R. (1970), *Crime, Police and Race Relations: A Study in Birmingham*, Institute of Race Relations/Oxford University Press.

Lawrence, E. (1982), 'Just plain common sense: the "roots" of racism', in CCCS, 47–94.

Lawrence, K. R. (ed.) (1992), *Decolonizing Tradition: New Views of Twentieth-Century 'British' Literary Canons*, Urbana, University of Illinois Press.

Lee, A. R. (1995), *Other Britain, Other British: Contemporary Multicultural Fiction*, Pluto Press.

Leerssen, J. (1996a), *Mere Irish and Fíor Gael: Studies in the Idea of Nationality, its Development and Literary Expression Prior to the Nineteenth Century*, 2nd ed., Cork University Press.

—— (1996b), *Remembrance and Imagination: Patterns in the Historical and Literary Representation of Ireland in the Nineteenth Century*, Cork University Press.

Leigh March, C. (1999a), 'Interview with Janice Galloway', *Edinburgh Review*, 101, 85–98.

—— (1999b), 'Interview with A. L. Kennedy', *Edinburgh Review*, 101, 99–119.

Leonard, T. (1984), *Intimate Voices: Selected Work 1965–1983*, Newcastle-upon-Tyne, Galloping Dog Press.

Levack, B. (1987), *The Formation of the British State: England, Scotland, and the Union, 1603–1707*, Oxford, Clarendon Press.

Levin, H. (ed.) (1977), *The Essential James Joyce*, St Albans, Granada.

Levitas, R. and W. Guy (eds) (1996), *Interpreting Official Statistics*, Routledge.

Lochhead, L. (1984), *Dreaming Frankenstein and Collected Poems*, Edinburgh, Polygon.

—— (1989), *Mary Queen of Scots Got Her Head Chopped Off*, Harmondsworth, Penguin.

—— (1990), 'Interview', in Somerville-Arjat and Wilson, 8–17.

Longley, E. (1988), 'Including the North', *Text and Context*, 3, 17–24.

—— (1991), 'Poetry in the wars', in Deane, vol. III, 648–54.

—— (1997), 'What do Protestants want?', *Irish Review* 20, 104–20.

Lucie-Smith, E. (1988), *The New British Painting*, Oxford, Phaidon.

Ludwig, H.-W. and L. Fietz (eds) (1995), *Poetry in the British Isles: Non-Metropolitan Perspectives*, Cardiff, University of Wales Press.

Lumsden, A. (1993), 'Innovation and reaction in the fiction of Alasdair Gray', in Wallace and Stevenson, 115–26.

Lydon, J. (with Keith and Kent Zimmerman) (1994), *Rotten: No Irish, No Blacks, No Dogs*, Hodder and Stoughton.

McCabe, P. (1995), *The Dead School*, Picador.

—— (1998), *Breakfast on Pluto*, Picador.

McCann, C. (1998), *This Side of Brightness*, Phoenix.

McClintock, A. (1993), 'The angel of progress: pitfalls of the term "post-colonialism"', in Williams and Chrisman, 291–304.

MacCormack, N. (ed.) (1969), *Government and Nationalism in Scotland*, Edinburgh University Press.

McCormack, W. J. (1994), *From Burke to Beckett: Ascendancy, Tradition and Betrayal in Literary History*, Cork University Press.

McCormack, W. J. and A. Stead (eds) (1982), *James Joyce and Modern Literature*, Routledge & Kegan Paul.

MacDiarmid, H. (1984 [1950]), *Aesthetics in Scotland*, Edinburgh, Mainstream.

Macdonald, M. (1990), 'Scotland, a paradox: catalogue essay for Alan Johnston Exhibit, *11 Cities, 11 Nations Exhibition*', Freislandhal Leeuwarden, Netherlands, 85–7.

—— (1994), 'An attitude problem based in London', *Edinburgh Review*, 91, 116–18.

McDowell, L. (1999), *Gender, Identity and Place: Understanding Feminist Geographies*, Oxford, Polity Press.

McGuckian, M. (1991), *Marconi's Cottage*, Newcastle-upon-Tyne, Bloodaxe Books, 1992.

McGuinness, F. (1997), *Mutabilitie*, Faber and Faber.

McKay, W. D. (1906), *The Scottish School of Painting*, Duckworth.

McLean, P. (1995), 'Curtain up on a dream', *The Western Mail* (25 February), 6.

McMillan, Dorothy (1995), 'Constructed out of bewilderment: stories of Scotland', in Bell, 80–99.

Macmillan, Duncan (1990), *Scottish Art 1460–1990*, Edinburgh, Mainstream.

Macmillan, J. (1998), 'Review of the *New Wales Trilogy* at Glasgow Tramway', (*Guardian*, 21 October 1992) reprinted in Davies (1998a), 225–6.

—— (1999), 'Britishness after devolution', in Hassan and Warhurst, 285–94.

Maconie, S. (1998), 'Everything must grow up', *Q*, 145 (October), 96–106.

—— (2000), 'One nation under a groove', *Q*, 165 (June), 82–4.

Macwhirter, I. (1995), 'Blinkered myth-makers of Middle England', *The Scotsman* (12 April).

Mahaffey, V. (1999), 'Sidereal writing: male refraction and malefactions in "Ithaca"', in Devlin and Reizbaum, 254–66.

Maley, W. (1998), 'Postcolonial Joyce?', in Marshall and Sammells, 59–69.

—— (2000a), 'Crossing the hyphen of history: the Scottish borders of Anglo-Irishness', in Bery and Murray, 31–42.

—— (2000b), '"Kilt by Kelt Shell Kithagain with Kinagain": Joyce and Scotland', in Attridge and Howes, 201–18.

Manic Street Preachers (1996), *Everything Must Go*, Epic CD, 4839302.

Markandaya, K. (1972), *The Nowhere Man*, Macmillan.

Markham, E.A. (ed.) (1989), *Hinterland: Caribbean Poetry from the West Indies and Britain*, Newcastle-upon-Tyne, Bloodaxe Books.

Marks, E. and I. de Courtivron (eds) (1981), *New French Feminisms: An Anthology*, New York, Harvester Wheatsheaf.

Marshall, A. and N. Sammells (eds) (1998), *Irish Encounters: Poetry, Politics and Prose Since 1880*, Bath, Sulis Press.

Martin, E. (1992), 'Body narratives, body boundaries', in Grossberg, Nelson and Treichler, 409–23.

Marzorati, G. (1989), 'Salman Rushdie: fiction's embattled infidel', *The New York Times Magazine* (29 January), 100–2.

Masters, J. (1983), *Bhowani Junction*, Sphere.

Melody Maker (1977), 'Street life' (4 June), 1.

Memmi, A. (1990 [1957]), *The Colonizer and the Colonized*, Earthscan.

Mercer, K. (1992), '"1968": periodizing politics and identity', in Grossberg, Nelson and Treichler, 424–49.

Milne, D. (1994), 'James Kelman: dialectics of urbanity', in Davies, 393–407.

Minhinnick, R. (1985), *The Dinosaur Park*, Bridgend, Poetry Wales Press.

—— (1989), *The Looters*, Bridgend, Seren Books.

Mohanti, P. (1985), *Through Brown Eyes*, Harmondsworth, Penguin.

Moore, R. (1990), *Paul Scott's Raj*, Heinemann.

Moriarty, M. (1991), *Roland Barthes*, Oxford, Polity Press.

Morley D. and K. Chen (eds) (1996), *Stuart Hall: Critical Dialogues in Cultural Studies*, Routledge.

Morrill, J. (1996), 'The British problem, 1534–1707', in Bradshaw and Morrill, 1–38.

Morrison, B. (1982), *The Penguin Book of Contemporary British Poetry*, Penguin.

Mort, G. (1992), *Snow from the North*, Coventry, Dangaroo Press.

Mosse, G. L. (1996), *The Image of Man: The Creation of Modern Masculinity*, New York and Oxford, Oxford University Press.

Muir, E. (1982 [1936]), *Scott and Scotland: The Predicament of the Scottish Writer*, Edinburgh, Polygon.

Muir, W. (1987 [1931]), *Imagined Corners*, Edinburgh, Canongate Classics.

Muldoon, P. (1990), *Madoc*, Faber and Faber.

Murdoch, A. (1998), *British History, 1660–1832*, Basingstoke, Macmillan.

Murdoch, I. (1969), *Bruno's Dream*, Penguin.

Murray, C. (1997), *Twentieth-Century Irish Drama: Mirror up to Nation*, Manchester University Press.

Murray, C. S. (1977a), 'We didn't know it was loaded…', *New Musical Express* (9 July), 27–9.

—— (1977b), 'John, Paul, Steve and Sidney: the social rehabilitation of the Sex Pistols', *New Musical Express* (6 August), 23–6.

Murray, S. and A. Riach (eds) (1995), *SPAN: Journal of the South Pacific Association for Commonwealth Literature and Language Studies, Special Issue: Celtic Nationalism and Postcoloniality*, 41.

Naess, A. (1989), *Ecology, Community and Lifestyle: Outline of an Ecosophy*, trans. D. Rothenberg, Cambridge University Press.

Naipaul, V. S. (1961), *A House for Mr Biswas*, Deutsch.

—— (1968 [1964]), *An Area of Darkness*, Harmondsworth, Penguin.

—— (1987 [1967]), *The Mimic Men*, Harmondsworth, Penguin.

Nairn, T. (1981), *The Break-up of Britain: Crisis and Neo-nationalism*, 2nd edn, Verso.

Narayan, R. K. (1990), *A Story-Teller's World*, New Delhi, Penguin.

Nehru, P. (1946), *The Discovery of India*, New York, John Day.

Nelson, C., P. A. Treichler, and L. Grossberg (1992), 'Cultural studies: an introduction', in Grossberg, Nelson and Treichler, 1–16.

Nicholson, C. (1992), *Poem, Purpose and Place: Shaping Identity in Contemporary Scottish Verse*, Edinburgh, Polygon.

Nicoll, L. (2000), '"This is not a nationalist position": James Kelman's existential voice', *Edinburgh Review*, 103, 79–84.

Nolan, E. (1995), *James Joyce and Nationalism*, Routledge.

Norquay, G. (2000), 'Fraudulent mooching: the novels of Janice Galloway', in Christianson and Lumsden, 131–43.

Norquay, G. and G. Smyth (eds) (1997), *Space and Place: The Geographies of Literature*, Liverpool John Moores University Press.

O'Connor, J. (1994), *Desperadoes*, Flamingo.

O'Keefe, T. (ed.) (1960), *Alienation*, Guildford and London, MacGibbon and Kee.

O'Rourke, D. (1994), *Dream State: The New Scottish Poets*, Edinburgh, Polygon.

Osborne, A. (1997), *Redemption Song*, in Clark, 102–21.

Osborne, J. (1956), *Look Back in Anger and Other Plays*, Faber and Faber, 1993.

Osmond, J. (1988), *The Divided Kingdom*, Constable.

O'Toole, F. (1994), *Black Hole, Green Card: The Disappearance of Ireland*, Dublin, New Island Books.

Parekh, B. *et al.* (The Commission on the Future of Multi-ethnic Britain) (2000), *The Future of Multi-ethnic Britain*, Profile Books.

Parker, P. and G. Hartman (eds) (1985), *Shakespeare and the Question of Theory*, Methuen.

Parry, J. (1999), 'Everything must go' (interview with Patrick Jones), *Buzz* (February), 6–7.

Paterson, L. (1996), 'Language and identity on the stage', in Stevenson and Wallace, 75–83.

Paul, K. (1997), *Whitewashing Britain: Race and Citizenship in the Postwar Era*, Ithaca, Cornell University Press.

Paulin, T. (1984), *Ireland and the English Crisis*, Newcastle-upon-Tyne, Bloodaxe Books.

Peach, L. (1996), 'Wales and the cultural politics of identity: Gillian Clarke, Robert Minhinnick, and Jeremy Hooker', in Acheson and Huk, 373–96.

—— (1997), 'Resisting postmodernity: the poetry of Mike Jenkins and Robert Minhinnick', in Norquay and Smyth, 333–46.

Pevsner, N. (1956), *The Englishness of English Art*, The Architectural Press.

Pittock, M. (1995), *The Myth of the Jacobite Clans*, Edinburgh University Press.

—— (1999), *Celtic Identity and the British Image*, Manchester University Press.

Plain, G. (1996), *Women's Fiction of the Second World War: Gender, Power and Resistance*, Edinburgh University Press.

Platt, L. (1998), *Joyce and the Anglo-Irish: A Study of Joyce and the Literary Revival*, Amsterdam, Rodopi.

Pocock, J. G. A. (1995), 'British history: a plea for a new subject', *Journal of Modern History*, 47, 601–21.

Porter, C. with C. Burke (eds and trans) (1985), *This Sex Which Is Not One*, Ithaca, New York, Cornell University Press.

Quiller-Couch, A. (1918), 'Patriotism in literature', *Studies in Literature*, Cambridge University Press.

Redhead, S. (2000), *Repetitive Beat Generation*, Edinburgh, Rebel Inc.

Reizbaum, M. (1992), 'Canonical double cross: Scottish and Irish women's writing', in Lawrence, 165–90.

Rhys, J. (1966), *Wide Sargasso Sea*, Harmondsworth, Penguin.

Richardson, A. (1995), 'The battle of Britpop', *New Musical Express* (12 August), 28–30.

Ricouer, P. (1992), *Oneself as Another*, trans. K. Blamey, University of Chicago Press.

Robbins, K. (1997), *Great Britain: Identities, Institutions and the Idea of Britishness*, Longman.

Roberts, J. H. (1970), 'James Joyce: from religion to art', in Denning, 612–15.

Rogan, J. (1994), *The Smiths: The Visual Documentary*, Omnibus Press.

Roms, H. (1998a), 'Caught in the act: on the theatricality of identity and politics in the dramatic works of Edward Thomas', in Davies (1998a), 131–44.

—— (1998b), 'Edward Thomas: a profile' (interview with Ed Thomas), in Davies (1998a), 186–91.

Rose, G. (1993), *Feminism and Geography: The Limits of Geographical Knowledge*, Routledge.

Ross, A. (ed.) (1989), *Universal Abandon? The Politics of Postmodernism*, University of Edinburgh Press.

Rushdie, S. (1983), *Shame*, Picador.

—— (1988), *The Satanic Verses*, Viking.

—— (1992), *Imaginary Homelands*, Granta.

Said, E. (1993), *Culture and Imperialism*, Chatto and Windus.

Salewicz, C. (1978), 'The poolside pronouncements of Johnny "No-Tan" Rotten', *New Musical Express* (18 March), 15.

Samuel, R. (ed.) (1989), *Patriotism: The Making and Unmaking of British National Identity. Vol. I, History and Politics; Vol. II, Minorities and Outsiders*, Routledge.

Savill, C. (1991), 'Wales is dead!', *Planet*, 85, 86–91.

Schama, S. (1995), *Landscape and Memory*, Alfred A. Knopf.

Schoene, B. (1998), '"Emerging as the others of our selves": Scottish multiculturalism and the challenge of the body in postcolonial representation', *Scottish Literary Journal*, 25:1, 54–72.

—— (1999), 'Dams burst: devolving gender in Iain Banks's *The Wasp Factory*', *Ariel: A Review of International English Literature*, 30:1, 131–48.

—— (2000), *Writing Men: Literary Masculinities from Frankenstein to the New Man*, Edinburgh University Press.

The Scotsman (2000), 'Huge jobs boost as Edinburgh economy thrives' (17 January), 1.

Scott, P. (1976a [1973]), *The Day of the Scorpion*, in *The Raj Quartet*, Heinemann.

—— (1976b), *A Division of the Spoils*, in *The Raj Quartet*, Heinemann.

—— (1978), *Staying On*, Grafton.

—— (1990 [1973]), 'Letter to Roland Gant', quoted in Moore, 114.

Scott, W. (1969 [1814]), *Waverley*, Everyman.

Scullion, A. (1995), 'Feminine pleasures and masculine indignities: gender and community in Scottish drama', in Whyte (1995a), 169–204.

Segal, L. (1990), *Slow Motion: Changing Masculinities, Changing Men*, Virago.

Shapcott, J. (1992), *Phrase Book*, Oxford University Press.

—— (1999), *Her Book: Poems 1988–1998*, Faber and Faber.

Sharkey, S. (1997), 'A view of the present state of Irish Studies', in Bassnett, 113–34.

Sharp, A. (1965), *A Green Tree in Gedde*, Michael Joseph.

Shepherd, N. (1996a), *The Quarry Wood*, in Watson.

—— (1996a), *The Weatherhouse* (1930), in Watson.

Shuker, R. (1998), *Key Concepts in Popular Music*, Routledge.

Silverman, K. (1992), *Male Subjectivity at the Margins*, Routledge.

Simpson, D. (1996), 'Why two's company', *Guardian* (13 July), 30.

Sissay, L. (1992), *Rebel Without Applause*, Newcastle-upon-Tyne, Bloodaxe Books.

Smyth, G. (1997), *The Novel and the Nation: Studies in the New Irish Fiction*, Pluto Press.

—— (2000), 'The right to the city: re-presentations of Dublin in contemporary Irish fiction', in Harte and Parker, 13–34.

—— (2001), *Space and the Irish Cultural Imagination*, Basingstoke, Palgrave.

Snell, K. D. M. (ed.) (1998), *The Regional Novel in Britain and Ireland, 1800–1990*, Cambridge University Press.

Soja, E. (1989), *Postmodern Geographies: The Reassertion of Space in Critical Social Theory*, Verso.

Somerville-Arjat, G. and R. E. Wilson (eds) (1990), *Sleeping with Monsters: Conversations with Scottish and Irish Women Poets, with Research and Interviews by Rebecca Wilson*, Edinburgh, Polygon.

Spark, M. (1992), *Curriculum Vitae*, Constable.

Spivak, G. C. (1993), 'Can the subaltern speak?', in Williams and Chrisman, 66–111.

Stephens, M. (ed.) (1991), *The Bright Field: An Anthology of Contemporary Poetry From Wales*, Manchester, Carcanet Press.

Stephenson, A. (1989), 'Regarding postmodernism – a conversation with Fredric Jameson', in Ross, 3–30.

Stevenson, R. and G. Wallace (eds) (1996), *Scottish Theatre Since the Seventies*, Edinburgh University Press.

Stevenson, R. L. (1999), *Dr Jekyll and Mr Hyde*, ed. by M. A. Danahay, Peterborough, Ont., Broadview.

Stopford Green, A. (1909), *The Making of Ireland and its Undoing, 1200–1600*, Macmillan.

Storey, M. (ed.) (1988), *Poetry and Ireland Since 1800: A Source Book*, Routledge.

Stratton, J. and I. Ang (1996), 'On the impossibility of a global cultural studies: "British" cultural studies in an "international" frame', in Morley and Chen, 361–91.

Stringer, J. (1992), 'The Smiths: repressed (but remarkably dressed)', *Popular Music*, 11:1 (January), 15–26.

Stubbs, D. (1998), 'Combat rock', *Uncut*, 15 (August), 44–7.

Syal, M. (1996), *Anita and Me*, HarperCollins.

Tagore, R. (1976), *Nationalism*, Macmillan.

Tavernor, R. (1991), *Palladio and Palladianism*, Thames and Hudson.

Taylor, A. (1994), 'Prize fight', *Scotland on Sunday Spectrum* (16 October), 1–2.

Thomas, C. (1996), *Male Matters: Masculinity, Anxiety, and the Male Body on the Line*, Urbana and Chicago, University of Illinois Press.

Thomas, E. (1994a), *Three Plays*, Bridgend, Seren Books.

—— (1994b), *House of America*, in Thomas (1994a), 11–100.

—— (1994c), *Flowers of the Dead Red Sea*, in Thomas (1994a), 101–66.

—— (1994d), *East from the Gantry*, in Thomas (1994a), 167–213.

—— (1994e), *Fallen Sons*, dir. C. Sherlock, a Teliesyn production for BBC Wales.

—— (1995), *Song from a Forgotten City*, draft.

—— (1997), 'A land fit for heroes (Max Boyce excluded)', *Observer* (20 July), 18.

—— (1998), *Gas Station Angel*, Methuen.

Thompson, E. P. (1963), *The Making of the English Working Class*, Penguin.

Tighe, C. (1986), 'Theatre (or not) in Wales', in Curtis, 241–60.

Todd, L. (1989), *The Language of Irish Literature*, Basingstoke, Macmillan.

Todorov, T. (1994), *An Other Tongue: Nation and Ethnicity in the Linguistic Borderlands*, Duke University Press.

Tóibín, C. (1990), *The South*, Picador.

Tonge, J. (1938), *The Arts of Scotland*, Kegan Paul.

van Toorn, P. and D. English (eds) (1995), *Speaking Positions: Aboriginality, Gender and Ethnicity in Australian Cultural Studies*, Melbourne, University of Technology Press.

Toynbee, P. (1996), 'True patriotism is nothing to be ashamed of … it bears with it no ill will towards other cultures', *Radio Times* (13–19 July), 11.

Travis, A. (2000), 'British tag is "coded racism"', *Guardian* (11 October), 1.

Trott, L. (1998 [1995]), '*Socialist Campaign Group News* (March), Review of *Song from a Forgotten City*', reproduced in Davies (1998a), 235–6.

Tuan, Y. (1977), *Space and Place: The Perspective of Experience*, Edward Arnold.

Turner, G. (1996), *British Cultural Studies: An Introduction*, 2nd edn, Routledge.

Ullah, P. (1981), 'The ethnic identity of the second generation Irish in Britain', unpublished MSc thesis, University of Birmingham.

—— (1983), 'Second generation Irish youth: a social psychological investigation of a hidden minority', unpublished PhD thesis, University of Birmingham.

—— (1985), 'Second-generation Irish youth: identity and ethnicity', *New Community*, 12:2, 310–20.

Vaughan Jones, Y. (1997/8), 'Playing on the world stage', *Agenda: The Journal of the Institute of Welsh Affairs* (Winter), 45–6.

Vermorel, F. and J. Vermorel (1978), *Sex Pistols: The Inside Story*, Omnibus.

Wadham-Smith, N. (ed.) (1995), *British Studies Now* (anthology of volumes 1–5), British Council.

Wales, K. (1992), *The Language of James Joyce*, Basingstoke, Macmillan.

Wallace, G. and R. Stevenson (eds) (1993), *The Scottish Novel Since the Seventies: New Visions, Old Dreams*, Edinburgh University Press.

Wallace, N. (ed.) (1991), *Thoughts and Fragments about Theatres and Nations*, Glasgow, Guardian Newspaper Publications.

Walter, B. (1999), 'Gendered Irishness in Britain: changing constructions', in Graham and Kirkland, 77–98.

Warner, A. (1996 [1995]), *Morvern Callar*, Vintage.

Watson, R. (ed.) (1996), *The Grampian Quartet*, Edinburgh, Canongate Classics.

Waugh, E. (1937 [1928]), *Decline and Fall*, Harmondsworth, Penguin.

Welsh, I. (1993), *Trainspotting*, Secker and Warburg.

—— (1996 [1995]), *Marabou Stork Nightmares*, Vintage.

Wesling, D. (1997), 'Scottish narrative since 1979: monologism and the contradictions of a stateless nation', *Scotlands*, 4:2, 81–98.

West, C. (1992), 'The postmodern crisis of the black intellectuals', in Grossberg, Nelson and Treichler, 689–705.

Whale, J. (ed.) (2000), *Edmund Burke's 'Reflections on the Revolution in France': New Interdisciplinary Essays*, Manchester University Press.

Whyte, C. (ed.) (1995a), *Gendering the Nation: Studies in Modern Scottish Literature*, Edinburgh University Press.

—— (1995b), 'Not(e) from the margin', *Chapman*, 80, 28–33.

—— (1998), 'Masculinities in contemporary Scottish fiction', *Forum for Modern Language Studies*, 34:3, 274–85.

Williams, G. A. (1985), *When Was Wales?: A History of the Welsh*, Harmondsworth, Penguin.

—— (1990/91), 'A pistol shot in a concert?', *Planet*, 84, 50–60.

Williams, I. (ed.) (1968), *Sir Walter Scott on Novelists and Fiction*, Routledge and Kegan Paul.

Williams, P. and L. Chrisman (eds) (1993), *Colonial Discourse and Post-Colonial Theory: A Reader*, Hemel Hempstead, Harvester Wheatsheaf.

Williams, R. (1958), *Culture and Society 1780–1950*, Penguin.

—— (1981), *Drama from Ibsen to Brecht*, Harmondsworth, Pelican.

—— (1989), *Resources of Hope*, Verso.

—— (1991), *Writing in Society*, Verso.

Williamson, J. (1988), 'Two kinds of otherness: black film and the avant-garde', *Screen*, 29:4 (Autumn), 106–12.

Williamson, K. (1996), *Children of Albion Rovers*, Edinburgh, Rebel Inc.

Willis, P. (1972), 'Popular music and youth culture groups in Birmingham', unpublished PhD thesis, University of Birmingham.

—— (1974), 'Symbolism and practice: a theory for the social meaning of pop music', Stencilled Occasional Paper, no. 13, University of Birmingham.

Wills, C. (1993), *Improprieties: Politics and Sexuality in Northern Irish Poetry*, Oxford University Press.

Woolf, V. (1993 [1929, 1938]), *A Room of One's Own and Three Guineas*, ed. M. Barnett, Penguin.

Wright, P. (1985), *On Living in an Old Country*, Verso.

Wynn Thomas, M. (1992), *Internal Difference: Literature in Twentieth-Century Wales*, Cardiff, University of Wales Press.

—— (1995a), 'Prints of Wales: contemporary Welsh poetry in English', in Ludwig and Fietz, 97–114.

—— (1995b), 'Hidden attachments: aspects of the two literatures of modern Wales', *Welsh Writing in English: A Yearbook of Critical Essays*, 1, 145–63.

Yeats, W. B. (1962), *Explorations*, Macmillan.

Yule, H. and A. C. Burnell (1996 [1886]), *Hobson-Jobson: The Anglo-Indian Dictionary*, Hertfordshire, Wordsworth.

Zephaniah, B. (1996), *Propa Propaganda*, Newcastle-upon-Tyne, Bloodaxe Books.

Ziesler, K. I. (1989), 'The Irish in Birmingham, 1830–1970', unpublished PhD thesis, University of Birmingham.

Index

Literary works can be found under authors' names; 'n.' after a page reference indicates a note number on that page.